I0127208

Attack the System
A New Anarchist Perspective
for the 21st Century
by
Keith Preston

Attack the System
A New Anarchist Perspective
for the 21st Century
by
Keith Preston

Copyright © 2017 Black House Publishing Ltd

All rights reserved. No part of this book may be reproduced
in any form by any electronic or mechanical means including
photocopying, recording, or information storage and retrieval
without permission in writing from the publisher.

ISBN-13: 978-1-910881-44-6

Black House Publishing Ltd
Kemp House
152 City Road
London
United Kingdom
EC1V 2NX

www.blackhousepublishing.com
Email: info@blackhousepublishing.com

To all enemies of the state, whoever they are

and wherever they may be.

Contents

Introduction

It has been said that anarchists are born and not made. Perhaps my own personal history serves as evidence to support such a claim. I still remember quite vividly the moment when I first came to understand that there really were people who stood for the abolition of the state and who seriously claimed the label of "anarchists" for themselves. I was a high school student at the time, about sixteen or seventeen years old. My senior level English literature textbook contained a brief biographical feature on the poet Percy Bysshe Shelley which mentioned that Shelley had been the son-in-law of William Godwin and that Godwin was an anarchist. I was instantly intrigued. The idea that there was actually a movement of those committed to anarchism as a philosophy and whose ranks included serious scholars and intellectuals was something that I found fascinating. Though I had never before heard of the concept of anarchism, it somehow felt very familiar as though I had discovered something that had already been a part of my life on a subconscious level all along. I had experienced similar feeling a short time earlier in the very same English literature class when I first encountered Thomas Jefferson's often-cited quote from a letter to James Madison concerning Shay's Rebellion, "A little rebellion now and then is a good thing."

Though my fascination with the notion of anarchism was immediate, it would be several more years before I would give the matter any serious reflection. For as a teenager living in a small town in the American state of Virginia in the early 1980s I was far more concerned with psychoactive substances and rock music than I was with philosophy or politics. My own early life was about as far removed from the world of the anarchist radical that I would later become as it could be. I came from an entirely conventional middle class American family and my own parents held impeccably conservative attitudes. The cultural revolution that Western civilization experienced during the 1960s had barely touched the Virginia community where I spent my 1970s childhood. Indeed, I was at the time part of the far fringes of the Christian fundamentalist subculture that looked with abject horror at the changes that were then transpiring in the outside world. The subculture from which I came attempted to isolate itself from that world and I spent my earliest years as a pupil under the tutelage of evangelical Protestant ideologues.

Being an obstreperous adolescent and rebellious young man, I was soon enjoying quite a career as an up-and-coming delinquent that led ultimately to experiences involving crashed cars, encounters with the police, and time spent behind bars. I graduated from high school only because of the generosity of the school administration and their probable desire to be rid of me, and began to attend college only for the sake of avoiding working for a living. But it was during my early years in the world of academia that I began to take ideas seriously and there was no idea that I took more seriously than the political philosophy of anarchism. I was an anarchist before I ever met any other actual anarchists and my earliest sources of information on anarchism were generic ones such as encyclopedias. It was through time spent in my college library that I first encountered names such as Proudhon, Bakunin, and Kropotkin, and terms such as syndicalism and mutualism. It was a short time later when, after transferring to another college and relocating to another city, I attended my first meeting of real life anarchists in the spring of 1988. I found them to be a strange lot indeed with their bizarre fashions, body piercings, and hairstyles, and orientations towards alternative lifestyles such as veganism, squatting, gender-bending, and habitual vagrancy.

It was through the anarchists that I was introduced to the subculture of the radical Left as it was in the United States of the 1980s. It was a subculture that in many ways seemed to be the polar opposite of the subculture in which I had spent my childhood and adolescence. The popular left-wing causes of the time were the growing environmentalist movement, the various expressions of identity politics and the related attitudes that later came to be known as "political correctness," and opposition to intervention by the United States in the civil wars that were then raging in the Central American nations. It was only the latter of these that ever made any particular impression on me. For it was through reading the works of leading critics of American imperialism from the time and, more importantly, hearing the personal stories of refugees from the US-backed regimes in Central America that I came to understand the true nature of the American empire and its impact on the poor nations of the earth. I became a committed revolutionary and have remained one ever since.

For a number of years in the late 1980s and early 1990s I was a hardcore participant in the radical left-wing movement though always with a strictly anarchist orientation. I regularly engaged in intense arguments and debates with Communists at leftist events. My weekly routine consisted of meetings, demonstrations, community projects, teaching at an alternative school, and writing articles for radical newsletters to the point where I was not able to remain in college and I would not complete my degrees until many years later. Meanwhile, I found myself having to arrange my radical activities around keeping a steady enough job to pay the rent. I also devoted myself to an intense study of anarchist history and theory. I became ever-more fascinated with the many varying sects of anarchism and related philosophies. The more my knowledge deepened the more dissatisfied I became with both the actually existing anarchist movement itself and the wider radical left-wing subculture. I came to believe that most leftists spoke in platitudes that lacked genuine substance, much like the Christian fundamentalists in whose company I had spent my earliest years. And I came to regard most anarchists as a collection of ne'er-do-well youth whose overall level of theoretical sophistication and competence as political organizers and activists was shabby beyond belief.

I began to distance myself from the left-wing circles I had previously been involved with and retreated into an ever-greater amount of private study. Meanwhile, I became increasingly concerned about the domestic American police state that began to rapidly expand itself during the 1990s under the guise of the wars on drugs and crime. It was during this time that the American patriot and militia movements began to develop and I found myself becoming increasingly interested in the growth of this indigenous American populist movement with a solidly anti-state bent. Through attending the events and reading the literature of these people I came to realize that many of them were anarchists in practice if not in name. I began to develop plans for a new anarchist movement that could move beyond the clichéd leftism and pretentious counterculturalism of the anarchist "establishment" towards an anarchist-led anti-state populism with an ever-more militant stance.

Fortunately, the advent of the internet provided me with a platform for the dissemination of my own ideas. I established the AttacktheSystem.Com website in January of 2001, the same month that George W. Bush assumed the presidency of the United States. In its early years AttacktheSystem.Com was primarily devoted to criticizing the massive police state expansion and imperialist aggression of the Bush regime. The name was originally suggested to me by a nineteen-year-old college student I met at a libertarian gathering. The nineteenth-century American individualist-anarchist Benjamin R. Tucker called his landmark work *Instead of a Book: By a Man Too Busy to Write One.* Likewise, I suppose I could refer to AttacktheSystem. Com as *Instead of a Magazine: By a Man Lacking the Resources to Publish One.* For the past twelve years, AttacktheSystem.Com has served as a de facto online journal through which I have been able to communicate with an ever-growing audience. In the meantime, I have been published in an ever-greater number of other forums, from literary compilations to online webzines. I have also more recently begun to engage in audio broadcasting through the internet and am increasingly invited to speak at academic conferences or to be interviewed by the international media. I am very grateful for the opportunities that have been granted to me in recent years to expound upon my own ideas and the movement that I wish to advance.

This anthology is a collection of twenty-six essays that were written between 2001 and 2013. My purpose in producing these works has been to create the theoretical foundation for a twenty-first-century anarchist movement that will constitute a third wave of anarchism that advances beyond the first wave classical anarchist movement of the late nineteenth and early twentieth century and the second wave of anarchism that emerged from the New Left in the late twentieth century and which continues to be the mainstream of anarchism at the present juncture. I have also sought to establish not only a theoretical basis for a new wave of anarchism but also a comprehensive strategic orientation for such a movement.

This work is divided into four parts, with each of these containing original writings dealing with the core issues that I wish to address. The first part considers the question of what the appropriate philosophical foundations for twenty-first-century anarchism might be. Like Emma Goldman, I find the philosophy of Nietzsche to be highly relevant to the anarchist struggle and I regard Nietzsche rather than Marx as the truly great radical thinker of nineteenth-century European intellectual culture. The introductory essay, "The Nietzschean Prophecies," addresses the existential crisis facing Western civilization and in which a twenty-first-century anarchist movement will necessarily be taking place. The second essay, "Our Struggle Is Neither Moral Nor Intellectual, But Physical," simply seeks to apply the philosophy of Max Stirner to the struggle ahead. It was Stirner more than any other of the great anarchist thinkers who really understood the nature of human existence and its

Introduction

philosophical implications. The final essay in the first part, "Ernst Jünger: The Resolute Life of an Anarch," examines the career of the legendary German soldier from the First World War and literary figure during the interwar period. Jünger is acknowledged as an ideal prototype for the model psychological makeup for a contemporary anarchist warrior.

The second part contains two essays which examine the enemy we face in contemporary times, the international plutocratic order and the American empire which upholds it. The first work, "Philosophical Anarchism and the Death of Empire," was written in 2003 as George W. Bush's war in Iraq was just beginning. It examines the role of the neoconservatives in escalating military aggression by the American regime and presciently argues that the neoconservatives would eventually be eclipsed by a more overtly internationalist liberal humanism and progressive imperialism of the kind now exhibited by the Obama regime. The second work, "Anti-Imperialists of the World, Unite!," calls for anarchists to reclaim their role as the leading resistance forces to imperialism which they held in the nineteenth century and reiterates the call for a worldwide anti-globalist struggle outlined in the previous essay.

The third part outlines the general theoretical framework for a new anarchist movement for the twenty-first century. The first writing, "Against the State," draws heavily on the "synthesist" tradition within classical anarchism and calls for a unified revolutionary front of anti-state radicals against common enemies. The next two pieces, "Why I Am an Anarcho-Pluralist," parts one and two, provide a practical discussion of the problems involved in reconciling the many contending schools of anarchism. The fourth essay, "Anarcho-Pluralism and Pan-Secessionism," attempts to clarify my general theoretical framework of "anarcho-pluralism" and the related strategic concept of "pan-secessionism" by examining misconceptions that have been associated with these.

The fourth and final part deals more broadly with strategic matters. The first essay in this part, "Liberty and Populism," was written in 2006 and is the most comprehensive exposition on my general strategic outlook that I have yet to produce. The second piece, "Smashing the State," was written in 2003 and at the time provided an initial introduction to my strategic paradigm as I was developing it. "Propaganda by the Deed, Fourth Generation Warfare, and the Decline of the State" examines how the armed wing of the classical anarchist movement were in many ways the originators of modern "terrorism" and how the model of non-state warfare they developed has since been adopted by other movements to the point where the state is losing its traditional monopoly on war. The final essay in the anthology, "Armed Struggle Against the State," provides an abstract discussion of how an armed insurgency might unfold in a modern society.

I would be remiss if I did not acknowledge those persons who have made this work possible through their contributions to my various endeavors over the years. I wish to thank my mentors during my early days as an anarchist nearly a quarter century ago, Ed Jahn and Jarama Bernstein, as it was they who provided me with the basic training in radical political organizing. I do not know if they would agree with every position I hold today, but I am in their debt nevertheless.

I wish to thank those, anarchists and non-anarchists alike, who have graciously published my various articles and essays over the years or endeavored in other ways to bring my ideas to a wider audience, especially Jeremy Sapienza, Lew Rockwell, Richard Spencer, Troy Southgate, Welf Herfurth, Dr. Paul Gottfried, Dr. Sean Gabb, Robert Stark, and Dr. Tomislav Sunic. I also wish to thank my current publisher, Karl Winn. I wish to thank the past producers of my internet radio program, Mike Conner and Matt Parrott. I am especially grateful to Matthew Peters for his diligent and meticulous efforts at editing and proofreading this work. His contribution to this project has been enormous. In particular I wish to thank my comrades at AttacktheSystem.

Com, especially R. J. Jacob, Jeremy Weiland, Vince Rinehart, Miles Joyner, Rodney Huber, Craig Fitzgerald, Peter Bjorn Perls, Daniel Acheampong, Lawrence J. Patti, and Michael Parish for their ongoing labor and support over the years. I am sure there are others whom I have neglected to mention and I apologize for any such omissions.

Lastly, I wish to thank all anarchists, libertarians, and anti-state radicals everywhere, whether they agree with my perspective or not, for their contributions to the struggle, large or small. You are all soldiers in the army of liberty.

Keith Preston

September 1, 2013

Part 1 - Philosophical Foundations

The Nietzschean Prophecies

Among the many great and enormously influential thinkers of the nineteenth century, it is Friedrich Wilhelm Nietzsche (1844–1900) who arguably stands the highest in terms of possessing both the most profound and penetrating criticisms of Western civilization as it was in his time, and the most prescient insights and predictions as to what the future course of the evolution of the West would involve. In our own day, Nietzsche has been a popular topic of academic discourse for some time, and the reading of his works has long been a popular pastime among trendy undergraduates. Yet Nietzsche remained obscure in his lifetime, and his works and ideas would not be widely read or accepted until after his death. Even with the abundance of Nietzsche scholarship that has been produced since his passing over a century ago, his core ideas remain widely misunderstood or misinterpreted. Indeed, Nietzsche has been largely appropriated by the academic Left, a great irony considering his own considerable contempt for the politics of the Left, and the prevailing academic philosophy of postmodernism includes the philosophy of Nietzsche as a direct ancestor in its genealogical line.

No thinker is more important or relevant to the ideas of the Conservative Revolution than Nietzsche. While Marx continues to retain his status as the most influential radical thinker of the nineteenth century, it was Nietzsche who was the more revolutionary of the two in the actual implications of his thought. Nietzsche also stands as a polar opposite of the conservative counter-revolutionaries that arose in opposition to the spread of the influence of the Enlightenment. Nietzsche is no mere traditionalist in the vein of Edmund Burke, Joseph de Maistre, or Louis de Bonald. His outlook involves a dramatic departure not only from traditional Western thought as it had unfolded since the time of the Socratics, but from the intellectual culture of even the most advanced or revolutionary thinkers of his own time.

The Historical Context of Nietzsche's Thought

An adequate understanding of Nietzsche is impossible without recognition of the historical context in which he wrote. Nietzsche's core works were produced between 1872 and 1888. By that time, the intellectual revolution of the Enlightenment was well-established among Western intellectual elites and among the rising educated middle classes. The Enlightenment intellectual revolution and its outgrowths were existential in nature. The most important aspect of the impact of the revolution was what Nietzsche characterized as the "death of God." Advancements in human knowledge in a wide variety of areas had the effect of undermining the credibility of traditional theological views on cosmology, moral philosophy, the meaning of human existence, and so forth. The overthrow of the Christian world view that had dominated Western civilization for fifteen hundred years left subsequent thinkers with a number of ultimately profound questions.[1] If the purpose of an individual's life is not to achieve salvation in an afterlife, then what is the purpose of life? If the king or established political authorities do not rule by divine right, then what is the basis of political legitimacy? How should society be organized? If morality is not to be understood according to the teachings of the Church, the Bible, or traditional religious authority, then what is the basis of justice, morality, truth, or "right and wrong"? Do such concepts have any intrinsic or objective meaning at all? If the observable universe was not the product of special creation by a divine power, and if humanity was not "created in the image of God," then what is the meaning of existence? Does it have any meaning beyond itself? If history is not guided by divine providence, then how is the process of historical unfolding to be understood? These are the questions

---

1   Peter Gay, *The Enlightenment: The Rise of Modern Paganism* (New York: W. W. Norton and Co., 1966), 8–9, 62–63.

that Western thinkers have been grappling with since the older, theological view of the universe and existence was demolished by the intellectual innovations of the Enlightenment.

The New Religion of Reason and Progress

Western civilization existed for millennia prior to the rise of Roman Christianity, so it is unsurprising that anti-Christian, Enlightenment intellectuals found inspiration in the classic works of antiquity. The Enlightenment thinkers (the *"philosophes"*) developed a world view and philosophical outlook relatively similar to that which prevailed among the great thinkers of Greco-Roman intellectual culture.[2] The traditional Christian emphasis on faith, revelation, mystery, and divine authority was rejected in favor of a new emphasis on the efficacy of human reason and ability to engage in rational criticism. The Enlightenment view of the universe mirrored the human-centered outlook of the Greeks, with the ideas of the *philosophes* reflecting the Greek adage that "man is the measure of all things" to a much greater degree than Christian thought had ever done. It was the view of the *philosophes* that human reason and rational thought alone possessed the capability for the discernment of profound insight into the workings of the universe through the use of science. This confidence had been generated by the scientific revolution of the seventeenth century. Human reason was likewise capable of discerning the workings of society and of discovering ways by which society and humanity could be improved upon. Out of this conviction emerged an intellectual optimism that expressed great confidence in the possibility and inevitability of progress. This intellectual framework that was bequeathed to subsequent generations of Europeans by the great thinkers of the Enlightenment formed the foundation for most of modern thought.

The concept of progress was a dominant feature of every major aspect of nineteenth-century thinking, whether in the areas

2   Ibid., 59–127.

of philosophy, politics, or science. Thinkers of the German Idealist school, such as Immanuel Kant and G. W. F. Hegel, attempted to retain the notion of justice, morality, and virtue as concepts possessing transcendent characteristics in a manner similar to that found in earlier Christian approaches to moral philosophy. Hegel developed a philosophical doctrine known as "historicism" that characterized the process of human historical development as one by which reason unfolds towards a higher state of rational unity that contains within itself the collection of prior expressions of, and resolved contradictions within, human thought. Hegel gave a metaphysical and quasi-theological gloss to his philosophical system in a way that is still debated and subject to various interpretations. Yet, this linear, progressive view of history postulated by Hegel established the framework for historical interpretation that would dominate Western thought for the next century.[3]

Karl Marx and Friedrich Engels developed a materialist conception of Hegel's interpretation of history as a dialectical process. The core component of the Marxist interpretation of history is a kind of economic determinism. According to Marxism, history is the manifestation of the struggle between competing socio-economic classes. Other aspects of human life such as politics, religion, culture, family, and philosophy are merely expressions or outgrowths of the material foundations of a given society. Marxism regards history as an evolutionary process whereby class conflict serves as the dialectical process whose impact is the advancement of humanity to a higher stage of social development.[4]

The nineteenth-century idea of progress was further strengthened by the scientific advances of the time. Evolutionary thinking became dominant in the natural sciences as the older,

---

3   Georg W. F. Hegel, *The Philosophy of History*, trans. J. Sibree (Amherst, NY: Prometheus Books, 1991).

4   Karl Marx and Friedrich Engels, *The Communist Manifesto* (New York: International Publishers, 1948).

religious views on the origins of humanity and the universe fell into intellectual disrepute. The prevailing model of evolutionary theory of the era was the "developmental" model. This framework suggested that the evolutionary process was a manifestation of a linear drive towards a particular end. The analogy often used was that of the growth of an individual. The conventional view was that evolution transpires in a way that demonstrates direction and purpose. This particular rendition of evolution, most famously represented by the theories of Jean-Baptiste Lamarck, was exploded by Charles Darwin. Darwin argued that evolution takes place through a process of adaption by means of natural selection.[5]

Darwin's actual theory indicated that the process of natural biological evolution exhibits a great deal of randomness, and unfolds in a haphazard way with no specific outcome being inevitable regarding the ends of the evolutionary process. The actual implications of authentic Darwinian evolutionary theory severely detracted from the established "developmental" model of biological and social evolution.[6] Yet the publication of Darwin's work had the effect of popularizing evolutionary thinking, even if his ideas were misunderstood or misinterpreted. Subsequent thinkers would attempt to find justification for their preferred social or political views in Darwinian evolutionary biology.[7] Marx considered Darwin to have found a scientific justification for his own views on socio-economic evolution, and Darwin was also appropriated by racists and proponents of chauvinistic nationalism. Indeed, efforts to interpret human social evolution within the context of a pseudo-Darwinian biological framework became rather open-ended in nature. Proponents of social reform, humanitarians, advocates of predatory capitalism, utopians, racial supremacy theorists, and proponents of class warfare all appealed to Darwin as a justification for their beliefs, all of which

---

5   Peter J. Bowler, *The Non-Darwinian Revolution: Reinterpreting a Historical Myth* (Baltimore: Johns Hopkins University Press, 1988), 9–10, 43–44, 24–28, 40–45.

6   Ibid., 9–14.

7   Ibid., 132–58.

were rooted in fundamental misunderstandings of Darwin's actual ideas.[8] It was the philosophy of Nietzsche that provided the interpretive framework of human history that was the most compatible with the implications of genuine Darwinism.

The Revolt Against Reason and Progress: The Philosophy of Nietzsche

If Darwinian evolutionary biology exploded the nineteenth-century idea of progress in the realm of the natural sciences, it was the thought of Nietzsche that provided the most far-reaching assault on the presumptions of the time in the world of philosophy. Nietzsche is perhaps most well-known for his statements concerning the "death of God," but the meaning of the "death of God" in Nietzschean philosophy involves a good deal more than mere conventional atheism. Other prominent intellectual atheists had come before Nietzsche such as Diderot, Baron d'Holbach, and (by implication) Hume, and he was by no means the inventor of modern atheism.[9] While Nietzsche was certainly an "anti-theological" thinker in the sense of rejecting a theistic world view in a conventional religious sense, his notion of the "death of God" was also intended as a critique of the intellectual presumptions of his own era, including those of intellectual elites who had rejected conventional religious faith. While Nietzsche was an atheist, materialist, and rationalist of a kind comparable to the most radical Enlightenment thinkers, his outlook sharply diverges from the Enlightenment tradition with regards to the role of reason in human life and thought.

Nietzsche regarded the Enlightenment emphasis on reason as having the effect of denying the role of the passions in forming human character, and shaping human action and human societies. He contrasted the Enlightenment's orientation towards reason with the earlier manifestations and emphasis on the passions he considered to have been made manifest by the Renaissance. He

---

8   Ibid., 166–73.

9   Gay, *The Enlightenment*, 63–64, 103, 105, 407–19.

compared these two eras within the framework of his famous Apollonian/Dionysian dichotomy. The Apollonian aspect of human essence is the rational, logical, prudent, and restrained. The Dionysian is the instinctual, impulsive, and emotive. Nietzsche was not a skeptic of the passions in the manner of Hobbes or Burke, who regarded human passion and feeling as prone towards dangerous excesses and in need of restraint. Instead, he counseled human beings to live dangerously. Nietzsche regarded the passionate and the irrational (or non-rational) as the foundation of all high cultures, which he in turn considered to be apex of human existence. The Greeks had emphasized and explored the passions, rather than having feared or shunned them, and for this reason the Greeks had produced the highest of hitherto existing human civilizations. Nietzsche vehemently opposed the rising egalitarian sentiments and trends towards mass society and mass democracy of his era. Only an elite motivated by the passions can produce a high culture. An egalitarian society would be a society of weak and fearful mediocrities concerned only with comfort and safety.

The "death of God" was intended as an attack on philosophical idealism of the kind retained by Kant and Hegel as much as it was an attack on the Christian faith. Nietzsche's philosophy insisted that there is no transcendent or metaphysical foundation for ethics, morality, or justice. Values of this kind are mere human constructions. They have no meaning aside from what human beings, individually or collectively, assign to them. Nietzsche likewise rejected the view of history represented by Hegel's historicism. One of Nietzsche's earliest works, *The Use and Abuse of History*, is an attack on Hegel.[10] The linear view of history contained within Hegel's philosophical system had many precedents in Western thought, with roots going back as least as far as Aristotle. According to Nietzsche, history has no purpose. It is merely a series of events that have no meaning

10   Werner J. Dannhauser, "Friedrich Nietzsche," in *History of Political Philosophy*, 3rd ed., ed. Leo Strauss and Joseph Cropsey (Chicago: University of Chicago Press, 1987), 829–31.

in and of themselves, other than subjective meanings adopted by individuals and human groups relative to their own time, place, and experiences. Nietzsche's philosophy was an attack on virtually the entire legacy of Western metaphysics since the time of Plato.

Nietzsche regarded the nineteenth-century idea of progress, and the myriad of ideologies, movements, and causes of the time that were a manifestation of this idea to be superstitions every bit as much as the theological superstitions that dominated the Christian era. His parable of the madman found in *The Gay Science* is to be interpreted in this way.[11] Nietzsche is ridiculing the intellectuals of his time who believe they have attained a superior state of enlightenment, and who regard themselves as the progenitors of a higher civilization. He is instead arguing that the thinkers of his time have not yet fully recognized the consequences of the "death of God" for Western civilization. Instead, they are simply trying to replace old dogmas and pieties with new ones. Among these new gods are socialism, liberalism, utopianism, humanism, nationalism, democracy, pseudo-scientific racism of the kind represented by thinkers such as Houston Stewart Chamberlain,[12] and the anti-Semitism of his former friend Richard Wagner. Such efforts are dismissed by Nietzsche as methods of avoiding or postponing the existential crisis that Western civilization would ultimately have to face. Nietzsche attacked even the conservatives of his era for making too many concessions to rising egalitarian movements such as democracy and socialism, and for retaining their allegiance to the corpse of Christianity. He dismissed the traditional European aristocracies as weak and in a state of decay, and he also opposed the rising nationalist movements of his time as symptomatic of the egalitarian mass societies of mediocre individuals he saw on the horizon. Nietzsche presciently suggested that the

---

11   Friedrich Nietzsche, *A Nietzsche Reader*, ed. and trans. R. J. Hollingdale (London: Penguin Books, 1977), 202–3.

12   Houston Stewart Chamberlain, *Foundations of the Nineteenth Century*, 2 vols., trans. John Lees (New York: Howard Fertig, 1968 [1899]).

twentieth century would be a time of great wars between the rising ideological mass movements of his own time, and that the existential crisis of civilization would be fully realized only in the twenty-first century.

Nietzsche's prophecy that the twentieth century would be a time of war on an unprecedented scale between polarized ideological forces found its realization in the Great War and then the Second World War, and the destructiveness of the latter surpassed even the shocking brutality of the former. The suffering and death generated by the two world wars, and the invention of weapons technology with the capacity to destroy all of mankind demolished the nineteenth-century faith in progress and pushed postwar intellectuals towards a confrontation with the nihilistic implications of modern science and philosophy of the kind Nietzsche had previously written about. Existentialism, with its implicitly or explicitly Nietzschean roots, became the prevailing philosophical outlook for intellectuals in the mid to late twentieth century. Existentialism represents an effort to confront the crisis of nihilism suggested by Nietzsche and the serious problems this crisis poses for human ethics and the question of meaning. If existence has no meaning, then what is the basis for proper human behavior? If God is dead, is everything permitted, as Dostoevsky suggested? The struggles of existentialist thinkers with these questions are famously illustrated, for instance, by the efforts of the feminist-existentialist Simone de Beauvoir to establish a framework of ethics in the face of the meaninglessness of existence by pointing to the commonness of the human experience, and the possibility of creating shared virtues and values that advance human interests in the realm of lived experience, even if these values ultimately have no objective or cosmic foundation or meaning.[13] Her companion Jean-Paul Sartre argued that one could create one's own meaning by participating in the social or political activities of one's time or even by embracing the irrational by, for example, becoming a devout Christian or a militant Communist. Sartre himself chose the latter.

---

13   Simone de Beauvoir, *The Ethics of Ambiguity* (Secaucus, NJ: Citadel Press, 1948).

The Future

Nietzsche predicted that it would be well into the twenty-first century before Western thought fully confronted the crisis of nihilism. It would thus far appear that he was correct. Western thought since the Enlightenment has attempted to compensate for the loss of the old faith by replacing the discredited Christian world view with new faiths and new pieties. As these have become increasingly difficult to justify within a framework of rationality and a belief in inevitable "progress," Western intellectuals have increasingly retreated into the irrational. This is illustrated by the curious phenomena of the present efforts by Western intellectual elites to embrace postmodernism, with its accompanying moral and cultural relativism, while simultaneously embracing the egalitarian-universalist-humanist moralistic zealotry popularly labeled "political correctness" and espousing with great piousness such liberal crusades as "human rights," "anti-racism," "gay liberation," feminism, environmentalism, and the like. Such an outlook, which combines extreme moralism in the cultural and political realm, complete moral relativism in the philosophical or metaphysical realm, and at times even falls into subjectivism in the epistemological realm,[14] is fundamentally irrational, of course. That such an outlook has become so deeply entrenched indicates that Western intellectuals are desperately working to avoid a full confrontation with the crisis of nihilism.

Vilfredo Pareto argued that civilizations die when their elites lose faith in their own civilization to such a degree that the will to survive no longer exists. Western political and cultural elites presently exhibit abiding contempt for the legacy of their civilization, as demonstrated by their attachment to anti-Western ideologies such as "multiculturalism" and support for political policies, such as permitting mass immigration into the West from the Third World, that ultimately mean the demographic overrun and death of Western civilization. The presumption of present-

---

14   Michel Foucault, *Madness and Civilization: A History of Insanity in the Age of Reason* (New York: Vintage Books, 1965 [1961]).

day elites is that dramatic demographic alteration can transpire without consequences of significance, or that the overthrow of Western civilization itself may even be desirable. The prevalence of such attitudes once again indicates that cultural nihilism has become rather deeply entrenched. Yet this nihilism has been thus far masked by liberal-humanist platitudes of escalating silliness. It remains to be seen what will eventually bring this crisis to the forefront. Genuine threats to the survival of Western civilization itself may well force such a confrontation. These might include the threat of nuclear terrorism, economic collapse, or ecological catastrophe, the depletion of resources on which civilization has become dependent, or confrontation with an ideological rival that poses an existential threat. As demographic change on a magnitude that threatens cultural dispossession becomes increasingly imminent, and as the consequences of such become increasingly undeniable, perhaps a belated cultural awakening and renewal will begin. Otherwise, it may well the case that Western modernity and post-modernity will eventually suffer the same fate as the classical Greco-Roman civilization of antiquity.

Max Stirner Revisited

Our Struggle Is Neither Moral Nor Intellectual, But Physical

The notion that there is any inherent relationship between one's views on moral philosophy and one's views on political philosophy is an idea that I tend to be rather skeptical of. For example, political conservatives can be either devout Christians who cling to one or another conception of divinely decreed morality or materialists and moral skeptics. Likewise, political liberals can be found among both adherents of the Social Gospel and secular humanists. For those such as I who reject the state entirely, the question remains of what sort of approach to moral philosophy, if any, serves as the basis for our political perspective.

Much of classical anarchist thought is implicitly rooted in the egalitarian humanist thought of the likes of Jean-Jacques Rousseau and the progressive, evolutionary view of history formulated by G. W. F. Hegel and some of the social Darwinists, notably Herbert Spencer. According to this view, human nature is essentially benign but has been corrupted or stifled by less than optimal social institutions or lack of education. As human knowledge increases and social institutions evolve, the benign, benevolent, and cooperative qualities of human nature will, according to this theory, eventually shine through. This kind of uniquely naive utopianism emerged during the eighteenth and nineteenth centuries, a time of immensely rapid political, economic, and scientific development. The achievements of that era unfortunately led to the foolish belief that virtually anything is possible so long as human beings maintained the proper commitment and applied themselves. Today, when we hear leftists talk about their ideals of a "world without hunger" or a "world without hate," and their constant rhetoric about "commitment," "awareness," and "raising consciousness," we know that the ghost of Rousseau walks among us. The problem, of course, is that not a shred of evidence exists to support this sort of outlook. There is no indication of human moral improvement, however defined, throughout the ages. The recently expired twentieth century produced some of the worst horrors in history—world wars, genocides, and nuclear weapons. Is this any sort of improvement over the cannibals and perpetrators of human sacrifice of ancient times?

Some anti-statists, such as the disciples of Murray Rothbard and Ayn Rand, attempt to justify their beliefs with some sort of "natural law" theory. This is largely a more consistent and well-developed version of the Lockean philosophy employed by the American revolutionaries. According to this view, the inalienable right of individuals to life, liberty, property, or the pursuit of happiness has somehow been decreed by nature. While this may have been a useful myth at the time of the ascendancy of classical liberalism, its seems on its surface to be little more than an arbitrary, quasi-religious, mystical doctrine that simply asserts what it wishes to prove. Historically, natural law doctrines have just as often been used to justify various types of authoritarianism, such as the "natural" superiority of some races over others or Catholic opposition to "unnatural" acts like contraception, than any sort of liberty.

Other anti-statists are utilitarian ethicists who defend liberty on the grounds that it brings about the "best" results. While it is certainly important to be able to demonstrate that anarchism is workable in practice and that free market economics produces results which most people would find favorable, utilitarianism as a moral outlook seems rather arbitrary as well. Why the greatest good for the greatest number? Why not the greatest good for the smartest, the strongest, the healthiest, the most creative, or the most attractive, or the members of some particular racial or religious group? The Benthamite calculus involving the attempt to weigh the overall balance of pleasure over pain seems impossible to measure in the real world. Why prioritize pleasure? What about people who argue that "suffering is good for the soul"? And why should I care if everyone else is miserable so long as I am happy?

Those who attempt to make a religious case for liberty seem to have the weakest position of all. Even if one accepts religious belief as legitimate, this says nothing about the problem of power. No religious denomination that has ever obtained political power has ever created anything even remotely approaching a free society. An occasional religious anarchist or libertarian can be found, but most seriously religious people tend towards theocracy more than anything else. Even those who support formal church/state separation usually believe that the state should legislate or regulate with regards to matters of personal or religious "morality" (abortion, homosexuality, drug use, pornography, etc.). Many espouse statist economic views and/or a militarist/imperialist foreign policy outlook as well.

The natural tendency of nearly all human beings is to favor themselves over others. Most people develop the views on politics, philosophy, ethics, morality, etc., that are most consistent with their own needs and desires and the interests of their peer groups or culture of origin. Most people exhibit very little capacity for independent thinking or moral perception beyond self-interest and the influence of peers and leaders. Because different individuals and groups have conflicting interests and value systems, social conflict inevitably results. Hobbes believed that the only solution to this dilemma was an all-powerful state that would restrain the predatory inclinations of individuals and competing social forces for the sake of preserving order and civilization. The problem with Hobbes' position should be obvious enough. Who restrains the restrainers? Hobbes saw the choices as either chaos or tyranny. He opted for the latter.

I largely agree with Hobbes' analysis but I reject his conclusion. There seems to me to be a third way between absolutism and disorder. I am referring to the "spontaneous order" described by Hayek that naturally accompanies freedom and decentralization. Because human beings are predators by nature, no one should ever hold power over another. Freedom allows individuals the means to cooperate with others for the sake of their own mutual self-interest without resorting to force or coercion. Anarchism is the political philosophy most capable of accommodating the greatest diversity of value systems, thereby minimizing the harm generated by social conflict. The idea of dispersion of power inherent in anarchism serves to erect a safeguard against the disasters that typically accompany concentrations of power. The result is a natural, organic order that tends towards the stabilization and harmonization of society. However, I do not regard this realization as grounds for any sort of objective morality. None of this has anything to say concerning the matter as to whether economic prosperity, social peace, and individual freedom are desirable ends in and of themselves. The conservative icon Russell Kirk regarded liberty as defensible only as a means to "virtue," however defined. Some argue that peace and prosperity breed weakness, mediocrity, and selfishness. Mussolini maintained that war is good because it advances the strong and eliminates the weak thereby contributing to the overall improvement of the species.

Like Bertrand Russell, I tend to regard moral questions as matters of subjective individual emotions and opinions. Ultimately, existence is predicated on Stirner's amoral war of each against all. Does this absence of any objective morality mean that "everything is permitted" as Nietzsche insisted? While there may be no abstract, metaphysical, cosmic source of moral imperatives, human beings are still bound by natural and physical laws (though some postmodern thinkers seem to deny even this). Means have to be consistent with the ends one wishes to pursue. Machiavelli regarded "morality" as a matter of simple expediency in the maintenance of power. The flip side of this, and a matter of supreme importance for anarchists, involves those who would resist power. Here a type of "reverse Machiavellianism" comes into play where the moral means is that which furthers resistance to power. The implication of this is that our struggle against the state is neither moral nor intellectual but physical. Does this mean that "might makes right"? No, it means that "might makes might" with "right" being an individual value judgment. Those among us who have decided that freedom and anarchism are "right," for whatever reason, need to acquire the might necessary to achieve our objectives.

This is a question that I struggled with for some years. When I first started out in this fight, I was a much more orthodox leftist that I am now and held views not unlike the Rousseauian-Hegelian perspective described above. When I became interested in free market economics, I was initially attracted to Rothbard's natural rights theory but eventually dismissed it as wishful thinking. The way I finally worked it out was when I watched a documentary on public television concerning the early 1960s trial of Nazi mass murderer and war criminal Adolf Eichmann. I kept asking myself, what made me right and what made Eichmann wrong? The matter of sheer self-interest? I would not want to live under a Nazi state. Natural sympathy? I had a certain empathic regard for those exterminated in the ovens and gas chambers. Logical principles? I could see no basis for the extermination programs as far as matters of expediency were concerned. Yet Eichmann's self-interest and sympathies were clearly much different from mine and irrationalism is a core tenet of Nazism.

The theologian C. S. Lewis once remarked:

> What was the sense in saying the enemy [i.e., the Nazis] were in the wrong unless Right is a real thing which the Nazis at bottom knew as well as we did and ought to have practised? If they had no notion of what we mean by right, then, though we might still have had to fight them, we could no more have blamed them for that than for the colour of their hair.

25

Yet, as Noam Chomsky has repeatedly pointed out, the Nazi archives provide ample evidence of the Nazis' conviction of the rightness of their cause. The key part of Lewis' statement is "we might still have had to fight them." Questions of self-interest, natural sympathies, and practical social considerations are in and of themselves sufficient reason to resist phenomenon such as Nazism. No objective morality is necessary.

As mentioned, our struggle against the state is primarily physical in nature. If someone is motivated to fight the state because they believe in "natural rights" or that anarchism will produce "the greatest good for the greatest number," then more power to them. Myths can be a source of inspiration in any conflict.

However, the real issue involves the need for our anarchist popular organizations, intermediary institutions, citizen militias, economic enterprises, common law courts, and other forms of organization needed to obtain the resources, influence, and raw social power, in the Nockian sense, to bring down the state and prevent its return by violent means if necessary. All of the moral theory and academic analysis in the universe will be insufficient if we cannot physically resist our enemies.

Ernst Jünger: The Resolute Life of an Anarch

Perhaps the most interesting, poignant, and, possibly, threatening type of writer and thinker is the one who not only defies conventional categorizations of thought but also offers a deeply penetrating critique of those illusions many hold to be the most sacred. Ernst Jünger (1895–1998), who first came to literary prominence during Germany's Weimar era as a diarist of the experiences of a front line storm trooper during the Great War, is one such writer. Both the controversial nature of his writing and its staying power are demonstrated by the fact that he remains one of the most important yet widely disliked literary and cultural figures of twentieth-century Germany. As recently as 1993, when Jünger was ninety-eight years of age, he was the subject of an intensely hostile exchange in the *New York Review of Books* between an admirer and a detractor of his work.[1] On the occasion of his hundredth birthday in 1995, Jünger was the subject of a scathing, derisive musical performed in East Berlin. Yet Jünger was also the recipient of Germany's most prestigious literary awards, the Goethe Prize and the Schiller Memorial Prize. Jünger, who converted to Catholicism at the age of 101, received a commendation from Pope John Paul II and was an honored guest of French President François Mitterrand and German Chancellor Helmut Kohl at the Franco-German reconciliation ceremony at Verdun in 1984. Though he was an exceptional achiever during virtually every stage of his extraordinarily long life, it was his work during the Weimar period that not only secured for a Jünger a presence in German cultural and political history, but also became

---

1   Ian Buruma, "The Anarch at Twilight," *New York Review of Books* 40, no. 12 (June 24, 1993); Hilary Barr, "An Exchange on Ernst Jünger," *New York Review of Books* 40, no. 21 (December 16, 1993).

the standard by which much of his later work was evaluated and by which his reputation was, and still is, debated.[2]

Ernst Jünger was born on March 29, 1895, in Heidelberg and raised in Hanover. His father, also named Ernst, was an academically trained chemist who became wealthy as the owner of a pharmaceutical manufacturing business, becoming successful enough to effectively retire while he was still in his forties. Though raised as an evangelical Protestant, Jünger's father did not believe in any formal religion, nor did his mother, Karoline, an educated middle class German woman whose interests included Germany's rich literary tradition and the cause of women's emancipation. His parents' politics seem to have been liberal, though not radical, in the manner not uncommon to the rising bourgeoisie of Germany's upper middle class during the pre-war period. It was in this affluent, secure bourgeois environment that Ernst Jünger grew up. Indeed, many of Jünger's later activities and professed beliefs are easily understood as a revolt against the comfort and safety of his upbringing. As a child, he was an avid reader of the tales of adventurers and soldiers, but an indifferent student who did not adjust well to the regimented Prussian educational system. Jünger's instructors consistently complained of his inattentiveness. As an adolescent, he became involved with the *Wandervogel*, roughly the German equivalent of the Boy Scouts.[3]

It was while attending a boarding school near his parents' home in 1913, at the age of seventeen, that Jünger first demonstrated his first propensity for what might be called an "adventurous" way of life. With only six months left before graduation, Jünger left school, leaving no word to his family as to his destination. Using money given to him for school-related fees and expenses to buy a firearm and a railroad ticket to Verdun, Jünger subsequently enlisted in the French Foreign Legion, an elite military unit of

---

2   Thomas R. Nevin, *Ernst Jünger and Germany: Into the Abyss, 1914-1945* (Durham, NC: Duke University Press, 1996), 1–7; Gerhard Loose, *Ernst Jünger* (New York: Twayne Publishers, 1974), preface.

3   Nevin, *Ernst Jünger and Germany*, 9–26; Loose, *Ernst Jünger*, 21.

the French armed forces that accepted enlistees of any nationality and had a reputation for attracting fugitives, criminals, and mercenaries. Jünger had no intention of staying with the Legion. He only wanted to be posted to Africa, as he eventually was. Jünger then deserted, only to be captured and sentenced to jail. Eventually his father found a capable lawyer for his wayward son and secured his release. Jünger then returned to his studies and underwent a belated high school graduation. However, it was only a very short time later that Jünger was back in uniform.[4]

Warrior and War Diarist

Ernst Jünger immediately volunteered for military service when he heard the news that Germany was at war in the summer of 1914. After two months of training, Jünger was assigned to a reserve unit stationed at Champagne. He was afraid the war would end before he had the opportunity to see any action. This attitude was not uncommon among many recruits or conscripts who fought in the war for their respective states. The question immediately arises at to why so many young people would wish to look into the face of death with such enthusiasm. Perhaps they really did not understand the horrors that awaited them. In Jünger's case, his rebellion against the security and luxury of his bourgeois upbringing had already been amply demonstrated by his excursion with the French Foreign Legion. Because of his high school education, something that soldiers of more proletarian origins lacked, Jünger was selected to train to become an officer. Shortly before beginning his officer's training, Jünger was exposed to combat for the first time. From the start, he carried pocket-sized notebooks in which he recorded his observations on the front lines. His writings while at the front exhibit a distinctive tone of detachment, as though he is simply an observer watching while the enemy fires at others. In the middle part of 1915, Jünger suffered his first war wound, a bullet graze to the thigh that required only two weeks of recovery time. Afterwards, he was promoted to the rank of lieutenant.[5]

---

4   Loose, *Ernst Jünger*, 22; Nevin, *Ernst Jünger and Germany*, 27–37.

5   Nevin, *Ernst Jünger and Germany*, 49.

At age twenty-one, Jünger was the leader of a reconnaissance team at the Somme whose purpose was to go out at night and search for British landmines. Early on, he acquired the reputation of a brave soldier who lacked the preoccupation with personal safety common to most of the fighting men. The introduction of steel artifacts into the war, tanks for the British side and steel helmets for the Germans, made a deep impression on Jünger. Wounded three times at the Somme, Jünger was awarded the Iron Cross, First Class. Upon recovery, he returned to the front lines. A combat daredevil, he once held out against a much larger British force with only twenty men. After being transferred to fight the French at Flanders, he lost ten of his fourteen men and was wounded in the left hand by a blast from a French shell. After being harshly criticized by a superior officer for the number of men lost on that particular mission, Jünger began to develop contempt for the military hierarchy whom he regarded as having achieved their status as a result of their class position, frequently lacking combat experience of their own. In late 1917, having already experienced nearly three full years of combat, Jünger was wounded for the fifth time during a surprise assault by the British. He was grazed in the head by a bullet, acquiring two holes in his helmet in the process. His performance in this battle won him the Knight's Cross of the Hohenzollerns. In March 1918, Jünger participated in another fierce battle with the British, losing 87 of his 150 men.[6]

Nothing impressed Jünger more than personal bravery and endurance on the part of soldiers. He once "fell to the ground in tears" at the sight of a young recruit who had only days earlier been unable to carry an ammunition case by himself suddenly being able to carry two cases of ammunition after surviving an attack of British shells.

A recurring theme in Jünger's writings on his war experiences is the way in which war brings out the most savage human impulses. Essentially, human beings are given full license to

6   Ibid., 57.

engage in behavior that would be considered criminal during peacetime. He wrote casually about burning occupied towns during the course of retreat or a shift of position. However, Jünger also demonstrated a capacity for merciful behavior during his combat efforts. He refrained from shooting a cornered British soldier after the foe displayed a portrait of his family to Jünger. He was wounded yet again in August of 1918. Having been shot in the chest and directly through a lung, this was his most serious wound yet. After being hit, he still managed to shoot dead yet another British officer. As Jünger was being carried off the battlefield on a stretcher, one of the stretcher carriers was killed by a British bullet. Another German soldier attempted to carry Jünger on his back, but the soldier was shot dead himself and Jünger fell to the ground. Finally, a medic recovered him and pulled him out of harm's way. This episode would be the end of his battle experiences during the Great War.[7]

In Storms of Steel

Jünger's keeping of his wartime diaries paid off quite well in the long run. They were to become the basis of his first and most famous book, *In Storms of Steel*, published in 1920. The title was given to the book by Jünger himself, having found the phrase in an old Icelandic saga. It was at the suggestion of his father that Jünger first sought to have his wartime memoirs published. Initially, he found no takers, antiwar sentiment being extremely high in Germany at the time, until his father at last arranged to have the work published privately. *In Storms of Steel* differs considerably from similar works published by war veterans during the same era, such as Erich Maria Remarque's *All Quiet on the Western Front* and John Dos Passos' *Three Soldiers*. Jünger's book reflects none of the disillusionment with war by those experienced in its horrors of the kind found in these other works. Instead, Jünger depicted warfare as an adventure in which the soldier faced the highest possible challenge, a battle to the death with a mortal enemy. Though Jünger certainly regarded himself as a patriot

---

7   Ibid., 61.

and, under the influence of Maurice Barrès,[8] eventually became a strident German nationalist, his depiction of military combat as an idyllic setting where human wills face the supreme test rose far above ordinary nationalist sentiments. Jünger's warrior ideal was not merely the patriot with a profound sense of loyalty to his country, nor the stereotype of the dutiful soldier whose sense of honor and obedience compels him to follow the orders of his superiors in a headlong march towards death. Nor was the warrior prototype exalted by Jünger necessarily an idealist fighting for some alleged greater good such as a political ideal or religious devotion. Instead, war itself is the ideal for Jünger. On this question, he was profoundly influenced by Nietzsche, whose dictum "a good war justifies any cause," provides an apt characterization of Jünger's depiction of the life (and death) of the combat soldier.[9]

This aspect of Jünger's outlook is illustrated quite well by the ending he chose to give to the first edition of *In Storms of Steel*. Although the second edition (published in 1926) ends with the nationalist rallying cry, "Germany lives and shall never go under!," a sentiment that was deleted for the third edition published in 1934 at the onset of the Nazi era, the original edition ends simply with Jünger in the hospital after being wounded for the final time and receiving word that he has received yet another commendation for his valor as a combat soldier. There is no mention of Germany's defeat a few months later. Nationalism aside, the book is clearly about Jünger and not about Germany. Jünger's depiction of the war displays an extraordinary level of detachment for someone who lived in the face of death for four years. It is a highly personalized account of the war where battle is first and foremost about the assertion of one's own "will to power." Clichéd patriotic pieties are, at most, a secondary concern.

---

8   Maurice Barrès (1862–1923) was a French novelist, journalist, anti-Semite, and nationalist politician and agitator.

9   Nevin, *Ernst Jünger and Germany*, 58, 71, 97.

Indeed, Jünger goes so far as to say there were winners and losers on both sides of the war. The true winners were not those who fought in a particular army or for a particular country, but who rose to the challenge placed before them and essentially achieved what Jünger regarded as a higher state of enlightenment. He believed the war had revealed certain fundamental truths about the human condition. First, the illusions of the old bourgeois order concerning peace, progress, and prosperity had been irrevocably shattered. This was not an uncommon sentiment during that time, but it is a revelation that Jünger seems to revel in while others found it to be overwhelmingly devastating. Indeed, the lifelong champion of Enlightenment liberalism, Bertrand Russell, whose life was almost as long as Jünger's and who observed many of the same events from a very different philosophical perspective, once remarked that no one who had been born before 1914 knew what it was like to be truly happy.[10]

A second observation advanced by Jünger had to do with the role of technology in transforming the nature of war, not only in a purely mechanical sense, but on a much deeper existential level. Before, man had commanded weaponry in the course of combat. Now weaponry of the kind made possible by modern technology and industrial civilization essentially commanded man. The machines did the fighting. Man simply resisted this external domination. Lastly, the supremacy of might and the ruthless nature of human existence had been demonstrated. Nietzsche was right. The tragic, Darwinian nature of the human condition had been revealed as an irrevocable law.

In Storms of Steel was only the first of several works based on his experiences as a combat officer that were produced by Jünger during the 1920s. *Copse 125* described a battle between two small groups of combatants. In this work, Jünger continued to explore the philosophical themes present in his first work. The type of technologically driven warfare that emerged during the Great

10 Hermann Weyl, review of *The Philosophy of Bertrand Russell*, edited by P. A. Schilpp, *The American Mathematical Monthly* 53, no. 4 (April 1946): 208–14.

33

War is characterized as reducing men to automatons driven by airplanes, tanks, and machine guns. Once again, jingoistic nationalism is downplayed as a contributing factor to the essence of combat soldier's spirit.

Another work of Jünger's from the early 1920s, *Battle as Inner Experience*, explored the psychology of war. Jünger suggested that civilization itself was but a mere mask for the "primordial" nature of humanity that once again reveals itself during war. Indeed, war had the effect of elevating humanity to a higher level. The warrior becomes a kind of godlike animal, divine in his superhuman qualities, but animalistic in his bloodlust. The constant threat of imminent death is a kind of intoxicant. Life is at its finest when death is closest. Jünger described war as a struggle for a cause that overshadows the respective political or cultural ideals of the combatants. This overarching cause is courage. The fighter is honor bound to respect the courage of his mortal enemy. Drawing on the philosophy of Nietzsche, Jünger argued that the war had produced a "new race" that had replaced the old pieties, such as those drawn from religion, with a new recognition of the primacy of the "will to power."[11]

Conservative Revolutionary

Jünger's writings about the war quickly earned him the status of a celebrity during the Weimar period. *Battle as Inner Experience* contained the prescient suggestion that the young men who had experienced the greatest war the world had yet to see at that point could never be successfully reintegrated into the old bourgeois order from which they came. For these fighters, the war had been a spiritual experience. Having endured so much only to see their side lose on humiliating terms, the veterans of the war were hostile to the rationalistic, anti-militarist, liberal republic that emerged in 1918 at the close of the war. Jünger was at his parents' home recovering from war wounds during the time of the attempted coup by the leftist workers' and soldiers'

11   Nevin, *Ernst Jünger and Germany*, 122, 125, 134, 136, 140, 173.

councils and its subsequent suppression by the Freikorps. He experimented with psychoactive drugs such as cocaine and opium during this time, something that he would continue to do much later in life. Upon recovery, he went back into active duty in the much diminished Germany army. Jünger's earliest works, such as *In Storms of Steel*, were published during this time and he also wrote for military journals on the more technical and specialized aspects of combat and military technology. Interestingly, Jünger attributed Germany's defeat in the war simply to poor military and civilian leadership, and rejected the "stab in the back" legend that consoled other veterans.

After leaving the army in 1923, Jünger continued to write, producing a novella about a soldier during the war titled *Sturm*, and also began to study the philosophy of Oswald Spengler. His first work as a philosopher of nationalism appeared in the *Völkischer Beobachter*, a Nazi newspaper, in September 1923. Critiquing the failed Marxist revolution of 1918, Jünger argued that the leftist coup failed because of its lack of fresh ideas. It was simply a regurgitation of the egalitarian outlook of the French Revolution. In Jünger's view, the revolutionary left appealed only to the material wants of the German people. A successful revolution would have to do much more than that. It would have to appeal to their spiritual or "folkish" instincts as well. Over the next few years Jünger studied the natural sciences at the University of Leipzig and in 1925, at age thirty, he married nineteen-year-old Gretha von Jeinsen. Around this time, he also became a full-time political writer. Jünger was hostile to Weimar democracy and its commercially oriented society. His emerging political ideal was one of an elite warrior caste that stood above petty partisan politics and the middle class obsession with material acquisition. Jünger became involved with the Stahlhelm, a right-wing veterans group, and was a contributor to its newspaper, *Die Standarte*. He associated himself with the younger, more militant members of the organization who favored an uncompromising nationalist revolution and rejected the parliamentary system. Jünger's weekly column in *Die Standarte* disseminated his nationalist ideology to his less educated readers. Jünger's views at this point were a mixture of Spengler, social Darwinism, the traditionalist philosophy of the French rightist Maurice Barrès, opposition to the internationalism of the left that had seemingly been discredited by the events of 1914, anti-rationalism, and anti-parliamentarianism. He took a favorable view of the working class and praised the Nazis' efforts to win proletarian support. Jünger also argued that a nationalist outlook need not be attached to one particular form of government, even suggesting that a liberal monarchy would be inferior to a nationalist republic.[12]

In an essay for *Die Standarte* titled "The Machine," Jünger argued that the principal struggle was not between social classes or political parties but between man and technology. He was not anti-technological in a Luddite sense, but regarded the technological apparatus of modernity to have achieved a position of superiority over mankind which needed to be reversed. He was concerned that the mechanized efficiency of modern life produced a corrosive effect on the human spirit. Jünger considered the Nazis' glorification of peasant life to be antiquated. Ever the realist, he believed the rural world to be in a state of irreversible decline. Instead, Jünger espoused a "metropolitan nationalism" centered on the urban working class. Nationalism was the antidote to the anti-particular materialism of the Marxists who, in Jünger's views, simply mirrored the liberals in their efforts to reduce the individual to a component of a mechanized mass society. Jünger dismissed the humanitarian rhetoric of the left as the hypocritical cant of power-seekers feigning benevolence. He began to pin his hopes for a nationalist revolution on the younger veterans who comprised much of the urban working class.

In 1926, Jünger became the editor of *Arminius*, which also featured the writings of Nazi leaders like Alfred Rosenberg and Joseph Goebbels. In 1927, he contributed his final article to the *Völkischer Beobachter*, calling for a new definition of the "worker," one not rooted in Marxist ideology but the idea of the worker as

12   Ibid., 75–91.

a civilian counterpart to the soldier who struggles fervently for the nationalist ideal. Jünger and Hitler had exchanged copies of their respective writings and a scheduled meeting between the two was canceled due to a change in Hitler's itinerary. Jünger respected Hitler's abilities as an orator, but came to feel he lacked the ability to become a true leader. He also regarded Nazi ideology as intellectually shallow and many Nazi leaders as talentless, and was displeased by the vulgarity, crassly opportunistic, and overly theatrical aspects of Nazi public rallies. Always an elitist, Jünger considered the Nazis' pandering to the common people to be debased. As he became more skeptical of the Nazis, Jünger began writing for a wider circle of readers beyond that of the militant nationalist right wing. His works began to appear in the Jewish liberal Leopold Schwarzschild's *Das Tagebuch* and the "national-bolshevik" Ernst Niekisch's *Widerstand*.

Jünger began to assemble around himself an elite corps of bohemian, eccentric intellectuals who would meet regularly on Friday evenings. This group included some of the most interesting personalities of the Weimar period. Among them were the Freikorps veteran Ernst von Salomon, the anti-Hitler Nazi Otto Strasser, the national-bolshevik Niekisch, the Jewish anarchist Erich Mühsam, who had figured prominently in the early phase of the failed leftist revolution of 1918, the American writer Thomas Wolfe, and the expressionist writer Arnolt Bronnen. Many among this group espoused a type of revolutionary socialism based on nationalism rather than class, disdaining the Nazis' opportunistic outreach efforts to the middle class. Some, like Niekisch, favored an alliance between Germany and Soviet Russia against the liberal-capitalist powers of the West. Occasionally, Joseph Goebbels would turn up at these meetings hoping to convert members of the group, particularly Jünger himself, whose war writings he had admired, to the Nazi cause. These efforts by the Nazi propaganda master proved unsuccessful. Jünger regarded Goebbels as a shallow ideologue who spoke in platitudes even in private conversation.[13]

---

13   Ibid., 107.

The final break between Ernst Jünger and the NSDAP occurred in September 1929. Jünger published an article in Schwarzschild's *Tagebuch* attacking and ridiculing the Nazis as sell-outs for having reinvented themselves as a parliamentary party. He also ridiculed their racism and anti-Semitism, stating that according to the Nazis a nationalist is simply someone who "eats three Jews for breakfast." He condemned the Nazis for pandering to the liberal middle class and reactionary traditional conservatives "with lengthy tirades against the decline in morals, against abortion, strikes, lockouts, and the reduction of police and military forces." Goebbels responded by attacking Jünger in the Nazi press, accusing him of being motivated by personal literary ambition, and insisting this had caused him "to vilify the national socialist movement, probably so as to make himself popular in his new kosher surroundings" and dismissing Jünger's attacks by proclaiming the Nazis did not "debate with renegades who abuse us in the smutty press of Jewish traitors."[14]

Jünger on the Jewish Question

Jünger held complicated views on the question of German Jews. He considered anti-Semitism of the type espoused by Hitler to be crude and reactionary. Yet his own version of nationalism required a level of homogeneity that was difficult to reconcile with the sub-national status of Germany Jewry. Jünger suggested that Jews should assimilate and pledge their loyalty to Germany once and for all. Yet he expressed admiration for Orthodox Judaism and indifference to Zionism. Jünger maintained personal friendships with Jews and wrote for a Jewish-owned publication. During this time his Jewish publisher Schwarzschild published an article examining Jünger's views on the Jews of Germany. Schwarzschild insisted that Jünger was nothing like his Nazi rivals on the far right. Jünger's nationalism was based on an aristocratic warrior ethos, while Hitler's movement was more comparable to the criminal underworld. Hitler's men were "plebeian alley scum." However, Schwarzschild also characterized Jünger's rendition of

---

14   Ibid., 108.

nationalism as motivated by little more than a fervent rejection of bourgeois society and lacking in attention to political realities and serious economic questions.[15]

The Worker

Other than *In Storms of Steel*, Jünger's *The Worker: Mastery and Form* was his most significant work from the Weimar era. Jünger would later distance himself from this work, which was first published in 1932 and reprinted in 1963 only after Jünger was prompted to do so by Martin Heidegger. In *The Worker*, Jünger outlines his vision of a future state ordered as a technocracy based on workers and soldiers led by a warrior elite. Workers are no longer simply components of an industrial machine, either capitalist or communist, but have become a kind of civilian-soldier operating as an economic warrior. Just as the soldier glories in his accomplishments in battle, so does the worker glory in the achievements expressed through his work. Jünger predicted that continued technological advancements would render the worker/capitalist dichotomy obsolete. He also incorporated the political philosophy of his friend Carl Schmitt into his world view. As Schmitt saw international relations as a Hobbesian battle between rival powers, Jünger believed each state would eventually adopt a system not unlike what he described in *The Worker*. Each state would maintain its own technocratic order with the workers and soldiers of each country playing essentially the same role on behalf of their respective nations. International affairs would be a crucible where the will to power of the different nations would be tested. Jünger's vision contains certain amounts of prescience. The general trend in politics at the time was a movement towards the kind of technocratic state Jünger described. These took on many varied forms, including German National Socialism, Italian Fascism, Soviet Communism, the emerging welfare states of Western Europe, and America's New Deal. Coming on the eve of the Second World War, Jünger's prediction of a global Hobbesian

15   Ibid., 109–11.

struggle between national collectivities possessing previously unimagined levels of technological sophistication also seems rather prophetic. Jünger once again attacked the bourgeoisie as anachronistic, regarding its values of luxury and safety as unfit for the violent world of the future.[16]

The National Socialist Era

By the time Hitler came to power in 1933, Jünger's war writings had become commonly used in high schools and universities as examples of wartime literature, and Jünger enjoyed success within the context of German popular culture as well. Excerpts of Jünger's works were featured in military journals. The Nazis tried to co-opt his semi-celebrity status, but he was uncooperative. Jünger was nominated for the Nazified German Academy of Poetry, but declined the position. When the *Völkischer Beobachter* published some of his work in 1934, Jünger wrote a letter of protest. The Nazi regime, despite its best efforts to capitalize on his reputation, viewed Jünger with suspicion. His past association with the national-bolshevik Ernst Niekisch, the Jewish anarchist Erich Mühsam, and the anti-Hitler Nazi Otto Strasser, all of whom were either eventually imprisoned, killed, or exiled by the Third Reich, led the Nazis to regard Jünger as a potential subversive. On several occasions, Jünger received visits from the Gestapo in search of some of his former friends. During the early years of the Nazi regime, Jünger was in the fortunate position of being able to afford travel outside of Germany. He journeyed to Norway, Brazil, Greece, and Morocco during this time, and published several works based on his travels.[17]

Jünger's most significant work from the Nazi period is the novel *On the Marble Cliffs*. The book is an allegorical attack on the Hitler regime. It was written in 1939, the same year that Jünger re-entered the German army. The book describes a mysterious villain who threatens a community, a sinister warlord called

16   Ibid., 114–40.

17   Ibid., 145.

the "Head Ranger." This character is never featured in the plot of the novel, but maintains a universally foreboding presence (much like "Big Brother" in George Orwell's *1984*). Another character in the novel, "Braquemart," is described as having physical characteristics remarkably similar to those of Goebbels. The book sold fourteen thousand copies during its first two weeks in publication. Swiss reviewers immediately recognized the allegorical references to the Nazi state in the novel. The Nazi Party's organ, the *Völkischer Beobachter*, stated that Ernst Jünger was inviting a bullet to the head. Goebbels urged Hitler to ban the book, but Hitler refused, probably not wanting to show his hand. Indeed, Hitler gave orders that Jünger not be harmed.[18]

Jünger was stationed in France for most of the Second World War. Once again, he kept diaries of the experience. Once again, he expressed concern that he might not get to see any action before the war was over. While Jünger did not have the opportunity to experience the level of danger and daredevil heroics he had during the Great War, he did receive yet another medal, the Iron Cross, for retrieving the body of a dead lance-corporal while under heavy fire. Jünger also published some of his war diaries during this time. However, the German government took a dim view of these, viewing them as too sympathetic to the occupied French. Jünger's duties included censorship of the mail coming into France from German civilians. He took a rather liberal approach to this responsibility and simply disposed of incriminating documents rather than turn them over for investigation. In doing so, he probably saved lives. He also encountered members of France's literary and cultural elite, among them the author Louis-Ferdinand Céline, a raving anti-Semite who suggested Hitler's harsh measures against the Jews had not been heavy-handed enough. As rumors of the Nazi extermination programs began to spread, Jünger wrote in his diary that the mechanization of the human spirit of the type he had written about in the past had apparently generated a higher level of human depravity. When he saw three young French-

18   Ibid., 162.

Jewish girls wearing the yellow stars required by the Nazis, he wrote that he felt embarrassed to be in the Nazi army. In July of 1942, Jünger observed the mass arrest of French Jews, the beginning of the implementation of the "Final Solution." He described the scene as follows:

> Parents were first separated from their children, so there was wailing to be heard in the streets. At no moment may I forget that I am surrounded by the unfortunate, by those suffering to the very depths, else what sort of person, what sort of officer would I be? The uniform obliges one to grant protection wherever it goes. Of course one has the impression that one must also, like Don Quixote, take on millions.[19]

An entry into Jünger's diary from October 16, 1943, suggests that an unnamed army officer had told Jünger about the use of crematoria and poison gas to murder Jews en masse. Rumors of plots against Hitler circulated among the officers with whom Jünger maintained contact. His son, Ernstel, was arrested after an informant claimed he had spoken critically of Hitler. Ernstel Jünger was imprisoned for three months and then placed in a penal battalion, where he was killed in action in Italy. On July 20, 1944, an unsuccessful assassination attempt was carried out against Hitler. It is still disputed as to whether or not Jünger knew of the plot or had a role in its planning. Among those arrested for their role in the attempt on Hitler's life were members of Jünger's immediate circle of associates and superior officers within the German army. Jünger was dishonorably discharged shortly afterward.[20]

Following the close of the Second World War, Jünger came under suspicion from the Allied occupational authorities because of his far right-wing nationalist and militarist past. He refused to cooperate with the Allied denazification program and was barred

19 Ibid., 189.

20 Ibid., 209.

from publishing for four years. He would go on to live another half century, producing many more literary works, becoming a close friend of Albert Hofmann, the inventor of the hallucinogen LSD, with which he experimented. In a 1977 novel, *Eumeswil*, he took his tendency towards viewing the world around him with detachment to a newer, more clearly articulated level with his invention of the concept of the "Anarch." This idea, heavily influenced by the writings of the early nineteenth-century German philosopher Max Stirner, championed the solitary individual who remains true to himself within the context of whatever external circumstances happen to be present. Some sample quotations from this work illustrate the philosophy and world view of the elderly Jünger quite well:

> For the anarch, things are not so simple, especially when he has a background in history. If he remains free of being ruled, whether by sovereigns or by society, this does not mean that he refuses to serve in any way. In general, he serves no worse than anyone else, and sometimes even better, if he likes the game. He only holds back from the pledge, the sacrifice, the ultimate devotion. . . . I serve in the Casbah; if, while so doing, I die for the Condor, it would be an accident, perhaps even an obliging gesture, but nothing more.[21]

> The egalitarian mania of demagogues is even more dangerous than the brutality of men in gallooned coats. For the anarch, this remains theoretical, because he avoids both sides. Anyone who has been oppressed can get back on his feet if the oppression has not cost him his life. A man who has been equalized is physically and morally ruined. Anyone who is different is not equal; that is one of the reasons why the Jews are so often targeted.[22]

---

21 Ernst Jünger, *Eumeswil*, trans. Joachim Neugroschel (New York: Marsilio Publishers, 1993 [1977]), 148.

22 Ibid., 188.

The anarch, recognizing no government, but not indulging in paradisal dreams as the anarchist does, is, for that very reason, a neutral observer.[23]

Opposition is collaboration.[24]

A basic theme for the anarch is how man, left to his own devices, can defy superior forces—whether state, society, or the elements—by making use of their rules without submitting to them.[25]

...malcontents...prowl through the institutions, eternally dissatisfied, always disappointed. Connected with this is their love of cellars and rooftops, exile and prisons, and also banishment, on which they actually pride themselves. When the structure finally caves in, they are the first to be killed in the collapse. Why do they not know that the world remains unalterable in change? Because they never find their way down to its real depth, their own. That is the sole place of essence, safety. And so they do themselves in.[26]

The anarch may . . . not be spared prisons—as one fluke of existence among others. He will then find the fault in himself.[27]

We are touching upon a . . . distinction between anarch and anarchist; the relation to authority, to legislative power. The anarchist is their mortal enemy while the anarch refuses to acknowledge them. He seeks neither to gain hold of them, nor to topple them, nor to alter them—their impact bypasses him. He must resign himself only to the whirlwinds they generate.[28]

The anarch is no individualist, either. He wishes to present

---

23   Ibid.
24   Ibid., 227.
25   Ibid., 241.
26   Ibid., 279.
27   Ibid.
28   Ibid., 280.

himself neither as a Great Man nor as a Free Spirit. His own measure is enough for him; freedom is not his goal; it is his property. He does not come on as a foe or reformer: one can get along nicely with him in shacks or in palaces. Life is too short and too beautiful to sacrifice it for ideas, although contamination is not always avoidable. But hats off to the martyrs.[29]

We can expect as little from society as from the state. Salvation lies in the individual.[30]

29   Ibid.
30   Ibid

Part 2 - Critiquing the Global Order of Neoliberal Imperialism

Philosophical Anarchism and the Death of Empire

Note: What follows is an effort, however humble, to apply traditional anarchist theory to the world situation we contemporary radicals currently find ourselves in, particularly the emergence of the New World Order, the ongoing dilemma of the Leviathan state, and the uniquely subtle form of totalitarianism that has caught the fancy of the elites of the First World nations, so-called "political correctness." What I have tried to develop is a kind of "big picture" anarchism, an anarchism that confronts the aforementioned issues head-on, without the distractions that preoccupy most of those in conventional anarchist circles (anti-racism, ecology, popular left-wing causes, particular economic positions, etc.).

I have developed something of a reputation for myself as a staunch proponent of jettisoning the conventional "left/right" model of the political spectrum. In this article, I attempt to carry this idea even further. Specifically, I reject the linear, "progressive" view of history implicit in much contemporary political thought in favor of an approach that somewhat approximates the cyclical view suggested by Nietzsche. Additionally, I am increasingly drawn to the view that the most serious intellectual problem of our time, at least with regards to political philosophy and social theory, is the universalist presumption adhered to by virtually all modern political thinkers, whether they be of the liberal,

47

Marxist, conservative, neoconservative, libertarian, or left-anarchist variety. Additionally, the world's two largest religions, Christianity and Islam, along with the increasing monistic humanism that dominates the intellectual culture of the West, include fairly powerful universalist strands as well.

Lawrence Dennis considered the most negative attribute of the Enlightenment era to be the tendency to interpret the world from the perspective of abstract ideological principles regarded as above and beyond the lived experience of real world human beings. The influence of such thinking on the Jacobins during the period of the French Revolution, the perpetrators of the Napoleonic Wars, and the ideologies of the imperial powers that came to a head in the Second World War (liberalism, fascism, communism) has been previously noted by certain scholars. The French New Right theorist Alain de Benoist goes even further, arguing that the monotheistic orientation of the Judeo-Christian traditions, and the concurrent negating of all other gods and traditions, along with the supplanting by these of the earlier pagan views of divinity, provided the historical foundation for the universalist conceptions of the modern era.[1] Whatever the

---

1   Some clarification on this point is needed. While the term "Judeo-Christian" has become fashionable in modern times, Judaism and Christianity are two separate and distinct traditions. With regards to the question of universalism, Judaism is far less so than Christianity. Foundational Torah Judaism, the type still practiced by some sects like the Neturei Karta, is a profoundly particularistic religion—of the Jews, for the Jews, and by the Jews. Although Gentiles are allowed to convert, Judaism in this form is frequently regarded as being in many ways irrelevant to outsiders. Also, evidence exists that the early Hebrews were henotheistic rather than monotheistic, but simply recognized Yahweh as their ethnic god, in the same way that other eastern Mediterranean peoples recognized Baal. It was the apostate Jew Saul of Tarsus (later known as St. Paul the Apostle) who brought overtly universalistic conceptions into Judaism, apparently against the wishes of some of the earliest disciples of Jesus (Galatians 2:11–14). It could also be argued that the current showdown between Islam and the West, the "clash of civilizations" referred to by Samuel P. Huntington, is best understood as a religious war between two offshoots of Judaism and Christianity—Islam and Humanism. Says Tomislav Sunic: "Undoubtedly, many would admit that in the realm of ethics all men and women of the world are the children of Abraham. Indeed, even the bolder ones who somewhat self-righteously claim to have rejected the Christian or Jewish theologies, and who claim to have replaced them with 'secular humanism,' frequently ignore that their self-styled secular beliefs are firmly grounded in Judeo-Christian ethics. Abraham and Moses may be dethroned today, but their

case may be, it seems clear enough that the key to mounting an effective resistance to the New World Order is the cultivation of a cross-cultural ethic whereby a taboo is erected against the insistence that a specific world view be universalized. It would seem that philosophical anarchism is the political paradigm most compatible with the establishment of such a taboo.

The history of human civilization can be divided into three primary phases when considering the evolution of political institutions. The first of these involves an idea that might be described as "the divinity of kings." In the ancient civilizations of Egypt, Babylon, and Rome, the head of state was assigned a godlike status by custom, tradition, law, theology, and popular folklore alike. The early Roman Christians were sent to the lions for the crime of "atheism" which, in the theology of the Roman state religion, meant denial of the divinity of the emperor.[2] When Christianity went on to conquer Greco-Roman civilization, a new political theology evolved in the form of the "divine right of kings," meaning that the king ruled, not as a god himself, but as an earthly appointee of a Divine Other who had been providentially chosen to rule in the political realm just as the Pope ruled in the religious realm. A principal achievement of the Enlightenment of the seventeenth and eighteenth centuries was the demolition of the notion of the divine right of kings. Beginning with the American and French Revolutions of the eighteenth century, a third political paradigm has come to dominate human political life.

moral edicts and spiritual ordinances are very much alive. The global and disenchanted world, accompanied by the litany of human rights, ecumenical society, and the rule of law—are these not principles that can be directly traced to the Judeo-Christian messianic outlook that resurfaces today in its secular version under the elegant garb of modern 'progressive' ideologies?" ("Monotheism vs. Polytheism," by Alain de Benoist, Introduction and translation by Tomislav Sunic, Chronicles: A Magazine of American Culture, April 1996.)

2   Mosheim says of second-century Christians: "The simplicity of the worship which the Christians offered to the Deity gave occasion to certain calumnies maintained by both the Jews and the pagan priests. The Christians were pronounced atheists because they were destitute of temples, altars, victims, priests, and of all that pomp in which the vulgar suppose the essence of religion to consist." (Mosheim, *Ecclesiastical History*, bk. 1, chap. 4, par. 3.)

Against Democratism

This paradigm that is now nearly universal, at least in the advanced countries, is the paradigm of liberal democracy. It might be said that liberal democracy discards the "divine right of kings" for the "democratic right of the state." Most people in the modern world recognize the illegitimacy of fascist, Nazi, communist, monarchical, theocratic, aristocratic, and military forms of government. It is assumed by persons on all points of the political spectrum that a government is only legitimate if periodic elections are held, opposition parties are allowed to organize, and something resembling a "free press" exists. For example, American political culture includes Christian fundamentalists, economic nationalists, and anti-immigration proponents on the "far right," and Marxists, radical feminists, and postmodernists on the "far left." Yet all of these parties claim the banner of "democracy." Those who wish to censor speech that is deemed "hateful" or "obscene" do so under the guise of seemingly venerable democratic notions like "community standards," majoritarian preference, or social equality. Likewise, those who champion "free speech" do so under the seemingly democratic principle of free exchange of ideas and beliefs. Those favoring racial quotas or preferences cite the allegedly democratic principle of equal opportunity while those opposed to such preferences claim that individual responsibility and merit are essential to democracy. Both socialists and "free market" economists claim to be advocates of "economic democracy."

The underlying presumption behind all of these points of view is that virtually any course of action that the state pursues is acceptable so long as the state meets a few bare minimum standards of democracy like "free elections," "free speech," and so on.[3] It is said that the state exists on the basis of a "social contract"

3   For example, the renowned British historian Paul Johnson, a darling of
    neoconservatives, says of Jean-Paul Sartre: "Sartre never showed any real knowledge
    of or interest in—let alone enthusiasm for—parliamentary democracy. Having the
    vote in a multi-party society was not at all what he meant by freedom. What did he
    mean then?" (Paul Johnson, *Intellectuals* [New York: Harper and Row, 1988], 243.) It

and is a reflection of the "popular will." For these reasons, it is widely believed that individuals have an obligation to comply with the decrees of the state, whether in the matter of the payment of taxes, military conscription, weapons confiscation, the prohibition of particular social or cultural practices, or whatever. This common notion is what is meant by the "democratic right of the state." Behind the shield of "democracy," the state may do what it wishes to its subjects, who in turn have no one to blame for their predicament but themselves as they comprise the state, an expression of the "general will." The absurdity and illogic of this view ought to be obvious enough. Clearly, the dominant political paradigm of "democracy" is severely flawed.[4] A new paradigm is surely needed.

Philosophical anarchism holds that the institution of the state is undesirable and unnecessary, and that it should be eliminated in favor of voluntary association and cooperation among groups and individuals. A coherent anarchist would seek to replace the current political paradigm of liberal democracy with a new paradigm in the form of philosophical anarchism or, more specifically, a social order grounded on the principle of voluntary association. The traditional anarchist position regards the state as nothing more than a criminal organization that exists for no genuine purpose beyond the control of territory, the protection of an artificially privileged ruling class, the exploitation of its subjects, and the expansion of its own power. This perspective is consistent with numerous philosophical, ethical, and religious traditions. This was the position of both the classical anarchist theoreticians and modern libertarian-anarchists like Murray

---

is interesting that a figure as eminent as Johnson apparently cannot conceive of any form of freedom greater than run of the mill parliamentarianism. Has he ever read Mill, Spencer, Stirner, Proudhon, Mencken, Rothbard, Rand, or even Milton Friedman? Sartre's views could be muddled and inchoate at times, to say the least. But Johnson, a former Laborite journalist who went to neoconservatism in the 1970s, seems to have no more capacity for independent thinking than the typical Soviet commissar.

4   Hans-Hermann Hoppe virtually destroys the intellectual house of cards that modern democratist ideology is built on in *Democracy: The God That Failed* (New Brunswick: Transaction Publishers, 2001). See my "Democracy as Tyranny," http://attackthesystem.com/democracy-as-tyranny/.

Rothbard.[5] The anarchist position on the state is also supported by the sociologist Franz Oppenheimer's landmark study on the origin of the state and its roots in plunder and conquest.[6] Democratists have attempted to respond to the anarchist critique of the state by claiming that their preferred form of state is somehow different from older expressions of the state, usually rooting their claims in some sort of constitutionalist or majoritarian doctrine. Yet, the constitutionalist theory of the state has been comprehensively refuted by Lysander Spooner and his critique of "social contract" theory.[7] And virtually all reasonable political thinkers from Plato and Aristotle onward have recognized majoritarianism as nothing more than a form of mob rule.

The classical liberal economist William Graham Sumner once remarked that the day would come when men would be divided into only two political camps, anarchists and socialists, or, more descriptively of Sumner's views, statists and anti-statists.[8] Sumner's prediction is in the process of being realized as the statist ideology of mass democracy is becoming more and more universalized throughout the modern world. This process has produced some rather silly intellectual offshoots in the form of Francis Fukuyama's "End of History" theory and the "democratic

5   During the late twentieth century, Murray N. Rothbard (1926–95) developed a highly consistent and systematic version of "free-market" anarchism. The pillars of his outlook are Lockean natural rights theory, the Austrian school of economics developed by Ludwig von Mises and others, nineteenth-century individualist anarchism as espoused by Benjamin R. Tucker, and the isolationist foreign policy views championed by the America First Committee in the period leading up to the Second World War. Rothbard was a brilliant thinker and painstaking logician, though he tended towards dogmatism at times, and his insights into political economy carried with them implications even more radical than even he seemed to realize. The best introductions to Rothbard's outlook would likely be his Man, Economy and State (1962), Power and Market (1970), For a New Liberty (1974) and The Ethics of Liberty (1982). See also Justin Raimondo's biography of Rothbard, An Enemy of the State: The Life of Murray Rothbard (Amherst, NY: Prometheus Books, 2000).

6   Franz Oppenheimer, The State: Its History and Development Viewed Sociologically, trans. John M. Gitterman (New Brunswick: Transaction Publishers, 1999).

7   Lysander Spooner, No Treason: The Constitution of No Authority.

8   Pierre Lemieux, "Give Me Libertarianism," Financial Post, August 29, 2002.

imperialism" of the neoconservatives.[9] So pervasive is democratist ideology that even some anti-statists cannot separate "democracy" from their own critique of the state. For example, many left-wing anarchists claim "direct" or "consensus-based" democracy as their ideal.[10] So be it. The voluntary associations that would form the basis of an anarchist social order could indeed have democratic internal structures of some type. But anarchist theory no more mandates that an association have a democratic form of organization than it mandates an autocratic one. Similarly, aside from avowed anti-democrats like Hans-Hermann Hoppe, many libertarians speak of "democratic processes" and "democratic ideals," often going so far as to claim that the current system of electoral democracy is fundamentally legitimate but has only been corrupted by an excess of statism brought on by self-serving public interest groups, crooked politicians, a disproportionate amount of power in the hands of statist intellectuals, etc.[11]

Bob Black has noted that one of the foremost obstacles to the realization of anarchism is the anarchists themselves.[12] Frankly, many professed anarchists could not give a coherent description of anarchist theory or what an anarchist society, realistically

9   Francis Fukuyama, *The End of History and the Last Man* (New York: Free Press, 1992); Joshua Micah Marshall, "Remaking the World: Bush and the Neoconservatives," *Foreign Affairs* 82, no. 6 (November–December 2003); Lee McCracken, "The End of Conservatism," http://www.strike-the-root.com/3/mccracken/mccracken6.html.

10   I am consistently amazed at the large number of left-libertarians who somehow believe that "decentralized direct democracy" would be the realization their own sociocultural ideals. In many communities, such a system would likely result in the establishment of theocracy or a racialist or nationalist enclave, just as the establishment of conventional parliamentary democracy in contemporary Iraq would no doubt result in a Shiite fundamentalist regime. It is important that anarchists work to develop a critique of modern societies whose depth surpasses that of conventional leftist or left-liberal analysis and emphasis. "Democracy" is not a universal cure-all or absolute, nor is "peace," "justice," "freedom," feminism, environmentalism, anti-racism, or any other left-wing shibboleth. These ideals and tendencies are defined in different ways by different people, many times arising in response to specific historical or cultural situations that are inapplicable to other situations.

11   It should not take a genius of political science to understand that mobocracy and individualism are incompatible, but many libertarians make a tortured effort to reconcile these two.

12   Bob Black, "Anarchism and Other Impediments to Anarchy," http://www.primitivism.com/impediments.htm.

speaking, might look like to save their lives.[13] If anarchism is to be
defined by the principle of voluntary association, then a system
of radical individual autonomy is implied. Individual autonomy
of this type should not be confused with either licentiousness
or egocentrism. Instead, individual autonomy involves a social
order where individual persons choose for themselves the kinds
of associations, communities, and institutions they wish to be
connected to. Persons with different values, beliefs, interests,
or needs will form different kinds of associations. Elitists will
form elitist associations. Egalitarians will form egalitarian
associations. Socialists will form socialist associations. Racialists
will form racialist associations. A continuing theme of traditional
anarchism is Kropotkin's concept of "mutual aid," whereby people
cooperate with one another towards common ends.[14] But mutual
aid can occur only among people with common values and
objectives. Consequently, the overarching principle of voluntary
association implies that individuals and groups with conflicting
interests or goals will naturally separate themselves from one
another and practice mutual self-segregation. This in turn
implies a radically decentralized social system where different
kinds of cultural and ideological groups exercise sovereignty
within their own communities. Of course, a social order based
on perfect voluntarism or sovereignty may never be achieved
in the real world, which is why insightful libertarian theorists
including Pierre-Joseph Proudhon, Bertrand Russell, and Paul
Goodman have regarded "anarchy" as an ideal, like "peace" and
"justice," that humanity can only strive for.[15]

13   Keith Preston, "Anarchism or Anarcho-Social Democracy?," chapter 10 of this
     volume. For most contemporary anarchists, "anarchism" is a muddled utopian
     ideology implicitly influenced by Rousseauian or Fourierist ideas, often mixed with
     bits of Dadaist nihilism or a romantic attachment to the Old Left. Contemporary left-
     anarchism is also heavily influenced by Gramscian cultural Marxism, whereby racial
     minorities, feminists, and homosexuals take the place of the proletariat as the focus of
     the class struggle.

14   One of the founding fathers of classical anarchism, Peter Kropotkin was a pioneer if
     often unrecognized sociologist. Although a formidable social scientist and philosopher,
     he had a strong inclination towards the delusional utopianism that characterizes much
     nineteenth-century political thought. His best works are *Mutual Aid, The Conquest of
     Bread*, and *Ethics*.

15   Pierre-Joseph Proudhon, the first thinker to call himself an anarchist, in many ways

It is interesting to explore the objections that anti-anarchists raise against the anarchist position and equally interesting to review the criticisms that different schools of anarchism have of one another. Most reasonable criticisms of the anarchist position are rooted, at least implicitly, in the ideas of Hobbes. In the classical Hobbesian view, human beings left to their own devices exist only in a "state of nature," the essence of which is characterized as "a war of each against all." The Hobbesian "solution" to humanity's predicament is the establishment of a "sovereign" who wields absolute power for the sake of achieving order and making civilization possible.[16] One need not reject Hobbes' overall view of human nature (and I do not) in order to recognize the circular nature of his argument for the supremacy of the sovereign. If human beings cannot be trusted to manage their own affairs in a non-predatory manner, how then is a state comprised of mere human beings to be trusted with power over others? Will not the state, the members of which ostensibly rule on behalf of "order," use its power for predatory purposes of its own? Of course it will. As Errico Malatesta noted:

We do not believe in the infallibility, nor even in the general goodness of the masses; on the contrary. But we believe even less in the infallibility and goodness of those who seize power and legislate, who consolidate and perpetuate the ideas and interests which prevail at any given moment.[17]

... the nature of government does not change. If it assumes

---

had more in common with Jeffersonian liberals or Burkean traditional conservatives than the revolutionary socialist tradition that classical anarchism is typically identified with. His application of anarchism was entirely practical, favoring decentralist confederations of local communities, each retaining their own cultural identity, and an economy ordered on worker cooperatives and mutual banks. Bertrand Russell, an unceasing radical during his nearly a century-long life, sometimes expressed sympathy for the ideals of the classical anarchists, but regarded them as impractical. Instead, he clung to the Old Liberalism of his godfather, John Stuart Mill, and the Guild Socialism of G. D. H. Cole and R. H. Tawney. Paul Goodman called himself a "conservative-anarchist," believing anarchism to require a gradual, evolutionary process.

16   Thomas Hobbes, *Leviathan* (Harmondsworth: Penguin Books, 1985).

17   Errico Malatesta, "Crime and Punishment," http://flag.blackened.net/daver/anarchism/crime_and_punishment.html.

the role of controller and guarantor of the rights and duties of everyone, it perverts the sentiment of justice; it qualifies as a crime and punishes every action which violates or threatens the privileges of the rulers and the property owners ... If it appoints itself as the administrator of public services ... it looks after the interests of the rulers and the property owners and does not attend to those of the working people except where it has to because the people agree to pay.[18]

Throughout history, just as in our time, government is either the brutal, violent, arbitrary rule of the few over the many or it is an organised instrument to ensure that dominion and privilege will be in the hands of those who by force, by cunning, or by inheritance, have cornered all the means of life ...[19]

Malatesta had no illusions that democracy was an improvement over any other kind of state and essentially agreed with George Bernard Shaw's adage that "democracy substitutes election by the incompetent many for appointment by the corrupt few."[20] Said Malatesta of democracy:

... if you consider these worthy electors as unable to look after their own interests themselves, how is it that they will know how to choose for themselves the shepherds who must guide them? And how will they be able to solve this problem of social alchemy, of producing the election of a genius from the votes of a mass of fools?[21]

Democracy is simply a system whereby A and B conspire against C, B and C conspire against A, and A and C conspire against B. As Max Stirner noted, "In a republic, all are masters, and each tyrannizes over the others."[22]

18   Errico Malatesta, *Anarchy*, trans. Vernon Richards (London: Freedom Press, 1974), 22–23.

19   Ibid., 17–18.

20   George Bernard Shaw, *Man and Superman*.

21   Malatesta, *Anarchy*, 53.

22   Max Stirner, *The Ego and His Own*.

Anarchists have never been able to agree among themselves on the question of what an ideal anarchist society would look like. The adherents of virtually all of the schools of anarchism accuse the other anarchist sects of statism and authoritarianism. Anarchists of the leftist or socialist variation are accused of favoring what, in practice, would amount to little more than a decentralized form of social democracy or state communism (and some of this not so decentralized).[23] Libertarian anarchists are condemned for favoring a form of industrialized feudalism that would amount to little more than aristocratic rule by local elites by means of private courts, police, and armies.[24] A newer school of anarchism called "national-anarchism" includes among its adherents believers in racial separatism (as opposed to racial supremacy) and resolute opponents of social practices dear to the hearts of leftists like abortion and homosexuality.[25] Consequently,

23   A particularly grotesque example of left-wing anarcho-statism can be found in the Northeastern Anarchist: Magazine of the Northeastern Federation of Anarcho-Communists, a publication that favors a global communist government with a central planned economy, which will allegedly be anarchistic because the central planners will be delegates chosen by local communities. Even this last point is not exactly clear. Apparently delegates from factory floors from all over the world are to meet in one big workers' parliament to plan production for the whole planet.

24   Hans-Hermann Hoppe even goes so far as to claim that feudal society was stateless, a dubious proposition at best.

25   For some in the national-anarchist milieu, the ideal community would be a Nazi-like racialist homeland, an arrangement that might be acceptable so long as membership was voluntary, but characterizing such an arrangement as anarchistic would certainly cause confusion on the part of outsiders. Such arrangements do indeed exist, such as the former Aryan Nations compound at Hayden Lake, Idaho. One of the interesting things about national-anarchism is its ability to accommodate everything from neo-Nazis to radical leftists to Jewish separatists. See my "National-Anarchism and the American Idea," http://attackthesystem.com/national-anarchism-and-the-american-idea/. I believe national-anarchism to be, in many ways, the most advanced form of contemporary anarchist thought. Classical anarchism positioned itself as the most radical wing of the international labor movement, the dominant social struggle of the day, and incorporated a lot of quasi-Marxist ideas into its overall analysis. Neo-anarchism, emerging in the heyday of the New Left of the 1960s, similarly attached itself to the black power movement, feminism, environmentalism, and the gay movement. Yet, today, these currents have become safely mainstream and, to some degree, a reactionary force. Libertarian-anarchism makes the same mistake as the Marxists with its narrow economic determinism, its often rigid focus on bourgeois class values (much libertarian thought amounts to replacing the proletariat and the bourgeoisie with the bourgeoisie and the regulatory welfare state as the antagonists in the class struggle), and its universalist and moralistic tendencies rooted in Enlightenment rationalism. National-anarchism properly focuses on the most crucial

national-anarchists are accused by their left-wing counterparts of advocating a type of "village fascism." Those of the "primitivist" variant of anarchism are denounced for condemning the bulk of mankind to disease and starvation because of their rejection of modern technology and industrial civilization.[26] And traditional anarcho-syndicalists have long been attacked by individualists for promoting an alternative form of state where the government is simply replaced by labor unions.[27] All of the criticisms that these contending schools of anarchism have of one another are legitimate. Like any other philosophy or ideology, anarchism is imperfect and cannot provide universal solutions to all of mankind's problems.

The differing schools of anarchism each bring to the table a valuable perspective often not found among the other schools. Classical anarchism continues to emphasize the class struggle against international state capitalism, and correctly so, but unfortunately often falls into the trap of economic determinism in the same manner as Marxists and libertarians.[28] Also, many classical anarchist groups resemble nothing quite so much as history clubs or archivist societies, continually adorning their activities with the symbolism of European anarchism of a century ago, an action whose propagandistic value to the modern world is at best quite dubious.[29] Neo-anarchism of the post-New

---

issue of the era—the New World Order—and rejects the universalism common to both the liberal and socialist traditions in favor of particularism and traditionalism, sort of a mixture of Bakunin and Joseph de Maistre.

26   The classic "Unabomber Manifesto" is as good an introduction as any to the primitivist perspective.

27   Unions have shown themselves to be just as oppressive when they come into state power as any other type of organization or institution. The British trade unions that include print workers have been known to censor newspaper articles critical of union activities.

28   For an interesting discussion of the weaknesses of economic determinism, see M. Raphael Johnson, "Economics and Nationalist Theory," *The Idyllic*, August 1, 2003, http://www.theidyllic.com/php/article.php?article=21.

29   An experience I had some years ago serves as an illustration of the level of silliness this sometimes involves. I was at a continental anarchist conference in San Francisco in the summer of 1989 and sitting in on a workshop on labor organizing. The program broke down into a shouting match between members of the Industrial Workers of the

Left, post-1960s variety admirably opposes the mistreatment of traditionally disfavored or marginalized social groups—racial minorities, women, homosexuals, the handicapped, and so on. Yet neo-anarchism has also adopted for itself the dogmatic "political correctness" of the liberal establishment with a fervor that approaches self-parody. Libertarian anarchism champions the individual against the state, a refreshing approach given the incipient collectivism and crypto-statism often found on the left wing of anarchism, but sometimes ignores the role of community, culture, and non-economic influences in shaping the human personality.[30] National-anarchism focuses on the long neglected matter of the plight of traditional racial, national, and religious groupings under attack by the forces of modernist multicultural totalitarianism, yet often places a myopic emphasis on race as opposed to class, culture, the state qua the state, and other such matters.[31] Primitivist anarchism of the Zerzanite variety points to the inherently totalitarian potential of advanced technology (as evidenced by such phenomena as the Echelon system), yet ignores the potentially liberatory aspects of technology (which classical anarchists like Kropotkin pointed out) and, predictably, dogmatizes its critique to the level of absurdity.

World (IWW) and the Workers Solidarity Alliance (WSA) over the question of which group was most qualified to lead a workers revolution. The IWW is a historical relic composed mostly of students, bohemians, and post-1960s New Leftists. The WSA, which had less than forty members at the time, is the US section of the International Workers Association, which also includes the Spanish CNT described in George Orwell's Homage to Catalonia.

30   It should be pointed out that there is a branch of libertarianism called "paleolibertarianism" (after "paleoconservatism") that pays greater attention to the role of non-economic and non-state "intermediary" institutions in social development. While unfortunately holding to a rather narrow bourgeois, Euro-Christian outlook, this tendency admirably works to fills in the gaps in the reductionist materialism and utilitarianism to be found in much libertarian thought. For a critique of paleolibertarianism, see my "Why I Am Not a Cultural Conservative," http:// attackthesystem.com/why-i-am-not-a-cultural-conservative/, and "I'm Still Not a Cultural Conservative," http://www.attackthesystem.com/lancaster.html.

31   National-Anarchists are often demonized, quite unjustly in my view, as crypto-Nazis. Actually, national-anarchism is a quite substantive outlook. For a discussion of the important differences between national-anarchism and the traditional right wing, see David Michael, "On a Decisive Break With 'Far Right' Ideology," http://www. nationalanarchist.com/break1.html.

Where anarchism differs from other political philosophies is in its provision, through its enduring principles of voluntary association and radical decentralization, of a means for irreconcilable social or political disputes to be handled without tyranny or bloodshed. As this article is being written, an ongoing controversy is taking place in the American state of Alabama concerning the placement of a monument to the biblical "Ten Commandments" in the lobby of a local courthouse by a religiously devout local judge. Secularists and "civil liberties" groups are insisting that such a gesture intolerably compromises the distinction between church and state while religionists are insisting that the mandatory removal of the monument amounts to religious discrimination and persecution.[32] As the courthouse is state property, owned in theory by religionists and anti-religionists alike, there is no objective or principled manner by which the conflict can be resolved. However, in an anarchist social system, individual persons would be free to join whatever associations or communities they wished with members of different communities adopting whatever laws or customs they desired. Some communities might require a particular form of religious observance while others might ban all references to or acknowledgement of religion. Still others might adopt a "live and let live" approach.

Separation of Politics and State

There was a time when nearly all states maintained a particular state religion that every subject was expected to conform to. Those who did not conform faced severe persecution, banishment, imprisonment, torture, and death.[33] The social chaos that resulted from efforts to impose a uniform religious observance motivated some thinkers to consider such notions as "freedom of religion" or "separation of church and state." America was one of the first nations to formally institutionalize such ideas. Today, virtually

---

32   For a comprehensive review of this event, see http://www.reclaimamerica.org/Pages/10Commandments/MooreTime.asp.

33   See Stefan Zweig's classic, *The Right to Heresy*.

all religions are represented in the United States, and most of them conduct their affairs unmolested by the state most of the time. While some gray areas of controversy remain, such as the aforementioned matter of religious displays on state property, most people take for granted that religious pluralism is preferable to the theocratic absolutism of previous eras. Anarchism, properly understood, applies the same principle to politics. Just as the classical liberals Voltaire and Thomas Jefferson wished to separate religion and state, it might be said that traditional anarchism aims to separate politics and state. Instead of a uniform political system being coercively imposed upon all citizens alike, anarchism allows for individuals and groups to form their own voluntary political systems organized according to their own needs. The national-anarchist theoretician David Michael notes that the content of these voluntary political systems (or associations, or communities, depending on what one wishes to call them) might be quite diverse and include communities of a nationalist, communist, Christian, Islamic, or some other variety.[34] It might be appropriate to think of anarchism as a type of meta-system capable of accommodating all sorts of political, economic, and cultural subsystems. Anarchism offers certain political tools—individual autonomy, voluntary association, mutual aid, free federation, radical decentralization, and community sovereignty—that provide diverse social groupings with the means of achieving self-determination.

An anarchist should be wary of teleological theories of society, whereby society is regarded as evolving towards some predetermined or prescribed end. This, of course, is a common characteristic of Marxist views on sociopolitical evolution and, indeed, of much progressive thought, rooted as much of this is in Hegelian metaphysics. Nevertheless, it is possible to make, with reasonable certainty, an elementary set of predictions as to what characteristics an anarchist social order would eventually display. Anarchist theory carries with it certain implications in the realm of economics, law, the prospects of the nation-state system that

34   "National Anarchist FAQ," http://www.nationalanarchist.com/faq.html.

has been predominant for the past five centuries, and a variety of sociocultural and demographic matters. The first order of business involved in the implementation of the anarchist program is an end to universalism. On this point, many anarchists, particularly those of the leftist-progressive and, to a lesser degree, libertarian schools, miss the boat. The victory of anarchism would, by its very nature, coincide with the triumph of particularism. The absence of centralism would naturally strengthen attachments of a regional, local, family, ethnic, religious, cultural, or linguistic nature.[35] The marshalling of atomized individuals into a herd of identity-less masses at the mercy of the predations of whatever aberrant social engineering schemes the latest gang of thugs to achieve political power wishes to impose would no longer be possible. Particularistic attachments of the sort that serve as a vital bulwark against such predations would naturally blossom. A myriad of thriving communities would emerge, each with it own ideological, cultural, and economic foundations, organically rooted in the aspirations and evolved norms of its members. The sham of mass democracy, which sets all sorts of varied sectional interests at the throats of one another, and herds these diverse sections into party hierarchies where they may be safely divided and conquered at the hands of rootless and predatory elites, would be rendered obsolete.[36]

The triumph of philosophical anarchism as a sociopolitical meta-system would likewise mean the simultaneous victory of an enormous variety of subsystems. Against the fake "diversity" and "multiculturalism" offered by the liberal and neoconservative establishments and the reactionary left, whereby the total state rules in the name of "progressive" platitudes like Equality, Social Justice, and Humanity, in the place of more traditional platitudes like God, Family, and Country, a victorious anarchism offers an authentic pluralism consisting not only of genuine diversity in matters of culture, religion, and ethnicity, but also in questions of

---

35 This is a point Hans-Hermann Hoppe effectively argues in *Democracy: The God That Failed*.

36 Hoppe, *Democracy*.

politics and ideology. If the heart and soul of the anarchist ideal is a social order where autonomous individuals voluntarily choose those types of institutions, communities, or associations that are most suited to their own needs or desires, then virtually the entire panoply of dissident factions stand to gain through the victory of anarchism. The enemies of the current international ruling class and its rapidly encroaching New World Order include among themselves followers of the teachings of Karl Marx, Murray Rothbard, Osama bin Laden, John Zerzan, Eduard Limonov, Saddam Hussein, Emilio Zapata, Bo Gritz, Israel Shamir, Muammar Qaddafi, Mao Tse-tung, Noam Chomsky, Russell Means, R. J. Rushdoony, Mikhail Bakunin, Adolf Hitler, Anton Szandor LaVey, Elijah Muhammad, Julius Evola, Michael Oakeshott, Che Guevara, Edmund Burke, V. I. Lenin, Hilaire Belloc, Thomas Aquinas, Michel Foucault, Barry Goldwater, and many others.[37] Such a dazzling array of dissidents might be characterized as constituting a type of "diversity on steroids." With the disintegration of centralized power, all of these (and other) dissident communities would gain greater opportunities for self-determination.

Some anarchist factions, particularly the leftist ones, will no doubt denounce the aforementioned program as "authoritarian," "reactionary," or whatever. It is said by some in the anarchist milieu that a "true" anarchist must also reject "hierarchy," "authority," or even "organization" and "structure" of any kind. While one could certainly be an anarchist and oppose all of these things as well (though it is doubtful a community of such anarchists would be very productive or enjoy much longevity), the insistence by some

---

37. It goes without saying that someone, somewhere will use this passage as evidence that I endorse the particular views of all of these figures. Nothing could be further from the truth. Rather, I am simply trying to give reality its proper reverence. The elimination of a power structure, in this case the New World Order, automatically results in the filling of the power vacuum by the best organized opposition groups. I believe that a real-world society influenced by anarchistic ideas would amount to a collection of decentralized social systems spanning the entire cultural, ideological, ethnic, and religious spectrum, with widely divergent political and economic systems. Therefore, anarcho-communist, mutualist, syndicalist, Objectivist, Maoist, neo-Nazi, and Ba'ath Party communities might all exist within the broader decentralist framework.

anarchists that rejection of "hierarchy" or "authority" is mandated by the anarchist position actually betrays the authentic anarchist ideal of voluntarism (although it is necessary to distinguish between natural and artificial hierarchies and authorities). If one chooses to join a Tibetan Buddhist monastery and endure its accompanying rigors, then is it not authoritarian for an anarchist to denounce such a choice? If one such as John Walker Lindh decides for himself to adopt the ascetic ways of the Taliban, then who is another, particularly an anarchist, to attack his choice? Which is more authoritarian: a Nazi community on the top of a mountain whose members voluntarily choose their way of life or a massive, centralist, "democratic" state that seeks to impose the narrow values of a self-serving elite on the whole of society? Of course, it is a near certainty that a world dominated politically by anarchist ideals would produce many, many types of communities beyond the narrowly "conservative" ones described here. There might also be thriving homosexual communities, even communities where homosexuals constituted a privileged social class of the type Foucault once speculated about.[38] Just as there might be associations or communities of such a puritanical nature as to put Calvin or Khomeini to shame, so might there be communities of libertines whose principal economic base involved the commercial trade in drugs, alcohol, pornography, gambling, cockfighting, gladiatorial contests, or whatever. Of course, this by no means implies that all value systems are equally "true," valid, or likely to produce desirable or equal results. Some of the institutions that would form in an anarchist world might be hallmarks in human progress and achievement while others might be hellholes of incomparable ghastliness. This is what authentic liberty and authentic diversity are all about. Individuals and communities alike must be left to succeed or fail on their own terms.

---

38   I once came across an interview with Foucault where he challenged the legitimacy of the cultural Marxist view of homosexuals as a social class within the bourgeois order. He went on to speculate about a type of society where homosexuals might be a social class, although without much elaboration, if I recall correctly. Unfortunately, I have not been able to locate a transcript of this interview for reference.

The Economic Implications of Anarchism

It is important that the implications of such a decentralized and pluralistic political order for the realm of economics be properly understood if, for no other reason, to clarify the boundless confusion that has often existed among anarchists on economic matters. Within the rich history of anarchist thought, one finds both "individualist" and "socialist" traditions as far as economic questions are concerned. The spectrum of economic thought among anarchists includes "anarcho-capitalists" on one end and "anarcho-communists" on the other. Both sides often prefer to act as if the others are heretics and pursue the symbolic excommunication of their opponents. However, "socialist" and "communist" interpretations or applications of anarchism are not incompatible with "capitalist" or "individualist" ones. Anarchistic thought of the libertarian-individualist-capitalist variety frequently regards itself as the proper ideological heir of classical liberalism of the type espoused by Adam Smith or John Stuart Mill. However, as Noam Chomsky points out, the early classical liberals embraced many of the same criticisms of the bourgeois state as the classical socialists.[39] Hence, Chomsky regards traditional socialist-anarchism, or "libertarian socialism," as the logical outgrowth of classical liberalism. From the opposite end of the spectrum, the anarcho-capitalist godfather Murray Rothbard expressed sympathy for many of the criticisms of state capitalism advanced by the classical socialists, including Marx and Bakunin, but attacked them for blaming the market rather than the state qua state for the exploitation inherent in state capitalism. For Rothbard, the principal error of most of traditional socialism was its effort to achieve socialism by the reactionary methods of statism and militarism.[40]

Clearly, the conflicting economic tendencies within anarchist

---

39   Noam Chomsky interviewed by David Barsamian, *Secrets, Lies and Democracy* (Tucson, AZ: Odonian Press, 2004), 17–18.

40   Murray N. Rothbard, "Left and Right: Prospects for Liberty," http://www.lewrockwell.com/rothbard/rothbard33.html.

thought are sorely in need of some sort of reconciliation. Fortunately, the work of Kevin Carson in the field of economics provides a means of doing so. Drawing upon both the Marxist and Austrian traditions within economics, Carson demonstrates that those who criticize the socialists for their carte blanche rejection of markets are correct in doing so.[41] After all, there is nothing inherently wrong, certainly not from an anarchist perspective, with the voluntary exchange of goods, services, and labor in the marketplace. Indeed, voluntary exchange is the cornerstone of anarchist social relations. Anti-market socialists have thrown out the baby with the bath water. However, pro-market, anti-state thinkers have quite frequently erred in failing to comprehend the degree to which market distortions resulting from state intervention are the source of genuine class exploitation. A principal problem is that many pro-market and anti-market observers alike consider the present system of international state capitalism to be an authentic product of the free market. The "left" tendency among anti-statists abhors this set of arrangements while the "right" tendency applauds it. Yet an authentic free market economy would produce institutional arrangements of a vastly different nature from those currently in existence.

The end of liberal democracy as a dominant political paradigm, and its replacement with philosophical anarchism, would naturally generate a brand new economic paradigm in the place of the current paradigm of state capitalism. Liberal democracy and state capitalism are considered by virtually all "mainstream" political theorists to be the natural corollaries of one another. Indeed, one often hears talk of "capitalist democracy" or "democratic capitalism" as some sort of ideal among establishment ideologists, particularly among (who else!) neoconservatives. On one hand, it is not exactly true that state capitalism and liberal democracy are natural complements to one another, as state capitalism preceded liberal democracy, and the mass democracy of the present era.

---

41   Kevin Carson, "Austrian and Marxist Theories of Monopoly
      Capital: A Mutualist Synthesis," http://kevin_carson.tripod.com/
      mutualistnetresourcesandinformationonmutualistanarchism/id10.html.

Carson, following the lead of both Marx and Rothbard, explains how the declining feudal aristocracy of the latter Middle Ages sought to reverse its own fleeting fortunes by reinventing itself as a class of bourgeois capitalists by means of state interventionist tools of the mercantilist variety in order to preserve the centralization of wealth.[42] Hence, the birth of the paradigm of state capitalism that has come to dominate all of the industrialized nations. However, it is true that liberal democracy came to power largely through the efforts of a mercantile class, a middle class in the traditional European sense, who resented having to share power with the monarchy, the church, the landed nobility, and other relics of the feudal era. Subsequently, liberal democracy took the shape of mass democracy in order to justify the expansion of the state needed to effectively buy off and pacify newly emergent power groups (intellectuals, professionals, union bosses, political interest groups) who went on to comprise the "new class" of managerial elites of whom George Orwell and James Burnham provided penetrating critiques.[43] At the present time, the corporate elites of state capitalism and the bureaucratic elites of the welfare-warfare state (i.e., liberal democracy) have largely become intertwined with one another in the form of a state-corporate ruling class. This ruling class has become dominant in all of the advanced nations and is currently reconstituting itself on an international level in the form of the New World Order.

Conventional theories of political economy typically portray "Big Business" and "Big Government" as natural antagonists of one another. The "left" champions the state as the protector of the little guy from the predatory corporation while the "right" champions the corporation as the hapless victim of predatory government bureaucrats.[44] However, the present corporate system

---

42   Kevin A. Carson, *The Iron Fist Behind the Invisible Hand: Corporate-Capitalism as a State-Guaranteed System of Privilege*, rev. ed. (Montreal: Red Lion Press, 2002).

43   Kevin A. Carson, "Liberalism and Social Control: The New Class' Will to Power," http://attackthesystem.com/liberalism-and-social-control-the-new-class-will-to-power/

44   Keith Preston, "Reply to Brian Oliver Sheppard's 'Anarchism vs. Right-Wing Anti-Statism,'" http://attackthesystem.com/reply-to-brian-oliver-shepards-anarchism-vs-right-wing-anti-statism/.

could not exist without the favors granted to corporations by the state in the form of subsidies, infrastructure, central banking, the state monopoly over the production of currency, tariffs, monopoly privilege, contracts, bailouts, guarantees, military intervention, patents, the suppression of labor, regulatory favors, protectionist trade legislation, limited liability and corporate personhood laws, and much else. Similarly, the state's legislative process and executive hierarchy is beholden to the corporate interests who fund the electoral system and provide the bureaucratic elite among the military, foreign policy, and "international trade" establishments. Condoleeza Rice's migration from Chevron to the National Security Council is no mere coincidence. The amalgam of Big Business and Big Government, consolidated on an international scale, represents a centralization of wealth and power of so great a degree as to jeopardize the future of humanity.

What sort of economic order would accompany the political victory of anarchism? Economic decentralization would naturally follow political decentralization. As the massive, bureaucratic nation-states currently being incorporated into the New World Order collapsed and disappeared, the corporate entities propped up and protected by these states would also vanish. Just as the dissolution of centralized political power would result in the sovereignty and self-determination of communities and associations, so would these entities be able to develop their own unique economic identities. Economic resources of all types, from land to industrial facilities to infrastructure to high technology, would fall into the hands of particular communities and popular organizations. Such entities would likely organize themselves into a myriad of economic institutions. It can be expected that workers would play a much greater leadership role in the formation of future economies as workers access to resources and bargaining power, both individually and collectively, would likely be greatly enhanced. The result would likely be an economic order where the worker-oriented enterprise replaces the capitalist corporation as the dominant mode of economic organization.[45]

---

45   Keith Preston, "What Would an Anarcho-Socialist Economy Look Like?," http://

The disappearance of massive, bureaucratic states would also result in the greater fluidity and dynamism of the marketplace, ushering in greater efficiency, more rapid innovation and, in the long term, rising living standards within the context of a more equitable overall distribution of wealth. Economic arrangements might include worker owned and operated enterprises, a proliferation of cooperatives and family businesses, mutual banks of the type envisioned by Greene, Proudhon, and Tucker, communal arrangements of the type envisioned by Kropotkin (and practiced, to some degree, by the kibbutzim of Israel), co-determined enterprises operating as a partnership between labor and management and industries operated by unions or workers councils in the manner envisioned by traditional anarcho-syndicalists, guild socialists, distributists, or council communists. The Mondragon workers' cooperatives of Spain have achieved some degree of success in this area.[46] Of course, if some groups of workers or entrepreneurs wished to organize themselves into giant, hierarchical formations similar to the traditional corporate model, that would be their prerogative. In addition, there would likely be an increase in the number of small to medium sized businesses of an individual or private nature, farmers, craftsmen, artisans, and the self-employed. The culture of particular regions or communities would shape the emerging economic arrangements. Land would be worked communally in those locations, such as central Africa, where traditions of communal ownership are strong. Open marketplaces would abound in regions where cultural precedent existed. There might also be municipalized industries or enterprises in some quarters, as well as such endeavors being owned by political parties of a particular stripe and operated by party members. There may be communities run by the Revolutionary Communist Party or the National Socialist Workers Revolutionary Party, each with their own factories or farms, with adherents of party ideology

attackthesystem.com/what-would-an-anarcho-socialist-economy-look-like/.

46   William Foote Whyte and Kathleen King Whyte, *Making Mondragon: The Growth and Dynamics of the Worker Cooperative Complex* (Ithaca, NY: ILR Press, 1991); Roy Morrison, *We Build the Road as We Travel* (Philadelphia, PA: New Society Publishers, 1991).

providing the workforce. Still other communities might maintain economic arrangements modeled on the teachings of those figures their members find most inspirational, whether Gandhi or Qaddafi.[47] Kevin Carson provides a description of what a post-state capitalist economic order might look like:

1. an economy of self-employed artisans and farmers, small producers cooperatives, and worker-controlled large enterprises, all dealing with each other through the free market;

2. a money system based on labor exchanges or mutual banks, in which the producers associate to transform their own products into money and credit without relying on usurious banking monopolies;

3. a system of land ownership based on occupancy and use, with no enforcement of rights of absentee ownership;

4. a government based only on free association without initiating coercion against non-aggressors. This means all expenses are met by user fees and membership dues charged to willing participants. My own picture is . . . local government, minus compulsory payment for or consumption of its services.[48]

This vision is idealistic yet realistic, and Carson's overall economic analysis and objectives effectively reconcile the anti-statist traditions of classical liberalism and classical socialism. Of course, much variation on this broader theme is likely, as previously noted. For example, different sorts of communities might define "just" ownership or use of property in different ways, and the structure of local political institutions might be highly varied. The collapse of the New World Order and the corporate-social democratic

47 Satish Kumar, "Gandhi's Swadeshi: The Economics of Permanence," http://caravan. squat.net/ICC-en/Krrs-en/ghandi-econ-en.htm; Muammar Qaddafi, *The Green Book* (Tripoli: The World Center for Studies and Research of The Green Book, 1987).

48 Kevin Carson, "The Left Libertarian Vision of the Good Society," http://groups.yahoo. com/group/LeftLibertarian/message/6821.

bureaucracies that govern its core provinces would inevitably lead to the coming to local power of a good many political or cultural elements disagreeable to the liberal elites who dominate the current world order and those who ape their values. For example, the disappearance of the nation-states across Europe would likely lead to the proliferation of a wide assortment of self-assertive communities and enclaves led by Communists, nationalists, monarchists, racialists, Catholic or Orthodox traditionalists, Islamic fundamentalists, neo-Nazis, warlords, or ordinary criminal gangs. Similarly, an end to Anglo-Zionist imperialism in the Middle East would inevitably lead to the removal of the region's current regimes and national borders alike, as these are nothing more than a legacy of previous imperial eras. However, it is quite doubtful that the sociopolitical institutions that would evolve in the Middle East following the dissolution of the present order there would be of a particularly "progressive" nature, as far as Western definitions of "progressive" are concerned. Already, the embarrassment of the neoconservatives, who have discovered unexpectedly that the people of Iraq prefer an ayatollah to a Tony Blair, has been witnessed.

Just as political decentralization would naturally result in the greater influence of those sociocultural and ideological elements most disagreeable to the values of modern liberalism, so would economic decentralization inspire a regeneration of those communitarian values that have been suppressed by the forces of global corporatism and its materialist/consumerist ethos. Although an end to the gargantuan bureaucracies of the current nation-state system and the overarching system of international state capitalism would on one hand result in a greater economic dynamism of the type sought by many "free market" libertarians, the absence of powerful corporate entities would allow the emergence of economic institutions that would be much more rooted in organic local and regional cultures and therefore much more beholden to the values and norms of those cultures. Further, the wider dispersion of economic resources involved in economic decentralization would allow greater opportunities for self-determination and self-sufficiency among the neo-proletariat and provide the traditionally beleaguered classes with the means for self-emancipation.

The Death of the Nation-State System

The aforementioned predictions concerning what sort of politico-economic arrangements would follow the demise of the New World Order naturally assume an end to the five hundred year pre-eminence of the nation-state system. Simply put, the system of nation-states is one whose historical relevance has already expired. Traditional nations have largely devolved into provincial regions of the global order. Contrary to the sentiments of old-fashioned nationalists, this is not necessarily an unwelcome development. The principal function of the nation-state has been the greater concentration of political and economic power and the increased destructiveness of war and imperialism. Of course, the liberal "solution" to the horrors of international warfare has been even greater wars, imperialism, and centralization culminating in a Wilsonian global state that makes the world safe for corporate-mercantilist totalitarian-progressive "democracy." Against this liberal perversion, an authentic anarchism offers the radical dispersion of power as an antidote to the total wars generated by the modern state. As Joseph Sobran explains:

> . . . in the year 1500 there were about 500 distinct political entities in Europe; by 1800 the number had been reduced to a few dozen, and was soon further reduced by the unification of Italy and of Germany . . . Certain words, "secession" being one, are used in tones of horror that imply there is no point in discussing their possible merits. But, if secession is always bad, history can move in only one direction: toward a single global state, from which nobody must be allowed to withdraw, no matter how tyrannical it may become . . . In the twentieth century the great nation-

states (which were also empires) collided in the two most terrible wars of all time.

The explosion began with the assassination of a single man in Sarajevo in 1914. The alliances among the European states drew everyone into war, including, within three years, Midwestern farm boys who had never heard of the Archduke Ferdinand.

This would have been impossible if Europe had still consisted of those 500 independent political entities of the year 1500. Europe had seen many wars, but they had mostly been local. The "Great War" was something totally new, dwarfing even the Napoleonic Wars.

We have far more to fear from the consolidation of states than from secession and dispersion. With small states, there are sure to be local conflicts at almost all times, but it would be relatively easy to flee them. With only a few huge states, the danger of a general holocaust is constant.

Secession, small states, limited government, dispersion of power—these are the real paths to peace. The more political entities there are, the more rulers are forced to compete with each other for subjects, who can migrate to less oppressive domains. But when only huge states exist, with monopolies of power extending for thousands of miles, escape is difficult.[49]

One of the few positive features of the New World Order is that the enemy is now much more clearly identified.[50] It is pointless for contending political, economic, and cultural tendencies to continue to bicker among themselves when all are rapidly being

---

49 Joseph Sobran, "Small States Are Path to Peace," *Wake-Up Call America*, January–February 1999.

50 As Eduard Limonov says: "There's no longer any left or right. There's the system and the enemies of the system."

subjugated by the forces of globalism. As there is now really only one government, the system of international state capitalism, the task of anarchists has become much more simplified. Globalism may well be the final stage in the historical evolution of the state. The global superstate represents the consolidation of conventional nation-states into an ever-more powerful entity. The annihilation of the global superstate may well be the catalyst that ultimately leads to the realization of the reign of anarchism, just as the execution of the French monarch became the cornerstone of the ultimate triumph of liberal democracy and the supremacy of the bourgeoisie.

Separation of Law and State

No discussion of what the end product of a particular political or economic order might be can ever be complete without substantial reflection on what sort of laws and legal systems such arrangements might produce.[51] Thus far, it has been argued that the practical effect of the full implementation of the anarchist program would be the proliferation of countless voluntary communities and associations whose primary function would be the provision of the means to sovereignty for many different types of ideological or cultural tendencies. The internal structures of such associations would likely span the entire spectrum of political preferences. There might well be communities of monarchists, fascists, communists, liberal capitalists, liberal multiculturalists, theocrats, black nationalists, white nationalists, anarchists (of every possible stripe), neo-Aztecs, UFO enthusiasts, or whatever. Obviously, all of these elements would have very different views on the meaning of life, the role of the human species in the universe, the nature of human beings, the proper relationship between the individual and external institutions or collective entities, the proper means of reproduction and child-rearing, the methods of handling deviants from community norms, and much else. Consequently, the laws and legal institutions would differ greatly from community to community.

---

51   Keith Preston, "Law and Anarchism," http://attackthesystem.com/law-and-order.

Many anarchists claim to categorically reject of the concept of "law," but this is simply a matter of semantics. Most anarchists believe that acts such as murder or robbery should be socially disallowed, although there may be considerable disagreement on what causes such antisocial behavior, and how offenders ought to be handled. Unless one prefers a hermitic existence in the Arctic or Andes (a reality that would be much more possible in an anarchist world), it is impossible for an individual to exist in the same manner as an asteroid floating about in the vacuum of space. As soon as a particular community is established, norms begin to develop concerning what is and what is not acceptable behavior. It is to be expected that the legal culture of a broader society organized along anarchistic lines would place a high emphasis on individual autonomy, or what the libertarians sometimes call the "non-aggression axiom." Such an emphasis would partly result from the prevalence of anarchistic thought in the broader society. However, it is to be expected, for reasons that will be explained below, that a radically decentralized politico-economic order would naturally evolve along such lines, regardless of the ideological inclinations of its inhabitants.

When surveying the history of past civilizations that eventually collapsed, it becomes clear political disintegration is rarely, if ever, accompanied by any sort of political liberation. The anarchist anthropologist Harold Barclay notes:

> Periods of so-called cultural or organizational decay in history may suggest this sort of trend [towards decentralization]. But what trends do occur in these situations is the creation of a number of petty despotisms out of one which had existed before. Decentralization is not accompanied by freedom. The revolutions and revolts of history and the decay of social systems have invariably entailed the replacement of one kind of despotism by another. Or what is a process of decay of one polity is the basis for the creation of another, so that, for example, the appearance of Clovis' Frankish kingdom and of the

Umayyad caliphate follow on the heels of the decline of Rome.[52]

It may be expected, then, that the eventual collapse and disintegration of the global superstate of the New World Order will result in the emergence of "petty despotisms" of various kinds as the new basis of political organization. Indeed, the parallels between the current era and Rome in its twilight period are obvious enough. Just as the end of the *Pax Romana* ushered in a whole new era of decentralized politics, technological regression (in the West but not quite so much in the East), and the coming to power of an apocalyptic otherworldly religious movement (Christianity), so might the end of the *Pax Americana* usher in a new era of decentralized politics, technological regression (at least initially) and the expanded influence of an apocalyptic otherworldly religious movement (Islamic fundamentalism). Just as it was the unwashed barbarians of the Germanic regions who sacked Rome, so it may well be the unwashed barbarians of the modern anti-globalization movement (accompanied by the barbarian hordes emanating from the trailer parks, ghettos, and barrios) who eventually sack Washington, D.C.

What are the implications of all this for the matter of law in an anarchistic social order? Following the collapse of the New World Order global superstate and the nation-states that comprise its provincial governments, the entire panoply of dissident factions who stand in opposition to the NWO will naturally achieve superiority or sovereignty in those geographic areas where they are best organized and have achieved the greatest level of popular support. These factions will then proceed to reorganize their internal political structures according to their own ideological inclinations. Such inclinations will range from the highly "liberal" or "progressive" on one hand to the very "conservative" or "reactionary" on the other. Remnants of the former system would likely continue in certain enclaves or be incorporated into newer

52   Harold Barclay, *People Without Government: An Anthropology of Anarchy* (London: Kahn and Averill, 1982), 148.

systems in the same manner that elements of contemporary American law include remnants of earlier English law. The laws of the communities, associations, and homelands that emerge following the demise of liberal democracy, state capitalism, the nation-state system, and the universalistic synthesis of these manifested by the New World Order will reflect the preferences and prejudices of organic regions and localities to a much greater degree than what is found in contemporary systems of parliamentary corporate-social democracy.

Fortunately, there exists in the contemporary world a working model of this type of decentralized legal order. The East African nation of Somalia experienced in the early 1990s the type of disintegration of central government that the entire world is likely to experience at some point in the future. Following this political collapse, the sixty clans that make up the Somali "nation" became largely sovereign entities unto themselves. The disappearance of the state has largely resulted in the resurrection of traditional society within Somalia. Political "leaders" are primarily the heads of extended families and religious leaders. Disputes among clans, families, businesses, and individuals alike are handled largely on the basis of mediation and arbitration. Crimes are dealt with in a manner similar to the handling of torts in Western society, with the emphasis being placed on compensating the wronged party. Since the implementation (or restoration) of this system, both economic prosperity and social peace have multiplied considerably in Somalia.[53]

While the laws regulating the subsystems to be found within an anarchistic meta-system would be highly diverse, certain common characteristics would likely evolve into a formally or customarily codified common law for the entire meta-system. This would stem from two factors. One, under a radically decentralized sociopolitical order migration from one polity to another becomes more feasible. If one finds a particular community unattractive, the natural solution is to find another

---

53   Michael van Notten, "From Nation-State to Stateless Nation," *Liberty*, April 2003.

community. This in turn means that communities that wished to prosper and preserve themselves would find it necessary to retain the allegiance of their more competent, productive, and valued members. Consequently, leaders of particular communities would be motivated to make their communities as attractive as possible to those whose loyalty they wished to obtain. Secondly, ordinary economic incentives would provide both individuals and collective entities with the desire to settle disputes in a cost-effective manner. Resolving conflicts through perpetual war is quite costly to polities that lack control over huge populations and resources that can be conscripted or taxed at will. Shifting the costs of obtaining advantages through political means (i.e., coercive legislation) onto a broader tax-paying public is also considerably more difficult in the absence of a centralized, tax-supported "democratic" state that can be lobbied towards such ends. This means that the residents of an anarchistic order will have every incentive to find both peaceful means of settling disputes between communities and individuals and limiting their own petitioning of legal institutions to matters of urgent self-interest, such as cases of violent or invasive crimes and serious breaches of contract.[54]

Although individual communities might maintain strong codified laws or informal social taboos and sanctions against behavior that departs drastically from community norms or ideals, the cultivation of an environment of stifling oppression would likely lead to little more than the departure of the communities' more desirable members. Consequently, the maintenance of communities as closed as those of the Nazis or the Taliban will take place only where ideological fervor is strong enough to trump virtually all other considerations, including prosperity and cordial relations with other communities. Likewise, communities would, out of the necessity of self-preservation, establish barriers to forms of social decay likely to be injurious to the overall stability

---

54   Bruce L. Benson, *Enterprise of Law: Justice Without the State* (San Francisco: Pacific Research Institute for Public Policy, 1990); Randy E. Barnett, *Structure of Liberty: Justice and the Rule of Law* (New York: Oxford University Press, 1998).

and prosperity of the community. As an example, predatory street crime of the type that the Western nations are increasingly famous for would likely find considerably less toleration among most communities in an anarchistic order, save those organized for the benefit of the criminals themselves, such as self-managed communities of exiles from other communities.[55]

It is likely that supra-community institutions or arrangements would eventually evolve for the purpose of resolving disputes between contending communities. This by no means implies the necessary re-emergence of the state in the traditional sense. Instead, it is more probable that evolved traditions would come into being according to which inter-community disputes might be dealt with through a process of negotiation, mediation, or arbitration. Such traditions might serve the same role as conventional "international law" in the current system. A process might also develop whereby individual citizens of one community would be able to effectively file grievances against citizens of another community. In traditional societies, such disputes are typically handled through the compensation of the injured party by the community of the offending party as a whole, thereby providing each community with the incentive to discipline their own members who act in injurious ways towards others, for the sake of preserving both the internal peace within their own community and external peace with other communities.

Disputes between communities or members of different communities would primarily involve ordinary conflicts over territory, resources, or common crimes (such as violence and theft) that are prohibited by all cultures and political entities out of necessity. As for the matter of deviation from community norms in a broader cultural sense, different types of communities would obviously handle such questions in their own ways. There already exists in modern states an endless amount of controversy over all sorts of social or cultural questions. Controversy of this

---

55   Keith Preston, "Dealing with Crime in a Free Society," http://attackthesystem.com/dealing-with-crime-in-a-free-society/.

type would likely escalate in the absence of conventional states as more and more sociocultural groups would begin to establish sovereign enclaves of their own. These enclaves might maintain wildly divergent cultural, religious, or ethical norms. A seemingly endless list of questions arises. Is abortion a woman's sacred right or the callous murder of an unborn child? Is homosexuality a natural, healthy expression of human intimacy or a vile perversion? Should the ownership of weapons be allowed for all citizens or only for those charged with specific functions related to security and defense? Is the open criticism or even ridicule of leaders and authority figures a vital check on incompetence or malfeasance among leaders or simply an invitation to disorder and disrespect for natural hierarchies? Is the process of reproduction a matter of societal interests to such a degree that external authorities are to have a say in such matters or are these questions simply a private issue between consenting parties? What is to be the proper allocation of resources and how is the just possession and use of such resources to be defined? Are beliefs regarded as blasphemous a simple matter of individual conviction or do these invite the wrath of supernatural powers towards the entire community? To what degree, if any, can be the individual be properly required to perform service towards the greater good of the community at large?

The important issue for this discussion is not so much the matter of how different communities might answer these questions but rather the manner in which deviations from established norms in these and other areas might be handled. Although it is certainly possible, and indeed likely, that at the initial stages of the formation of various communities the sanctions enacted against deviants would be quite harsh, it is unlikely this will continue indefinitely without alteration or modification. Initially, religious fundamentalist communities might stone heretics or adulterers to death. Communities of political correctness lunatics might engage in the summary execution of racists, sexists, homophobes, anti-Semites, or vivisectionists in a manner emulating the Red Guards of the Great Proletarian Cultural Revolution or the

Khmer Rouge during the Return to Year One. In the polities that would follow the demise of liberal democracy and its institutional appendages, a wave of repression and bloodletting would likely accompany systemic collapse. However, the broader decentralized meta-system would allow the subjects of individual communities to once again "vote with their feet" in the absence of centralized nation-states or the global superstate. This arrangement would have a moderating effect on communities seeking to retain the allegiance of members and subjects. Decentralism, easy migration, and a polycentric legal order rooted in negotiations between communities and associations would produce an eventual scenario whereby "diffuse" sanctions would serve as the primary method of enforcing community standards. These might include everything from ostracism and economic reprisals ("discrimination") to "private" forms of violence (such as fighting, dueling, or vigilantism) to public censure and reprimand of a non-coercive nature (the so-called "bully pulpit").

The Death of Modernity

In the early period of the post-NWO world, occurrences resembling those that followed the collapse of Rome would likely transpire. During that period, roving bands of Christian zealots traveled about destroying pagan monuments and artifacts.[56] Similar behavior on the part of various anti-NWO elements is likely as well. A case in point is the destruction of Buddhist monuments by the former Taliban government of Afghanistan. Another example might be the zeal for the destruction of monuments to the late Confederate society of the American South found among the left-wing elements in my own community of Richmond, Virginia. While revolution is usually accompanied by chaos, and followed by a period of reaction, eventually stabilization begins to take place and the ordinary process of natural social evolution resumes. Therefore, the purges, bloodletting, and waves of repression that would naturally follow the disorder involved in the destruction of the NWO would eventually give way to the establishment of a new type of decentralized order such as that which developed in Western Europe during the post-Roman, medieval era. Indeed, the destruction of international state capitalism would in many ways be nothing more than the restoration of pre-modern traditional society with its emphasis on localism, regionalism, tribalism, particularism, religion, polycentrism, and the like. The rapid growth, on a worldwide basis, of Islam in general and Islamic fundamentalism in particular, and the corresponding explosion of Christianity in Asia, Africa, and Latin America (and to a lesser degree, the growth of Christian fundamentalism in North America), attests to this.[56] The specific civilization that is commonly referred to as "modernism" is already approaching a stage of advanced decay. Therefore, the eventual disappearance of modernism in a way that parallels the disappearance of Greco-Roman civilization can be predicted with relative safety.

If current demographic trends continue, it can be expected that a "post-modern" (not postmodernism in the popularized sense) world would exhibit certain predictable characteristics. Islam may well become the world's largest religion, and continue to dominate the Middle East and many other parts of Asia, and eventually come to dominate Europe and parts of North America as well[57]. The future strongholds of Christianity will likely be found in the southern hemisphere and East Asia, particularly the Pacific rim region. The particularly primitive form of Christian fundamentalism found in North America may come to dominate much of that continent. These expanded or revitalized religions, along with revitalized regional or local organic communities or ethno-cultures, will likely be the basis of the social structures of

---

56 "The [Christian] zealots for conversion took to the streets or criss-crossed the countryside, destroying no doubt more of the [pagan] architectural and artistic treasure of their world than any passing barbarians thereafter." Ramsay MacMullen, *Christianizing the Roman Empire* (New Haven, CT: Yale University Press, 1984), 119.

57 The disparity in birth rates alone render it virtually certain that Muslims will outnumber indigenous Europeans within a century. For an interesting look at the growth of Christian fundamentalism in North America, see Dean M. Kelley, Why Conservative Churches Are Growing: A Study in Sociology of Religion (New York: Harper and Row, 1972). For a look at African Christianity, see Harvey J. Sindima, Drums of Redemption (Westport, CT: Greenwood Press, 1994).

the future world. This too would be a development that paralleled the society of the medieval period. Once the stabilization of this order became seriously rooted, the foundation for further human social evolution of a genuinely progressive nature would be established. Substantial historical precedent can be found for this simply by looking at the progression of medieval society in the period leading up to the Enlightenment. If classical Greece at its height can be compared with the intellectual culture of the Renaissance, then contemporary modern civilization can be compared with Rome in its geriatric years.

The Enlightenment would have been impossible without the Middle Ages, for it was the decentralized and polycentric order of medieval Europe that inadvertently provided the cultural framework for the intellectual development that characterized the Enlightenment.[58] The most important characteristic of medieval society was the lack of a significant concentration of power. The monarchs had to share power with the popes and vice versa. Different manors, fiefdoms, feudatories, kingdoms, tribes, and other political entities had to share power with one another as none were ever able to acquire the upper hand. This decentralization allowed the individual more latitude with which to "vote with his feet" and placed an enormous check on the power of rulers in the manner previously discussed, and so limited their predations. Perpetual negotiations and renegotiations between kings and commoners and between rival kingdoms led to the intellectual conceptualization of such ideas as "freedom," "liberty," and "rights" that eventually became intertwined with Enlightenment political culture.

The Demographic and Cultural Implications of Anarchism

It has been argued that the current world civilization ("modernism") is on its deathbed in a manner resembling the expiration of

---

58   For a discussion of traditions of decentralization in Western culture, see Clyde Wilson, "Devolution," http://www.lewrockwell.com/wilson/wilson15.html.

Greco-Roman civilization. It has been argued that the dominant political paradigm of modernism (liberal democracy) is doomed due to its own fatal contradictions. Drawing on the past historical experience of the collapse of Rome and the emergence of the decentralized polities of the medieval period, it has been argued that a similar decentralization is likely to transpire following the demise of the New World Order, which is simply the final stage of modernism, liberal democracy, the evolution of the modern state, and state capitalism. It has been argued that a principal characteristic of a post-NWO world will likely be the dramatic re-emergence of particularism. It has also been argued that out of this world order of decentralization and particularism, now matter how retrograde it may be in its initial stages, there might very likely evolve a new politico-economic paradigm whereby philosophical anarchism or voluntary association replaces liberal democracy and worker-oriented productive institutions come to replace capitalism and corporatism. Likewise, a decentralized political order and a polycentric legal order would generate a high level of individual autonomy and responsibility. The removal of parasitical state bureaucracies from human economic life would, in the long run, generate greater economic prosperity and corresponding increases in health and living standards and wider dispersion of economic resources. This type of scenario would then lay the intellectual, cultural, and material framework for the emergence of a new renaissance of human cultural achievement in a manner resembling that of the classical Greek or classical Renaissance periods, and a new revolution in science, philosophy, and politics of the type that occurred during the early stages of the Enlightenment.

There are still other interesting questions regarding sociological, cultural, and demographic matters that are certainly worth considering. One of these involves the matter of immigration.[59]

---

59 For a discussion of the implications of anarchist theory for ethnic matters, see my "A Calm Anarchist Look at Race, Culture and Immigration," http://attackthesystem. com/a-calm-anarchist-look-at-race-culture-and-immigration/. Interestingly, within contemporary anarchist thought two diametrically opposed schools have developed concerning the question of race. One of these, situated on the Far Left,

This is an issue that is becoming increasingly more controversial in the Western nations. Broadly described, immigration opponents regard unwanted migrants as a source of increased crime, competition for scarce employment opportunities, dilution and erosion of established culture, burdens on tax-financed social services and, in some instances, depletion of particular ethnic or regional identities. Pro-immigration forces regard immigration as a source of cultural diversity and enrichment, cheap labor for business interests, a source of strength for favored ethnic groups, humanitarian asylum for refugees from political oppression or deplorable socio-economic conditions, individual freedom of movement and travel, and economic progress derived from the importation of foreigners possessing valuable skills. Both sides on this conflict have a habit of oversimplifying the issues involved. Whatever one's views on the matter of immigration, it is interesting to look at how this issue might have been handled under anarchistic institutions and what the results would be.

As for my own views on the subject of immigration, let me say that I am in favor of the free migration of peoples. I oppose border police, passport laws, visa requirements, and customs inspectors.

has adopted doctrines rooted in the latter New Left of the 1960s, such as "white skin privilege," "whiteness" theory, and other similar perspectives of questionable intellectual character. On the other end, national-anarchism (or at least a subset of it), originating from the European Far Right, maintains a relief in racial separatism and ethnic "identity" theories more commonly associated with neo-Nazis and certain fundamentalist religious perspectives such as Christian Identity. As to which side is more authentically anarchistic, it would appear that national-anarchists are more strongly committed to the practice of voluntarism, wishing to set up their own sovereign ethnically homogeneous enclaves and allowing for similar communities among other ethnic groups and non-racial ideological tendencies. Left-wing anarchists frequently seem to have no conception of the principle of voluntarism when it comes to questions of social relations and often seem committed to eliminating those who oppose their rabid integrationist/left-multiculturalist agenda by violence. In many ways, these two diametrical opposites may be necessary counterparts to one another within the broader realm of anarchist theory. This conflict also illustrates the degree to which most contemporary anarchist factions are derived from the cultural fringes. Most people are neither racists nor racial separatists or "anti-racist" multicultural fanatics. Presumably, once the New World Order is defeated and modernism disappears, communities and regions will emerge that reflect the entire panoply of racial and ethnic identity. There will likely be homelands for racial separatists and/or supremacists, authoritarian multiculturalists, militant integrationists, and racially neutral persons such as myself alike.

I regard the INS as just another police state organization of the same type as the FBI, DEA, and BATF. However, I also believe that a system of genuine free migration would produce results more favorable to contemporary anti-immigration advocates. The current international system is about as far removed from a system of free migration as it could possibly be. The existence of passport laws or border police is only a minor aspect of the overall statism that currently dominates international travel. Indeed, current migration patterns represent the influence of the broader imperialistic and social engineering schemes of international state capitalism. First and foremost, it must be recognized that many Third World immigrants into First World nations are in fact refugees from political and economic conditions created by the imperialist policies towards the Third World established by the First World. The legacy of the colonialism of Old Europe has been the disruption and destruction of organic social structures of the indigenous societies of the Third World. Africa is an excellent case in point. The strategy of the colonialists was to destroy indigenous forms of self-rule on that continent and play off different ethnic factions against one another in a classic "divide and conquer" maneuver, thereby eradicating any and all popular resistance to the pillaging of the continent. The enduring legacy of this has been perpetual instability, bloody ethnic conflict, and terminal poverty on a continent with the greatest abundance of natural resources in the world. Similarly, much Latin American immigration into the United States has been inspired by the poverty and civil war perpetuated or aggravated by nearly a century of American imperialism in that region. Persons in First World nations are justified in criticizing Third World immigration into their own regions only to the degree that they recognize and oppose imperialist efforts on the part of their own states towards the Third World. The best bet for those wishing to reduce Third World immigration into the northern hemisphere would be the achievement of political, economic, and cultural sovereignty and eventual stability for the Third World.

It is also necessary to recognize the degree to which the domestic states of the First World encourage immigration into their own territories by means of social, as well as foreign, policy. As most Third World immigrants are poor and uneducated, their increased presence automatically necessitates the expansion of social and educational services, thereby justifying the further expansion of the state and higher levels of taxation. As poor immigrants are disproportionately prone to street crime, increased numbers of police, the construction of new prisons, and the expansion of the state's apparatus of control (the so-called "criminal justice system") can be sold more easily to the general public. Immigrants create an expanded demand for social welfare-related entitlements and therefore a larger social welfare bureaucracy with greater employment security for welfare bureaucrats. Various ethnic lobbies understandably wish to increase the size of their constituencies and push for increased immigration by members of their own ethnic, racial, or national group. Corporate lobbies view immigrants willing to work for lower wages as a means of reducing labor costs and the overall individual and collective bargaining power of workers and push for pro-immigration policies alongside left-wing "multiculturalists" who associate any and all opposition to immigration with fascism, Nazism, slavery, genocide, et al., *ad nauseum*. Additionally, the embarrassingly low quality of American education, particularly in the arts and sciences, virtually necessitates the importation of skilled technical and professional workers from other regions into the United States. The interests of the central state are served by the immigration of peoples possessing a drastically different cultural identity into the host nation. The standard tactic of states everywhere who rule over diverse populations—"divide and conquer"—can be employed must more easily and effectively in such a scenario. Of course, this can only work for so long. Eventually, such systems collapse and the ethno-cultural or religious antagonisms which have been kindled by the prior ruling elite ignite.

Those who favor "liberal" immigration policies on civil libertarian or humanitarian grounds have a point. As the international power of the New World Order continues to be consolidated and the First World nations degenerate into ever-greater authoritarianism, it is likely that attacks on those who dissent from the dictates of the Establishment will continue to expand. Being able to flee from one political jurisdiction to another is a vital means of countering such attacks. As the policing systems of the corporate-social democratic states of the West continue to more closely resemble paramilitary occupational forces, it can be expected that police units of this type charged with the enforcement of immigration law will be increasingly incorporated into consolidated state security units along with those charged with investigation or enforcement with regards to "terrorism," "diversity," "drugs," "firearms," "public morality," "sedition," and the like. Whatever one's views on immigration, it is not strategically advantageous to favor the expansion of the state's current enforcement apparatus as a means of curbing it.

Opponents of the New World Order and the state-corporate ruling class include both staunch anti-immigration and stanch pro-immigration thinkers. Anarchistic politics offers a way of dealing with this conflict. The first order of business would be to deny state entitlements to non-citizens or require a long waiting period (say, fifteen years) before immigrants could become eligible for such entitlements. This would go a long way towards resolving the pressures on social services resulting from massive immigration. Such a policy would also be very likely to generate overwhelming popular support, although much of the radical left would falsely regard such an effort as racist or xenophobic. Cultural conflicts and social antagonisms generated by immigration could be handled more effectively simply by removing legal barriers to "discrimination" against immigrants. Forced integration only exacerbates hostility between social groups. Allowing different groups to practice mutual self-segregation and sovereignty may be a partial way out of this predicament. Again, the liberal establishment and the reactionary left will regard such ideas as heresy, but this only demonstrates the intellectual bankruptcy of these elements. Another idea might be to decentralize the immigration and naturalization process to the local level, as is currently the case in Switzerland. This way, different communities could adopt for themselves immigration policies that were as restrictive or as permissive at they desired. Of course, such a decentralized immigration policy could only work if politics in general were to be decentralized. Otherwise, different regions and localities would simply view immigrants as a means of expanding the voting bloc for their own territory in order to obtain more subsidies and favors from the central government.

Economic decentralization would also help to stabilize international migration patterns. An economy ordered on the basis of localized production for local use would not involve the relocation of productive facilities to regions with more easily exploitable labor. If workers owned or operated their own economic institutions they would not be particularly inclined to fire themselves in favor of cheap imported labor or to ship their jobs abroad. Also, solidarity and cooperation among workers on an international level against the corporate powers that be would improve the situation of workers everywhere by preserving the economic stability of First World workers and reducing the exploitability of Third World workers. International labor unions and cooperatives organized on the old anarcho-syndicalist model might be the proper path with regards to these questions. There is also the matter of the responsibility of communities and private groups in the broader sense. Those who champion immigration on humanitarian grounds should be prepared to put their time and money where their mouth is. During the 1980s, the "sanctuary" movement in the Southwestern United States, composed mostly of Catholic and evangelical churches, provided asylum to refugees from the wars that were then raging in Central America, largely as a result of the imperialistic policies of the US regime. This was often done in defiance of US law, and those being assisted were genuine victims of political persecution and military aggression. At the same time, "asylum" laws in some countries are simply a means of creating clients for social welfare agencies and granting safe haven to criminals who happen to belong to favored social groups. Such abuses might be curbed by transferring responsibility for such matters to non-governmental organizations. Likewise, in some communities large-scale immigration is the source of a genuine crime problem. Reliance on local militias rather than the state's immigration enforcement and policing systems would likely prove to be more productive.

Immigration is only one issue in the broader "culture wars" that are currently being waged in the Western states, particularly America. Typically, the scenario is described as an impending showdown between "conservative" or "reactionary" forces on one end and "liberal" or "progressive" forces on the other. The stereotypical combatant on the liberal side is a tofu-munching, unkempt, unwashed neurotic railing hysterically against racism, sexism, homophobia, looksism, transphobia, producerism, et al., with his conservative counterpart being a flag-waving, Bible-banging, pious prig who issues warnings to Middle Americans concerning the imminent homo-doper menace to their children by day, while cruising for teenage male prostitutes by night. Somewhere in between is the stereotypical libertarian with his credit cards in one pocket and crack cocaine in the other. Stereotypes are usually derived from the generalization or exaggeration of perceptions that have some basis in actual facts. Unfortunately, the types of human waste material being discussed here are also very easy to find in various opposition movements from the Left and the Right. I suspect one of the reasons that anti-Establishment elements in American politics enjoy so little success is the tendency of these to adopt the most small-minded perspective on cultural matters imaginable. Populist-oriented tendencies have been more influential in European than American politics in recent times, probably because of the efforts of populist figures in Europe to transcend the conventional left/right cultural-ideological boundaries. Whatever one thinks of

Jean-Marie Le Pen, he comes across as an educated, worldly man unafraid to address working class issues and make common cause with the Left on such matters, as his attraction of considerable Communist cross-over votes demonstrates. The closest thing in American politics to Le Pen is Patrick Buchanan, a man who combines many sensible and thoughtful ideas with the standard right-wing American hysteria over the alleged threat posed by dirty books, flag-burners, and unisex toilets.

Even more interesting is the case of the late Pim Fortuyn, a truly original political figure who might have seriously shaken up the Establishment had he survived to do so.[60] It is indicative of the nature of the reactionary left that a man who sought to curb immigration from backward, feudal, theocratic Islamic nations into liberal Northern European nations, where gays and feminists enjoy considerable influence, would be assassinated, ironically, not by a Muslim but by a reactionary leftist, political correctness fanatic, who equated the gay libertarian Fortuyn with Adolf Hitler. This action as much as any other demonstrates that the guiding values of the reactionary left are absurdity, nihilism, and masochism rather than socialism or liberalism. Nevertheless, the Left includes many sincere and reasonable people in addition to riff-raff, just as the Right includes many authentic populists alongside Know-Nothings. A new political synthesis that transcends boundaries of Left, Right, and Center is necessary if the international ruling class is to be successfully combated. The first step is to begin to work around the cultural differences to be found among anti-Establishment elements. The key is to focus on issues that concern ordinary working people rather than the cultural fringes. Most people do not think that Nazis or Commies or homosexuals or homophobes are hiding under every bed. Most of the current anarchist factions originate from extremist elements of one kind or another. This situation is not wholly undesirable as it provides fertile ground for the evolution of a Left-Right anarcho-fusionism. Yet, for such a synthesis to reach

---

60   For background on the Fortuyn phenomenon, see Tjebbe van Tijen, "The Sorrow of the Netherlands," http://www.opendemocracy.net/ democracy-newright/article_382.jsp.

its full potential, the Centrist perspective, particularly on cultural matters, has to be included as well. Most people are cultural and social moderates rather than hard leftists or hard rightists. Any authentic populism has to appeal to the sensibilities of ordinary people and, as populism and anarchism are closely related, any authentic anarchism must do so as well.[61]

Anarcho-Populism: A New Political Force?

An effective political outlook or strategy requires the development of a certain hierarchy of priorities. Those issues that are the most pressing and on which there is the most common agreement should be the primary focus. Issues of this type come in two categories: those that are the most serious for the world as a whole but are often recognized only by the small number of people who are actually capable of independent thinking beyond the influence of peers and leaders, and those that are foremost on the mind of the common man.[62] The most important issue in the contemporary world is the consolidation of an international

---

61   Keith Preston, "Canning Reactionary Leftism," chapter 11 of this volume.

62   The adoption of some pseudo-Nietzschean concepts may be useful here. Nietzsche tended to categorize persons as slaves, masters, and "Übermenschen." A heterodox adoption of these categories may provide us with certain insights into modern social psychology. Most people appear to fall into the category of the "slaves," demonstrating an inability to think or act independently of group norms, directions provided by authority figures, and the values of their particular culture of origin. The dominant instincts for this category are those of survival and the herd. They are concerned primarily with obtaining their own day-to-day sustenance and look to peers and leaders for a sense of security and identity, hence the reflexive, non-reflective, and often quite irrational attachment of those in this category to particularistic notions like religion, tradition, "morality" as defined by their culture of origin, nationality, ethnicity, family, the orthodoxy of the official ideology of the state to which they are subjects, and so on. The category of the "masters" includes those who are more intelligent and perceptive than others, and also more ruthless and cunning. This element tends to see through established cultural, political, religious, national, or moral myths, and instead devote themselves to the pursuit of power, wealth, and pleasure. It is from this category that societal leaders in the political and economic realms are typically drawn. The final category, the Nietzschean "Übermenschen," are those genuinely superior individuals who find base concerns like the pursuit of wealth and power for its own sake to be unsatisfying. For this element, knowledge, creativity, and discovery are the highest values. It is from this category that the greatest achievers in the arts, sciences, and philosophy are drawn. It is those in this category who become the innovators and instigators of genuine human progress.

Leviathan in the form of the proto-state of the New World
Order under the boot of American imperialism and its Anglo-
Zionist allies. This is an issue that is more commonly recognized
in the Eastern world and in those Western nations outside of the
Anglosphere. Consequently, serious opposition to the New World
Order will have to originate from those parts of the world. The
international trend towards the universalization of American-style
"capitalist democracy" (welfare-warfare corporate statism) should
be countered by the emergence of an Eastern bloc whose members
assert their common independence from Washington and are
supported by an alliance of dissident forces within the Anglosphere
itself. The American conquest and annexation of Iraq under direct
colonial administration has been vehemently opposed by most of
the world, particularly France, Germany, Russia, Belgium, and the
Islamic world. Therefore, the natural leadership of an international
resistance to American imperialism should come from these nations.
The question is the matter of what type of strategic-ideological
formulation would get the job done.

Larry Gambone argues that a principal source of division
between the Anglosphere on one hand and the nations of
continental Europe and Asia on the other is the ideology
of neoconservatism. It is only in the Anglo nations that this
peculiar tendency has thrived. This is a highly elitist ideology
whose adherents are numerically small but whose core tenets
have become standard policy for the Anglo nations, particularly
the United States. Gambone attributes this to the "winner take
all" structure of Anglo-American electoral systems as opposed to
the proportional systems of the European continent.[63] This may
be true, but I suspect the success of the neocons is more likely
the result of their efforts to work their way into positions as
court intellectuals and the close-knit, cult-like, often family and
kinship based nature of the internal structure of their movement.
Many in the paleoconservative milieu (Paul Gottfried, for
instance) argue that the globalist ambitions of the neocons

63   Larry Gambone, "The Neocons in a Nutshell," http://attackthesystem.com/2013/09/05/
the-neocons-in-a-nutshell/#comment-53510.

originate from the Marxist or Trotskyist roots of some of their leading theoreticians.[64] According to this view, the neocons simply substitute global capitalist democracy for international socialism as the motivation for their messianic zeal. Gambone argues that the neocons have more in common with another messianic ideology from the twentieth century: fascism. Says Gambone:

> In its eclectic nature, its authoritarianism, militarism, statism, hostility for real democracy, centralism, Jacobinism, mercantilism, corporatism and Big Lie propaganda, neoconservatism is very similar to fascism. But of course, it is not fascism in the true sense, with its ambiguity about nationalism, and the lack of the party-army, mass mobilization of the population, leader-concept and a popular corporatist ideology. It could be seen as a moderate substitute for fascism . . .[65]

In other words, neoconservatism is as close to fascism as Anglo-American political culture will accept.

My own studies of the nature and origin of neoconservative ideology lead me to the conclusion that the Jewish ethnicity of most of the intellectual exponents of this perspective is essential to understanding their ambitions and beliefs. For the sake of avoiding the usual misunderstandings and accusations, let me say that I am not an "anti-Semite" and generally hold Judaism in higher regard than the other religions originating from the Near East.[66] Nor do I have any special objection to the nation of

---

64 Paul Gottfried, "The Trotsky Hour," http://www.lewrockwell.com/gottfried/gottfried46.html.

65 Gambone, "The Neocons in a Nutshell."

66 Ancient Hebraic religion seems to me to be more closely related to pre-biblical paganism than either Christianity or Islam. First, it is considerably more particularistic, the Jews having their god, Yahweh, with each of the other ethno-cultures having theirs, whether it be Shamash, Baal, Moloch, Zeus, or whomever. Also, biblical Judaism in considerably more "this-worldly" than its two offshoots, with this life and the nation of Israel being where the action is. Christianity seems to me be little more than an apostate, apocalyptic spin-off from Judaism intertwined with various ideas lifted from

Israel, beyond its vile oppression of the Palestinian people and its maintenance of a fifth column within domestic American politics. Yet to avoid the discussion of real and immensely important questions out of fear of giving the appearance of impropriety is foolish. Considering the ethnic or religious motivations of those pursuing particular aims is indispensable to sound political analysis. If there is any issue on which the neocons can be counted on to behave with absolute consistency, it is their rabid Zionism. It seems relatively unimportant as to whether the neocons draw their greatest inspiration from Robespierre, Trotsky, or Mussolini. Those who seek absolute power are likely to resemble all of these in certain ways. The more serious question involves the matter of why they seek such power in the first place (beyond ordinary pathology) and what they intend to do with it.

Since the neocons' takeover of the foreign policy apparatus of the United States, their political opponents have begun to examine the influence of Leo Strauss on the neoconservative world view. Virtually all of the leading neoconservative intellectuals, from Irving Kristol to David Horowitz, cite Strauss as a major influence. Some, like Paul Wolfowitz, are his former students. The left-wing scholar Shadia Drury describes Straussian thought as extremely elitist in nature, rooted in a belief in the unfitness of the masses for self-determination and the need for political authority to vested in Machiavellian leaders whose principal function is to preserve those myths and fairy tales, whether religious or national, by which the masses can be rallied to the defense of the state. The role of the intellectual is to serve as a court advisor to such leaders. Strauss' adoption of such views seems to be rooted in his experience as a German-Jewish refugee from the Hitler regime. Strauss blamed the liberal political climate of the Weimar Republic for allowing the ascendancy of the Nazis. In his view, this discredited political pluralism as a means of achieving sanctuary for the Jews. While he

---

paganism—virgin births, savior gods, resurrections from the dead, etc. Islam has always seemed to me to be a cheap imitation of Christianity, albeit one with superior warrior traditions.

may not have said so directly (a not surprising fact given his taste for esotericism), Strauss seems to have developed the idea that the best course for Jews would be to develop authoritarian states that they would either rule directly, such as Israel (Strauss was a rabid Zionist), or serve as court intellectuals and thereby influence the practice of statecraft, as in America. Hence, the development of neoconservative ideology by the students and admirers of Strauss.[67]

Of course, the neoconservatives could have never achieved their present level of power without accomplices, primarily the traditional right wing of the US ruling class—oil barons, armaments manufacturers, elite banking interests, etc.—and the Christian Zionist dullards who serve as their ground forces and shock troops. It might be said that the neocons play the role of the NSDAP with Halliburton, Boeing, et al., filling the position of Krupp and I. G. Farben. Perhaps the Christian Zionists are playing the role of the SA.[68] Just as the world united for the defeat of Fascism and National Socialism sixty years ago, so must the world unite for the defeat of the neocons and the New World Order of whom they are the most militant proponents. Outside the Anglosphere, the most successful opponents of the New World Order thus far have been adherents of what Kenneth J. Schmidt refers to as "populist nationalism":

In Europe, these days particularly, nationalism has replaced communism as the threat which unites the center-right and the center-left. In recent days all one needs to do is pick up a newspaper and the names jump out at you: Le Pen, Fortuyn, Haider, Kajarrlstad.

What are the reasons for the rise of a populist-tinged nationalism? In the so-called western world, a great rift has developed between the ordinary people and the elites that rule over them.

---

67   Shadia B. Drury, *Leo Strauss and the American Right* (New York: St. Martin's Press, 1997).

68   Preston, "Canning Reactionary Leftism."

The fact that the elites and the common people have always had different worldviews is a given. I contend, however, that never in the history of European civilization has there been such a large gap in the way our elites see the world and how the common folk see the world. The historian and social thinker Christopher Lasch had a term for this, he called it a "Revolt of the Elites." The people that rule over us—the big business managerial elite, the media barons, the Zionists and the Manhattan intelligentsia—adhere to values that are strongly at variance with those of working and middle-class whites.[69]

Schmidt notes that populist-nationalist parties in Europe have primarily eclipsed the radical left rather than the center-right. The center-right and center-left parties have essentially identical positions: neo-liberal economics and left-egalitarian cultural values. It is for this reason that, despite the relative vibrant nature of the anti-globalization movement, the far left will fail as a revolutionary force against the international ruling class. On cultural matters, the Far Left differs from the left wing of capital only with regards to the question of degree. The Libertarians are in a similar position, differing from the neo-liberal economics of the Establishment only on questions of degree rather than principle. Some have even gone so far as to endorse flagrantly mercantilist arrangements such as NAFTA. It should also be noted that most rank-and-file supporters of "populist nationalism" throw their allegiance behind those whom they perceive as representing their own interests, rather than some grand principle. While "populist nationalism" may have its roots in the Far Right, its ability to attract sympathy from mainstream working people, crossover leftists, and even some libertarians, such as those of the paleo variety, establishes it as a force with considerable potential.

---

69   Kenneth J. Schmidt, "Populist Nationalism Developing Across the Western World," *The Barnes Review* 9, no. 3 (May–June 2003), http://www.barnesreview.org/May_2003/Populist/populist.html.

I am not a nationalist and I regard the principal flaws in nationalism to be its tendency towards chauvinism and its usually inadequate critique of the state.[70] Leaders like Le Pen, Fortuyn, Haider, and Buchanan may have laid an important foundation but much, much more work needs to be done. I have argued in this article that philosophical anarchism represents a potential alternative paradigm to the contemporary paradigm of state-capitalist liberal democracy. Elsewhere, I have argued that populism is likely to be the proper means to anarchism.[71] Hence, what I am proposing is a new strategic paradigm and, to a certain extent, a new school of anarchist thought that I call "anarcho-populism." This new brand of anarchism would draw on the other schools in various ways. The classical anarchism originally developed by Proudhon would be its foundation. Like anarcho-socialism, anarcho-populism would be anti-capitalist and pro-class struggle. Like anarcho-capitalism, anarcho-populism would endorse property, markets, and the independent sector as an antidote to statism, corporatism, and welfarism. Along with leftist-anarchists, this new anarchist tendency would support political freedom and cultural self-determination for racial minorities, women, gays, and the like, but it would not seek to mindlessly glorify or privilege these groups or demonize white males. Along with primitivists and eco-anarchists, anarcho-populism would seek to preserve the natural environment, but without the misanthropy and anti-tech hysteria of much of modern environmentalism. Like national-anarchists, anarcho-populism would endorse the right of traditional racial, ethnic, religious, or cultural groups to self-preservation and political sovereignty and cross-cultural, cross-ideological alliances against the NWO, but would seek to branch out into "mainstream" society rather than seek out reclusive isolation from the modern world. The objective is revolution rather than withdrawal. On cultural matters, anarcho-populism would endorse social organicism, evolved and historic traditions, and natural evolution in

---

70   Keith Preston, "Conservatism Is Not Enough: Reclaiming the Legacy of the Anti-State Left," chapter 6 of this volume.

71   Preston, "Canning Reactionary Leftism."

opposition to either "cultural conservatism" (which implies stasis or chauvinism) or "progressivism" (with its incipient universalism or utopianism). Our icons would be Aristotle, Burke, Jefferson, Stirner, Proudhon, Nietzsche, Mencken, Dennis, Hayek, Nisbet, and Kirk, rather than Rousseau, Marx, and Adorno, or William F. Buckley, Margaret Thatcher, and Rush Limbaugh.[72]

Resisting the Empire

It has been mentioned that leadership in building a consensus and alliance against the New World Order and American imperialism would necessarily have to come from outside the Anglosphere. While admirably opposing imperial aggression against the Islamic nations, the nations of continental Western Europe are too influenced by American cultural values, political correctness being largely an American export, and their elite classes are too intertwined with American capitalism to initiate consistent leadership against these things. These nations are in a process of social and economic decay and are militarily weak. Also, their lengthy history of formal alliances with the US regime will be altered only with considerable struggle and difficulty. The Arab nations are too poor to lead such a resistance and the Asian nations are more interested in buying American consumer goods than resisting American imperialism. Ideally, leadership in the development of an anti-NWO, anti-Anglo-Zionist bloc would come from Russia. First, Russia is second only to the United States in military strength. Second, Russia has a long history of serving as a counterbalance to Western, particularly American, imperialisms, even if it was done under the decaying, backward regimes of the tsars or the political deformation of communism.

---

72 From Aristotle, we derive the core principles of logic against mysticism and irrationalism. From Burke and Jefferson, we understand the relationship of community to anti-statism. From Stirner and Nietzsche, we recognize the importance of the superior individual in the shaping of history. From Proudhon, we adopt the classical anarchist alternative to state-capitalism. From Mencken, we understand that no totems should be spared attack. From Lawrence Dennis, we know the importance of operational as opposed to ideological thinking. From Hayek, Kirk, and Nisbet, we champion evolved traditions, organic society, and natural social evolution against centralist social engineering schemes of any kind.

Archonis, a national-anarchist commentator, observes:

> The Russian people and politicians must forge ahead in
> the "Red-Brown" alliance of Left and Right populism and
> decentralization, and return Russia to a nation of small
> institutions, but with adequate defenses and an agrarian
> economy. The civil institutions must be made small . . .
> along the lines of farming and guild socialism. The military
> defenses including nuclear weapons must be built up.

> Russia should forge alliances with China and the Middle
> East, along with Europe, and be the center of power in a
> domain that embraces both the East and West . . . guard the
> resources of its former satellites . . . and . . . maintain control
> of the oil and mineral reserves . . . [T]he economic survival
> of Eurasia as a whole is predicated on the interdependence
> on all of the countries of Europe as well as China and India.
> . . . Without Europe unifying with Russia and Asia, along
> with the Middle East, . . . [these nations] will end up being
> a "Client-State-Network," dominated by U.S. hegemony.

> A united Eurasia could pressure [the Anglo-American-
> Zionist axis] with trade sanctions and disinvestment, . . .
> form an intra-net and cut off these countries from their
> portion of the Internet. The only recourse imperialist
> nations could turn to would be war, but as long as Eurasia
> has weapons of mass destruction this will not happen. U.S.
> imperialists . . . are greedy, decadent cowards who only
> care about keeping their wealth and nothing else. They
> cannot comprehend the honor-concept of war. They only
> understand war as a tool of "gunboat" diplomacy. . . .

> Even in conventional warfare, Russia and the large
> Eurasian landmass has an advantage over the balkanized
> sea-surrounded lands. Movement is quicker and there are
> more options for strategic deployment. There are hosts
> of areas with strange peoples and terrains in the former

Soviet Asia, and Chechens and the Turkic peoples . . .
have training in unconventional warfare. In the event of
war against Eurasia by the imperialists, Russia and China
and the peoples of the former Soviet Asia could provide
the fighting forces, whereas the European flank can levy
diplomatic and economic sanctions . . .[73]

While the downfall and disintegration of the USSR was, for
the most part, a positive occurrence, one of its negative side
effects has been the creation of power vacuum that American
imperialism has been all too eager to fill, thereby generating an
even greater concentration of power on a global scale. The sort
of revitalized Russia that Archonis hopes for, a Russia rooted
in its own traditional culture, a culture that produced Tolstoy
and Dostoevsky and Bakunin and Kropotkin, and minus the
crackpot ideology of Soviet communism and its accompanying
bureaucratic monolith, might indeed be the force needed to
successfully challenge the hegemony of the Anglo-American-
Zionist triumvirate, the genuine "Axis of Evil." Such an effort
within the Russian nation would require visionary leadership
founded on recognition of the necessity of looking beyond
conventional ideological, cultural, or national boundaries towards
the creation of an anti-imperialist bloc. The Russian philosopher
and political figure Alexander Dugin postulates the concept of
"Eurasianism" as the means to such ends. Dugin explains:

To whom are we addressing the call to enter and to back our
movement? To each Russian, educated or not, influential
and the last of the dispossessed, to the worker and to the
manager, to the needy and the well-off, to the Russian and
the Tatar, to the Orthodox and the Jew, to the conservative
and the modernist, to the student and the defender of the
law, to the soldier and the weaver, to the governor and the
rock musician. . . . The movement "Eurasian" is founded on
the principles of the radical centre. We are neither leftists

---

73   Archonis, "Onward Eurasia," http://www.rosenoire.org/essays/eurasia.php. See also
      Archonis, "The Hammer of Nihilation," http://www.rosenoire.org/essays/hammer.php.

nor rightists, we are neither slavishly compliant to the authorities, nor oppositionists barking with a reason and without at any costs . . .

Russia will seriously be faced with the purpose of rescuing itself and the rest of the world from the terrible threat which creeps from the West . . .

In the religious sphere it means constructive and solid dialogue between the traditional creeds of Russia: Orthodoxy, Islam, Judaism, Buddhism . . . In the sphere of foreign policy, Eurasianism implies a wide process of strategic integration . . . spread to wider areas—to the countries of the Moscow-Teheran-Delhi-Beijing axis . . . priority relations with the European countries . . . active cooperation with the countries of the Pacific region . . . active and universal opposition to globalization . . .

Eurasianism defends the blossoming complexity of peoples, religions and nations . . . a combination of strategic unity and ethno-cultural (in definite cases, economic) autonomies. Different ways of life at the local level . . . Eurasianism is primarily addressed to the youth, to the people whose consciousness has not yet been spoiled by random leaps from one inadequate ideological pattern to another, even less adequate . . .[74]

Dugin mentions a number of ideological tendencies that are involved in the struggle against New World Order imperialism. These include Orthodoxy, Islam, Traditionalism, the Conservative Revolution, National Bolshevism, Third Positionism, Russian nationalism, Socialism, Islamic socialism, Eurasianism, Nationalism (in general), Anarchism (in its various manifestations), the New Left, the New Right, and a good

---

74   Alexander Dugin, "Manifesto of the Eurasia Movement," http://arctogaia.com/public/ eng/Manifesto.html.

number of others.[75] While it is true that there is a vast array of tendencies struggling against the common imperial enemy, and that tactical alliances between these forces are necessary and legitimate, there remains the practical matter of how such differences within the revolutionary ranks can be accommodated. Fortunately, the "national-anarchist" theories of Troy Southgate and David Michael provide some clues as to how to proceed.[76] Whatever one's views on the state, the ideal formation of the state, and the proper role of the state in human political or civil society, it is abundantly clear that, as a matter of expediency, statist centralization is simply incompatible with the formulation of solid tactical alliances against the common imperial enemy. The establishment of strong states in ostensible opposition to the NWO, but where the state is ordered on the basis of bitter factionalism with an ongoing danger of internal cannibalization, will inevitably have a corrupting effect on the resistance forces whereby one or another contending faction can be induced to stab the others in the back by means of bribery and offers of greater power on the part of the enemy. One need only look at the ruling classes of the so-called "moderate" Arab nations to see a graphic illustration of this point.

The conventional nation-state system has been rendered obsolete by the consolidation of the NWO global superstate. Therefore, old-style nationalisms are irrelevant. The proper form of social organization to be offered in opposition to the global superstate is the organic local, regional, cultural, or ideological community. Within all traditional nations, many tendencies stand in opposition to the NWO, from the Far Left to the Far Right to the Radical Center, to libertarians, anarchists, religious communities, Greens, "Beyond Left and Right," and others. Single-issue unity on the part of these forces for the purpose of pulling their respective nations out of the imperial system seems

75   From the Arctogaia website at http://www.arctogaia.com/public/engl1.htm.

76   For a look at the works of David Michael, visit his website at http://www.
     nationalanarchist.com. For an overview of national-anarchism, visit http://www.
     rosenoire.org and http://terrafirma.rosenoire.org.

to be the way to go. Points of contention can be dealt with more effectively through decentralization. For example, in the nation of France, opponents of American imperialism and the NWO include the Communists and Greens from the left, nationalists on the right along with Muslims and Catholic traditionalists. Yet there is considerable disagreement among these divergent forces on many issues, particularly immigration. Conversion to a decentralized political infrastructure, such as the Swiss canton system or the federalism of Old America, might allow different factions autonomy and self-determination within their own enclaves. There could be towns and cities governed by the National Front, the Greens, Islamists, Communists, or whomever. In many nations, forces such as these constitute a majority against the center-left/center-right, pro-NWO ruling classes.[77]

What about the fate of those countries currently enduring the greatest assault at the hands of the imperialists? The resistance forces in both Iraq and Afghanistan are notoriously divided and on the verge of civil war. Collaborators and traitors exist within their ranks. How much different would the fate of Iraq be, if the Sunnis, Shiites, and Kurds each agreed to sovereignty within their own historic regions, with internal sovereignty for individual tribes and clans, additional enclaves for minorities like the Assyrian Christians, and common unity and resistance to the imperial conqueror? If the contending tribes, religious, and ethnic factions of Afghanistan adopted a polycentric order of the Somali variety, Afghanistan's current status as a colony of Western oilmen might be drastically altered. Likewise, the relegation of the Palestinian people to the "One Big Concentration Camp" that the West Bank has become might be reversed if Anglo-Zionist imperial power had a decentralized but confederated Eurasian bloc, organized on the basis of a defensive, diplomatic, and economic tactical alliance, to contend with.

What about the struggle within the "belly of the beast" itself, the

---

77   Jaroslaw Tomasiewicz, "An Alternative to the American Empire of the New World Order," http://www.attackthesystem.com/alternative.html.

nations of the Anglosphere? If, as Kenneth J. Schmidt argues, the ideology of the ruling class is "libertarian in its economic views and left-wing multiculturalist in its social policies,"[78] then it stands to reason that the natural opposition would be the reverse: libertarian in social matters but "left-wing" (radical and revolutionary) in economics, i.e., "libertarian socialism." By "libertarian," I am not referring to utopian universalism of either the left-progressive or liberal-consumerist variety. Rather, I am referring to an authentic cultural diversity rooted in such anarchistic principles as individual autonomy, voluntary association, mutual aid, and decentralism. By "socialism," I do not mean statism of either a Marxist or nationalist variety but something more consistent with the original meaning of socialism—an economy of the producers, by the producers and for the producers. "Producerism," as the reactionary leftist Chip Berlet might call it.[79] The established schools of anarchism each have something to offer, as I pointed out earlier. However, there remains the question of how anarchism is to break out of its various ideological ghettos and into mainstream society. From classical anarchism and anarcho-syndicalism, we derive the class struggle. From libertarian-individualist anarchism, we champion the individual against the state. From eco-anarchism, we approach material and technological development with a watchful eye. With neo-anarchism, we champion the downtrodden and marginalized. With national-anarchism, we seek the preservation of indigenous cultures and ideological diversity. But the point remains that most people care little, if anything, about any of this.

To develop an effective anti-ruling class strategy, the structure and tactics of the ruling elite must first be understood. The Anglo nations, particularly America, are dominated by two largely identical parties that represent contending factions of

78   Schmidt, "Populist Nationalism Developing Across the Western World."

79   For an unintentionally comical discussion of "producerism" by a reactionary leftist, see "Right-Wing Populism in America: Too Close for Comfort," http://www.publiceye.org/tooclose/producerism.html.

the corrupt elites. The right wing of the ruling class consists primarily of "old money," i.e., banking, oil, agricultural cartels, arms merchants, etc. The left wing of the ruling class consists of newer, high-tech, capital-intensive industries such as media, entertainment, medical, and computer related corporate interests. Both principal factions cement their support base by appealing to contending cultural factions—"social conservatives," the dominant ethnic group, and religious fundamentalists on one end, and elite members of minority groups, union bosses, public sector workers, and environmentalists on the other end. Zionists appear to be rather influential within both camps. The key to building any sort of successful opposition would be to disrupt and neutralize existing ruling class coalitions.[80]

For an Anarchist Vanguard

It is interesting to note that existing ruling class factions and their constituencies include some rather bizarre alliances. What exactly do aristocratic country clubbers have in common with backwoods religious fundamentalists? Yet both are a part of the Republican coalition. What do traditional working class union members have in common with militants from the homosexual counterculture? Yet both are a part of the Democratic coalition. An effective oppositional coalition would draw away certain elements from both of the enemy coalitions, yielding them ineffectual. To achieve this objective, several strategies might need to be simultaneously employed. First, there is the question of leadership. Mark Gillespie postulates the idea of an "anarchist vanguard" whose primarily function is the construction of an anti-ruling class coalition. Says Gillespie:

Anarchists can work to foster alliances between disparate

---

80   Noam Chomsky has developed an interesting "investment theory" of US politics.
      Chomsky argues that the US political system operates on the basis of shifting coalitions
      of investors. These investors have previously acquired enough private wealth and
      power to make the acquisition of political power feasible. See Anthony Gancarski,
      "Does Noam Chomsky Hate America?," http://www.antiwar.com/gancarski/gan102403.
      html.

groups. As mediators and vision-holders, we can help each group to see that uniting for the common goal of freedom, trumps their own agendas. After all, once the government is gone, no one will care if you set up an all-black, all-white, all-Jew, all-Muslim, all-socialist, all-capitalist community. We should pick up the torch of unity and educate people into respecting the diverse views of others. I may like what you're doing, saying, being, etc. but I will defend to the death your right to do, say or be it.[81]

This kind of modern Voltairean outlook might serve as the core principle of the anarchist vanguard. In a sense, we should seek to emulate our deadly enemies, the neoconservatives, in an effort to become a highly influential element in great disproportion to our actual numbers. David Michael suggests that such an effort might be done through non-traditional political strategies such as resource acquisition, alliance building, and community formation.[82] This could include the establishment of self-sufficient intentional communities, alternative media, alternative economic institutions, and even alternative legal institutions or defense organizations as some in the US militia/patriot/constitutionalist movement have sought to do. Such communities and institutions might eventually develop a cultural presence and identity of their own in the same manner that the divergent ethnic groups in large cities currently do. These could in turn be the building blocks of localized political movements and, eventually, full-blown local and regional secessionist or autonomist movements.

Hans-Hermann Hoppe argues that the proliferation of independent or semi-independent free cities, such as those that emerged in the latter Middle Ages, might be the core institutional foundation for the subversion of modern centralist,

---

81   Mark Gillespie, "The Vanguard Idea," http://www.attackthesystem.com/the-vanguard-idea/. See also Keith Preston, "Smashing the State: Thoughts on Anarchist Strategy," chapter 24 of this volume.

82   David Michael, "On Strategy," http://www.nationalanarchist.com/strategy.html

imperialist states.[83] A core idea within the national-anarchist milieu is the creation of anti-establishment communities functioning on a largely autarchic basis, highly diverse in their cultural and ideological orientation, but mutually supportive of one another against the common enemy.[84] In this way, a common alliance of those wanting out of the System could develop. Divergent forces might form a common agreement to work to gain political pre-eminence in their own areas of influence with each agreeing to support the others in their efforts to do so as well. Thus, communities formed by the All-African Peoples' Revolutionary Party in the inner-city regions might be tactically aligned with similar communities formed by the Militia of Montana in rural areas.

While efforts of these types might go along way as far as dealing with "extremist" elements within the ranks of various oppositional tendencies, and such elements might form the core constituencies of an anti-ruling class coalition, there remains the question of how to reach mainstream working people not inclined towards any sort of clearly articulated ideological structures or any particular aspect of peripheral cultures. Troy Southgate argues that a tactic known as "entryism" might be appropriate as far as creating an organizational infrastructure that can be utilized as a political vehicle goes. Says Southgate:

> Entryism is the name given to the process of entering or infiltrating bona fide organizations, institutions and political parties with the intention of either gaining control of them for our own ends, misdirecting or disrupting them for our own purposes or converting sections of their memberships to our cause. . . . So what are we looking for? Any organization with a weak, apathetic or elderly leadership. An organization that has a youth section or a youthful membership . . . What we need is an organization that has idealists, people motivated by ideology and an

83   Hoppe, *Democracy*.

84   David Michael, "Unity in Diversity," http://www.nationalanarchist.com/unity.html.

organization that has—or could have—some sort of influence, given the right leadership in the community . . . It is the case that many organizations currently dominated by both Left and Right simply need turning away from their present ideology . . .[85]

Organizations of this type might include dissident or minor political parties, neighborhood or grassroots community organizations, single-issue pressure groups, territorial secession movements, labor unions, and educational institutions, particularly university humanities departments. Cadre of anarchists would seek seats on the board of directors of the National Rifle Association or the American Civil Liberties Union. Anarchists would obtain positions on the executive committees of "third parties" or local civic organizations. Anarchist educators would be teaching the history of the United States during the twentieth century from the perspective of Murray Rothbard, William Appleman Williams, or Lawrence Dennis rather than Arthur Schlesinger Jr. at the local university. Anarchists sitting on the advisory boards of local business associations, churches, or charities would do much more for the broader struggle than anarchist agitators who throw rocks through Starbucks windows currently do, although the latter is not necessarily without its place as well.

It is through achieving control of the kinds of institutions being described here, using the methods that Troy Southgate suggests, that anarchists could work their way into positions to influence the broader public. Indeed, a precedent for this does exist. In an excellent essay on the ideas of the classical anarchist godfather Pierre-Joseph Proudhon, Larry Gambone describes how the values of libertarian socialism had at one time begun to enter mainstream society:

Proudhon's criticism of the credit and monetary systems were an influence upon the Greenback Party. His concept of

85   Troy Southgate, "The Case for National-Anarchist Entryism," http://www.rosenoire.org/articles/entryism.php.

mutual associations and the Peoples' Bank were forerunners of the credit union and cooperative movements. . . . Support for labor and even "socialism" was found among the upper classes. The British Prime Minister, Disraeli, expressed sympathy for the workers, Lincoln corresponded with the International [Workingmen's Association] and the editor and publisher of the world's largest newspaper, the *New York Tribune*, Charles Dana and Horace Greely, were followers of Proudhon and Charles Fourier.[86]

Beyond Left and Right

The initial way for this new, modernized, revitalized version of traditional anarchism to publicize itself, once it has secured its position in the manner previously suggested, would be to vocally proclaim to be an alternative to the liberal establishment, the reactionary left, and mainstream "conservatism" alike. First, the matter of the culture wars has to be dealt with. This seems to be more of an issue in America that in other Anglo nations like England or Canada and, as I am an American and most familiar with the political landscape of my own country of origin, I will address this question from the perspective of the internal politics of America. A mainstream "conservative" commentator, Dennis Prager, describes some of the controversies that define the culture war:

> The Left believes in removing America's Judeo-Christian identity, e.g., removing "under God" from the Pledge, "In God We Trust" from the currency . . . The Right believes that destroying these symbols and this identity is tantamount is to destroying America.
>
> The Left regards America as morally inferior to many European societies with their abolition of the death penalty, cradle-to-grave-welfare and religion-free life;

---

86 Larry Gambone, "Proudhon and Anarchism: Proudhon's Libertarian Thought and the Anarchist Movement," http://www.spunk.org/library/writers/proudhon/sp001863.html.

and it does not believe that there are distinctive American values worth preserving. The Right regards America as the last best hope for humanity and believes that there are distinctive American values, the unique combination of a religious (Judeo-Christian) society, a secular government, personal liberty and capitalism—that are worth fighting and dying for.

The Left believes multiculturalism should be the ideal for American schools and American policy. The Right believes that the Americanization of all its citizens is indispensable to the survival of the United States.

The Left believes that "war is not the answer." The Right believes that war is often the only answer to governmental evil.[87]

Prager goes on to describe other aspects of the whole moronic "liberal-conservative" divide including condoms in schools, silicone breast implants, gays in the Boy Scouts, yadda, yadda, yadda. Some of his Prager's assertions are absurd to the point of comedy, such as his claim that "capitalism" is worth fighting and dying for. Yes, we can all envision the troops marching into battle singing: "If I die, at least I know, I gave my life for Texaco." Then there is the assertion that America is "the last best hope for humanity." Yes, an ethos of materialist-consumerism, false egalitarianism, and totalitarian therapeutic statism is most assuredly the road to Paradise. Essentially, these culture wars are between those who prefer that the New World Order take on a distinctively "Americanist" identity and those who prefer a global superstate with a more overtly internationalist face. Should the United States rule the world through the United Nations or through the Pentagon? The discrepancies are not

87   Dennis Prager, "The Second American Civil War: What It's About," http://townhall.com/columnists/dennisprager/2003/10/14/the_second_american_civil_war_what_its_about/page/full, and "The Second American Civil War: What It's About—Part II," http://townhall.com/columnists/dennisprager/2003/10/21/the_second_american_civil_war_what_its_about_part_ii/page/full.

nearly as significant as the partisans to this intramural battle insist. Joseph Sobran points out that the constitutional order that the allegedly "right-wing" or "conservative" Bush regime seeks to impose on Iraq includes provisions for ". . . democracy, non-violence, diversity and a role for women."[88] This sounds like something out of the mouth of Morris "Dildo" Dees or Hillary "It Takes a Police State to Raise a Child" Clinton. This is to be the conservative "solution" for a highly patriarchal, religious, militaristic society? Even Trotsky, who claimed that under Marxism the average man would reach the level of an Aristotle, would likely have been more practical.

The relevance of all of this for those of us who are involved in the struggle against the US regime is the question of which side in the "culture wars" will eventually win and, therefore, be our greatest enemy in the long run. I predict that the liberal-internationalist-multiculturalist wing of the US ruling class will win hands down. Even some of the proponents of the "Americanist" perspective agree. For example, John Fonte, a columnist for "Front Page Magazine," edited by the arch-propagandist for Anglo-Zionist imperialism David Horowitz, speculates:

> Thus, it is entirely possible that modernity—thirty or forty years hence—will witness not the final triumph of liberal democracy, but the emergence of a new transnational hybrid regime that is post-liberal democratic and, in the American context, post-Constitutional and post-American.[89]

The simple reason that the "Americanists" are destined to lose is that their ideology is even more utopian and constructivist than that of the "progressives" whom they so ardently despise. There is not, and can never be, an authentic American nationalism. Nationalism must be rooted in the organic culture of the people. This is impossible in a state whose common identity is rooted

---

88 Joseph Sobran, "A New Constitution—Coming Up!," http://www.sobran.com/columns/2003/030930.shtml.

89 John Fonte, "The Ideological War Within the West," September 9, 2002, http://www.frontpagemag.com/Articles/ReadArticle.asp?ID=2853.

in abstract ideological concepts, with the debate being over how these concepts are to be applied, and where whatever passes for a common culture is simply a constantly changing amalgam of all sorts of fractious and contradictory tendencies.[90] This is the so-called "melting pot." Some "Americanists" at least implicitly understand this. Robert Locke, a cynical but candid expositor of Straussian jingoism, observes:

> [T]he Constitution . . . is a curious mixture of Greco-Roman ideas, Christian ideas, Lockean natural-rights ideas, plus a few other odds and ends from Montesquieu and other sources . . . The idea that America was founded foursquare on liberty and inalienable rights is the Platonic noble lie of our republic, and as such is entirely appropriate for schoolchildren and most of the rest of us. It is not, however, the truth.[91]

Locke regards the ideological nationalism promulgated by most "Americanists" to be inadequate as a source of national cohesion and prefers to attempt to construct an American nationalism rooted in more conventional nationalist concepts like ethnicity (in a nation where nearly a third of the population are minorities), Judeo-Christian religious traditions (where did the "Judeo" part come from?), language (in an increasingly bilingual society), and "middle class values" (when most of the constituents of political correctness are middle class professionals and intellectuals). Like most crackpot reactionaries, Locke wants to return to an America that may have existed briefly in the early nineteenth century, if it ever existed at all. Modern America is an imperial empire, not a nation. Even the American state itself more closely resembles the old USSR than anything—a continent-wide regime composed of all sorts of sub-cultural and sub-national groupings absorbed into a bureaucratic monolith ordered on the basis of an imposed ideology. Like the Soviets, the Americanists wish to impose a

---

90   Joseph Sobran, "The Empire and Its Denizens," *The Wanderer,* May 15, 2003.

91   Robert Locke, "Why America Is Not a Propositional Nation," Front Page Magazine, June 4, 2002, http://archive.frontpagemag.com/readArticle.aspx?ARTID=24240.

regime of ideological homogeneity on a society ordered on the basis of extreme cultural diversity. It doesn't work that way.

It is likely, then, that the prevailing future ideology of the United States and therefore the international ruling class will be overt liberal corporatism, globalism, and multiculturalism. All contemporary trends point in that direction. Consequently, the primary target of the anarchist intellectual vanguard should be the liberal establishment and the reactionary left. The David Horowitzes and Ann Coulters are an amusing sideshow to the main event, the professional wrestling of the political/media elite. The liberal orientation of the supposedly "conservative" Bush administration—Keynesian economics, nationalized education, massive subsidies to "curing AIDS in Africa," the liberal "constitution" to be imposed on Iraq, proposed amnesty for illegal immigrants—attests to this. An interesting parallel might be invoked from certain pages in classical anarchist history. The classical anarchists fought for generations against the capitalists, only to be stabbed in the back by their Marxist arch-enemies when the "socialist" revolution actually came. This is the primary fight that authentic anarchists are in today. Old-style capitalism no longer exists. Modern societies are ruled by the "new class" or "managerial elite" observed by Burnham, Orwell, and Dennis. This class has long since made its peace with both capitalism and socialism (in the form of corporate-social democracy and neo-mercantilist "free trade") and has adopted "cultural Marxism" (whether of the neo-conservative or neo-liberal variety) as its social outlook. It is this element that is our principal enemy.

Tradition, Revolution, and Anarchism Without Hyphens

Whatever else could be said about the Straussians, one thing they get right is their understanding of the utility of national and cultural myths as a potent force for political mobilization. Although an actual American nationalism is contradictory and impossible, an appeal to classical American revolutionary ideals is entirely appropriate for opponents of the current American regime. Such venerable notions to be derived from historic Americana as inalienable rights, criticism of state power, decentralism, anti-imperialist revolution, authentic cultural and ideological pluralism (mythically personified by the "First Amendment"), anti-taxation protest, self-reliance, agrarianism, populism, "the right to bear arms," "give me liberty or give me death," and symbolized by such events as the Boston Tea Party, Lexington and Concord, the Whiskey Rebellion, the Confederate secession, the Underground Railroad, Haymarket, and much else provides a virtual fountain of cultural resources for modern enemies of the state to draw on. Larry Gambone provides instruction on how to begin:

> Anarchists should organize at the local level, i.e., neighborhood, village, municipality or county, around issues that affect the population . . . A city-wide organization could fight to decentralize the city government to the neighborhood level and gain greater autonomy for the municipality.[92]

In such an effort, we might look to the example of Norman Mailer's 1969 New York mayoral campaign. Mailer remembered:

> I ran for mayor of New York in the hope that a Left-Right coalition could be formed and this Left-Right pincers could make a dent in the entrenched power of the center . . . So, we called for Power to the Neighborhoods. We suggested that New York City become a state itself, the fifty-first. Its citizens would then have the power to create a variety of new neighborhoods, new townships, all built on separate concepts, core neighborhoods founded on one or another of our cherished notions from the Left or the Right. One could have egalitarian towns and privileged places, or, for those who did not wish to be bothered with living in so detailed (and demanding) a society, there would be the

92   Larry Gambone, *Sane Anarchy* (Montreal: Red Lion Press, 1995), 12.

more familiar and old way of doing things—the City of the State of New York—a government for those who did not care—just like old times.[93]

A number of local and regionalist movements have emerged in the United States in recent years. The ideological and cultural content of these is quite diverse. Some from the Left have suggested secession by the city of San Francisco, the Northeast corridor, and other bastions of "liberal" cultural values. The libertarian-capitalist Free State Project is working to become politically dominant in New Hampshire and radically scale back that state's government. Similar independence, separatist, or autonomist movements exist in the South, Texas, Alaska, Hawaii, New England, the Northwest, Puerto Rico, and elsewhere, including many localities. Some within the patriot/ constitutionalist milieu have sought to set up an alternative infrastructure, usually based on local or populist themes that can be put into place once central power is eradicated. Anarchists should get involved with these kinds of tendencies, and seek to influence the intellectual content and ideological orientation of such movements. It is of the utmost importance to recognize the need for authentic cultural and ideological diversity within the ranks of such resistance efforts. In the tradition of Voltairine de Cleyre, Larry Gambone calls for an unhyphenated anarchism where particular cultural, economic, or theoretical differences are subordinated to the struggle against the common enemy:

Read even the most superficial book on anarchism and you will discover that many forms of anarchism exist— anarchist-communism, individualist-anarchism, anarcho-syndicalism, free-market anarchism, anarcho-feminism and green-anarchism. This division results from people taking their favorite economic system or extrapolating from what they see as the most important social struggle and linking this to anarchism. . . . The hyphenation presents a danger.

---

93   Norman Mailer, "I Am Not for World Empire," *The American Conservative*, December 2, 2002, 18.

Like it or not, everyone, without exception, compromises, modifies or softens their beliefs at some point. Where they compromise is what is important. Do they give up on the anarchism of the other aspect? You can be sure that most hyphenated anarchists will prefer to drop the libertarian side of the hyphen. There are plenty examples of this occurring.[94]

Most existing anarchist tendencies tend to promote their preferred set of sociocultural, economic, or issue-based views over the broader struggle against the state. For example, anarchists with leftist cultural views to be more interested in anti-racism, feminism, and "gay liberation" than anarchism. At the other end, anarchists with nationalist or racialist tendencies are often likely to emphasize the latter rather than the former. Eco-anarchists are typically environmentalists first and anarchists second, or last. Anarcho-socialists and anarcho-capitalists usually put socialism or capitalism before anarchism. To some degree, this is understandable. Most people, including anarchists, tend to identify more strongly with their own culture and others who share their personal values than with ideological abstractions. One anarchist tendency, the national-anarchists, has attempted to deal with this problem. David Michael distinguishes between "core" issues and "peripheral" issues. Core issues involve the common struggle against the New World Order global superstate and the regional/national elites who are its benefactors and beneficiaries. Peripheral issues involve one's preferred cultural, intellectual, economic, or lifestyle interests.[95] These could include communism, capitalism, black nationalism, white nationalism, environmentalism, socialism, feminism, Christianity, Islam, monarchism, Satanism, injecting heroin, or whatever. Divisions of this type are certainly important, and cannot merely be swept under the rug for the sake of some fractious "unity," yet nothing will ever be achieved if these sorts of differences allow the opposition forces to be divided, conquered, or co-opted by the

94 Gambone, *Sane Anarchy*, 9.

95 David Michael, "National Anarchist FAQ," http://www.nationalanarchist.com/faq.html.

international ruling class. David Michael provides us with one poignant example after another of how the NWO imperialists have done just this to nations, cultures, and religions all over the world, including the communist countries of Eastern Europe, the Islamic nations of the Middle East, and the peoples (both white and black) of southern Africa.[96] As Larry Gambone says:

> . . . try as much as you like, you can't ignore the big one— Leviathan—the central state. Eventually it must be tackled head on and this can only be done by a nation-wide mass movement [or a global movement in the case of the NWO]. This does not mean an opposition between local organizations and the larger movement, on the contrary, the latter must be based upon the former. This must be a single issue movement, uniting everyone with a grievance against the state into a movement for the decentralization of power. It must not be allowed to be bogged down by secondary and therefore divisive issues. These can be dealt with by other groups.[97]

Indeed, domestic American politics tends to be driven by single-issue movements and organizations rather than ideological ones. Raw ideology pushers tend to find little success in US politics. With this consideration in mind, the question becomes one of how to best formulate a successful single-issue anti-state movement. Several possible constituents for such a movement have already been discussed. The emergence of a single-issue anti-state party or organization that included the agendas of each of the various local and regionalist movements would likely be a good start. There is no reason why there cannot be a party, or alliance of parties, that simultaneously favors the independence of Puerto Rico, Hawaii, Texas, the South, numerous local communities, and religion/ethnicity based separatists like the Nation of Islam, Christian Identity, Aztlán, indigenous peoples, and others. Such advocacy of regional/local autonomy should

96   Michael, "Unity in Diversity."

97   Gambone, *Sane Anarchy*, 12.

be accompanied by an emphasis on populist structural changes. Norman Mailer's suggestion of decentralizing the governments of large metropolitan areas down to the neighborhood level coincides nicely with the objective of sovereign townships or county supremacy found in the patriot/constitutionalist milieu.

The efforts of the American Civil Liberties Union to defend the civil rights of all sorts of groups which come under attack from the state, ranging from neo-Nazis to pornographers, might be emulated. There are many such groups who are currently ignored by mainstream political organizations. These include home schoolers, "cults" or marginal religious denominations, intentional communities, so-called "hate" groups, prisoners and their families, opponents of the war on drugs, gun rights militants, tax resisters, and many others. It is important to remember that a movement for political decentralization should employ a decentralized strategy. This means that the same tactics will not be appropriate in all situations. For example, anarchists working in urban or metropolitan areas should naturally take a political line that is considerable further to the left than anarchists working in rural areas or among more conservative population groups. The cultural paradigm of anti-racism, feminism, and gay rights that dominates the modern left might well be applicable in those communities that it is suited for, such as large cities with huge minority populations and where the prevailing values are cosmopolitan in nature. However, this would clearly not be an appropriate model for rural Kansas. For anarchists to persistently push "the right to bear arms" in liberal Connecticut would probably be a waste of time. For anarchists to agitate for gay causes in small Tennessee towns would likewise be rather futile.

So-called "extremists" from all points on the political spectrum might be rallied as the core constituents of the anti-System forces. It is essential to remember that the anarchist movement itself (properly and constructively organized) is not necessarily a mass movement per se but only the intellectual and activist vanguard of a broader populist movement containing many different tendencies. The role of the anarchists is to serve as the coordinating mediators conceived of by Mark Gillespie or the principled militants envisioned by Mikhail Bakunin. The decentralized organizational efforts of the anarchists would necessarily involve a scenario where the character of the anti-System movement varied considerably in its specific ideological, cultural, religious, or ethnic orientation on a geographical or institutional basis. Across the American heartland, in the Deep South and in the mountainous regions, the anarchists might assemble a coalition of tax resisters, home schoolers, gun nuts, conspiracy theorists, pro-lifers, Christian fundamentalists, common law enthusiasts, farmers rights advocates, land rights advocates, "cults," racists, libertarians, militiamen, and other elements common to the political culture of right-wing populism. In large metropolitan centers, inner cities, border areas, and coastal regions, a similar coalition might include militants and separatists from the various minority groups, advocates for all sorts of class-based social issues (gentrification, housing, environment), gays and other sexual minorities, all sorts of countercultural groups, students, street gangs and other official outlaws, communists, left-wing "anarchists," and others.

Among the affluent elements of American society, such as the realm of suburbia, it is probably best if the ranks of the revolutionaries draw heavily from the youth population. Opposition to the great oppressor of youth—the state's school systems—may well be the key issue. It is also important to note that class distinctions in modern liberal democratic states are somewhat more blurred than they may have been in previous times. Any authentic populist revolutionary movement would naturally have to include persons from all classes. The task of the genuine anarchists, who will always be a small minority, even in Official Anarchist circles, is to coordinate and guide formal and informal alliances among such disparate groups. The kinds of issue and ideology based constituent groups being described here would provide the grassroots base for the broader anarchist agenda. But there remains the question of how to appeal to the broader public. A party/organization that combined local and regional autonomy, defended social groups under attack by the state, recruited disparate elements from the cultural fringes as its activist/support base, and maintained a decentralized infrastructure would also have to develop a populist program for the masses.

Popular Front Anarchism and the Defense of Culture and Civilization Against Nihilism

It is essential to remember that not everything the state does is equally pernicious or equally in need of abolition. The most important issue is the need to defeat the New World Order internationally and the creeping police state domestically. All other considerations should be subordinated to these concerns. The ultimate objective is to bring down the corrupt, tyrannical US regime and to consequently implode the New World Order. The issues that motivate those on the margins— radical environmentalism, gun rights absolutism, racial nationalism, socialism, radical feminism, queer power, religious fundamentalism—mean nothing to most people. The ordinary citizen is concerned only with his own day-to-day business. His issues are unemployment, housing, taxes, health care, provisions for old age, and education.[98] Some people may also have one or two social issues like abortion or the environment that they are interested in or have strong opinions about. Most Americans have received something of a libertarian education from the Jeffersonian strand of traditional American politics. For this reason, populist rhetoric denouncing "big government" resonates well with the commoner. A populist movement that combined both libertarian and socialist themes, without explicitly describing itself as such, would likely go over well with the broad American working class.

Populist structural changes with a libertarian bent might be the first item on the agenda. Larry Gambone comments:

---

98   Ibid., 8.

In order to make significant structural changes to society, one must have a program consisting of, say, half a dozen or so key items which the majority of the population might support. The most important point, and the point upon which all populists agree, is the need to empower the ordinary person and their communities and the concurrent weakening of the authority of the politico-economic elite. This can be done by combining the traditional populist structural political reforms of proportional ballot, referenda, initiative and recall with radical decentralization of political power down to the natural community. The power of the economic elite can be clipped by the abolition of corporate welfare and all other government-granted privileges. All populist groups either do or would agree with these principles. Once empowered, the people and their communities could then seek any other social, political or economic reforms they chose, since they would now have the ability to make those decisions.[99]

This proposal seems to be as cogent as any. As the recent recall of the governor of California illustrates, populist fiscal reforms are also quite popular, even in havens of leftward-leaning politics. As taxes are the lifeblood of the state, and as the average American is familiar with the partial origins of the American Revolution in anti-taxation protest, a radical assault upon the state's taxing system seems warranted. Depicting Establishment politicians as corrupt squanderers of the public treasury is a tried and true American political tactic, and could almost certainly be utilized to the advantage of anarchists.

Kevin Carson provides us with a possible economic program.[100] On economic matters, an anarcho-populist, libertarian-decentralist, left-right, radical-center alliance should assert itself as a populist alternative to both the neoliberal economics of the Anglo-

---

99   Gambone, "The Neocons in a Nutshell."

100   Kevin Carson, "A 'Political' Program for Anarchists," http://attackthesystem.com/a-political-program-for-anarchists/.

American New Right (as opposed to the more populist New Right of the European continent) and the New Class welfare statism of the reactionary left. Carson offers three principal targets for such an alliance: the state's monopolistic currency and banking legislation, the monopoly privilege imposed by patent laws, and the concentration of control over land through the enforcement of absentee ownership. Elimination of barriers to the formation of credit unions, organization of tenants of public and private rental housing into unions organized on the old anarcho-syndicalist model, demands for the recognition of squatters rights, establishment of the right of local and regional political units and "private" groupings to issue alternative units of exchange, and the establishment of mutual aid societies for the provision of unemployment, medical, and old-age insurance might be a first step. These can be followed by the elimination of licensing regulations designed to prevent competition with established corporate or professional monopolies from small businesses and the self-employed and to concentrate control over the media.

The elimination of all corporate welfare and the establishment of worker cooperatives as an antidote to corporatism and the conversion of social or municipal services to consumer cooperatives should accompany the dismantling of the corporate-social democratic welfare state.[101] Measures such as these have been proposed by a wide variety of radical thinkers and would be fairly consistent with both the ideals of the "small is beautiful" social activist left along with the "anti-big government" right. Furthermore, the emerging presence and popularity of radicals advocating such a program would have the effect of further discrediting the common left/right divide. The reactionary left would be forced to abandon any populist or decentralist pretensions it might otherwise display and position itself as the defenders of the welfare state. Likewise, the reactionary right would be forced to abandon its libertarian pretensions and become the open, unabashed defenders of corporatism. Also, the anarchist/populist

101 Ibid.

forces would include a genuine cross-section of the cultural spectrum, ranging from patriarchal fundamentalists and racialists to gay, feminist, countercultural anarchists and communists, each of these seeking sovereignty within their own communities. In response, the totalitarian multicultural left would likely gravitate towards the corporatists. The ruling class enemy would be more greatly consolidated in the form of the corporate-social democratic welfare-warfare state, with reactionary multiculturalism and totalitarian progressivism as its ideological orientation, and would therefore be easier to identify and attack.

There remains yet another consideration regarding programmatic concerns. Any movement that aims to break up ruling class coalitions needs to recognize the importance of "wedge" issues to such efforts. These involve issues for which there is a constituency but where all established parties are committed to the other side.[102] Probably the most significant wedge issues in American politics are drug prohibition and the relationship between the United States and Israel. A growing and militant opposition is brewing on both of these matters, yet the political establishment cannot budge a bit as the "war on drugs" is an essential component of the police state apparatus, and involves a vast array of vested interests, and the Zionist lobby has a firm grip on both the center-left and the center-right. Anti-Zionism and anti-prohibition both have a considerable number of enthusiasts from across the spectrum of opinion and on the Far Left and Far Right alike. The one-time US Speaker of the House Thomas P. "Tip" O'Neill once remarked that "all politics is local." Localism as both a means and an end seems consistent with a broader anarchist perspective. Ideological and programmatic considerations aside, there remains the immensely complicated question of how the US regime is to be effectively challenged. Most of the "third-party" formations in the United States are oriented towards some particular ideological or cultural constituency that is sizable enough to form a minor party but not large enough to actually challenge the status quo. Examples of this include the theocratic

---

102 Opposition to the drug war as a wedge issue has been repeatedly suggested by R. W. Bradford of *Liberty* magazine.

"Constitution" Party and the highly ideological "Libertarian" Party. These types of party formations ultimately fail because of their inability to transcend ordinary cultural, ideological, ethnic, or religious boundaries. For an example of how to best proceed with this task, we might look to a nation with a long tradition of authentically progressive politics, the Netherlands, and the phenomenon of Pim Fortuyn. A Dutch commentator, Tjebbe van Tijen, observes:

> The shake-up . . . had its first expression in local elections, with many locally initiated parties—often called Leefbaar (Livable) followed by the name of a village or town. The issues raised by these parties varied depending on the particular area. But in general they focused on "quality of life" issues: recurring elements were environmental, housing, and traffic problems, and sometimes also questions about "foreigners," be it the influx of refugees or lamentations about the lack of adaptation of other nations, religions and cultures to Dutch society.

> After the success of such Leefbaar parties in some bigger cities in the mid-1990s, an initiative was made to try to bundle this locally dispersed force into a national Leefbaar Nederland party.

> The bundling of loose parts implies the use of a binding element, and little coherence could be found in the diverse assembly of many of those local parties. . . . So . . . they started looking for a leader . . . in the person of a commentator on Dutch social and economic affairs, a former professor of sociology . . ., a . . . homosexual, and a provocative public debater: Pim Fortuyn.[103]

It should be noted that Fortuyn's primary significance was rooted in his role as a symbolic figurehead of a grassroots, authentically populist movement. His appeal seems based on the fact that, as a gay, Marxist, social liberal opponent of immigration, he found a hearing

---

103   Tijen, "The Sorrow of the Netherlands."

among both the liberal cultural elite and the instinctively nationalist and xenophobic common people as well. Some might argue that Fortuyn's subsequent assassination by a reactionary leftist ideologue is indicative of his political failure. However, the martyrdom of John Hus did not prevent the Protestant Reformation.

Anarchist militants should begin to assemble diverse coalitions in local communities across the United States, tailoring their specific programs to the culture of the local community. Anarchists, as the intellectual and activist vanguard, should maintain communication with one another irrespective of local boundaries and formulate a common agenda and plan. The first goal is to become the dominant force at the local level, whether by electoral means, strikes, boycotts, armed insurrection, or whatever. Once established in local communities, the next step would be to issue formal declarations condemning central government as some communities have already done regarding such matters as the US invasion of Iraq and the USA PATRIOT Act. Alliances between such communities should then be formed with the eventual goal of secession from the national regime. Larry Gambone describes how such a revolution might take place:

> People begin taking control at the local level, developing or re-instituting forms of self-government and ignoring the state. Certain politicians at the national level become cognizant of the anti-statist sentiment, and for genuine or opportunist reasons, will help prevent the regime from attacking the decentralists. They may also pass certain "de-fanging" legislation which will weaken the state. Demonstrations accompanied by mass strikes will occur on an almost daily basis in the capital cities in support of the local movements and as means to keep up the pressure on the politicos. [Allies] . . . in other countries will also be developed to insure a massive outcry should the state choose to repress the libertarian upsurge. The outcome will be the development of genuine federal institutions.[104]

---

104 Gambone, *Sane Anarchy*, 13.

If history is any guide, such an insurgence is likely to occur following both an unpopular and failed war and a series of scandals leading to the loss of perceived legitimacy on the part of the state in the eyes of the public. One needs only to look at the loss of prestige suffered by the US regime following the combined Vietnam/Watergate fiasco and the fall of the Soviet Union in the aftermath of the disastrous Afghan war. The US regime is currently moving into such a scenario once again, thanks to the imperial ambitions of the neoconservatives, brewing scandals in the Bush administration, and impending economic collapse resulting from currency devaluation and outrageous levels of both private and public debt. In the likely scenario that armed confrontation with the regime becomes necessary, popular militias formed at the community level combined with defector units from the state's military forces will become the basis of the armed struggle. The task of anarchist and populist leaders will be to redirect the apparent natural zeal for war among the commoners towards the war against the illegitimate ruling class, appealing to American revolutionary traditions, and to redirect the natural patriotic inclinations of the masses towards the struggle against the state in defense of their own communities, regions, cultures, and religions.[105] Such efforts are apparently not as impossible as they may seem. After all, if a former *National Review* conservative like Joseph Sobran can be converted to the anarchist position, who couldn't be?[106]

The struggle against the Anglo-American-Zionist empire, the authentic Axis of Evil, is not simply a matter of idealism, advancing one's own social or political aesthetics, or humanitarian

---

105 One thing that will certainly be necessary in the broader struggle against the New World Order, particularly in the Western countries, is the cultivation of a warrior ethic appropriate to the battle at hand. Thus far, most Western radicals are heavily under the influence of the delusions of liberalism, humanism, pacifism, democratism, and other perspectives that look askance at any sort of warrior ethic. Traditions and cultural phenomenon we might look to for inspiration include the gladiators of ancient Rome, the Spartan warriors, the chivalry of medieval knights, the New Model Army, the Taiping rebels, the bushido warrior ethics of the samurai and the kamikaze, and, of course, modern Islamic jihadists.

106 Joseph Sobran, "The Reluctant Anarchist," http://www.lewrockwell.com/orig3/sobran-j1.html.

concern. Rather, it has become a matter of planetary survival (in a human, rather than eco-doomsday, sense). The conservative commentator Paul Craig Roberts points to the real agenda of the Empire and its neoconservative court intellectuals:

> . . . influential advisors at the Pentagon are backing the development of a new generation of low yield nuclear weapons . . . In the place of bad old nuclear weapons, the new good nukes will be easier to use and more "relevant to the threat environment" . . . The Pentagon report designates "terrorists" as the targets of the mini-nukes. New nuclear weapons are said to be necessary in order to destroy deeply buried biological weapons caches, terrorist cells and hidden weapons of mass destruction. Such weapons caches will exist wherever neoconservatives declare them to be. Obviously, nuclear weapons of any size are too destructive to use against terrorists . . . The only purpose of the "small nuclear weapons" is to incinerate Muslim cities. It looks as if the neocons intend a final solution to their "Muslim problem" and are organizing genocide for Arabs.[107]

The use of such weapons by the US regime will necessitate the development, deployment, and use of such weapons by other states, and the provision of such weapons to freelance military organizations by states. The neoconservatives' ambitions amount to little more than worldwide nuclear holocaust. Larry Gambone perceptively describes the neocons as "an American version of the Khmer Rouge . . . The possible roots of neocon nihilism? A mad desire to revolutionize the world, not for socialism, but for global corporatism, the Zionazi hatred of everything Arab, and the 'Christian' fundi's world-hating lust for an apocalypse."[108]

Whatever one's perception of Islamic "terrorists" and "suicide" bombers, the Muslims are fighting for the defense of their culture,

107   Paul Craig Roberts, "A Holocaust in the Making," http://www.antiwar.com/cs/roberts3.html.

108   Larry Gambone, Porcupine Blog, May 17, 2003.

religion, and homelands. The neocons have no excuse. Eminently destructive weaponry in the hands of such fanatics constitutes the greatest danger to the world yet to emerge, surpassing even the looming nuclear holocaust of the Cuban missile crisis and the apocalyptic showdown between the imperial powers during the Second World War. Therefore, the defeat of Empire and the development of a new political paradigm that is antithetical to Empire has become an imperative. Hopefully, philosophical anarchism will help to show the way.

Anti-Imperialists of the World, Unite!

Towards an Anarchist Theory of Geopolitics

In the century and a half that modern anarchist movements have been in existence, anarchism has thus far passed through two distinct phases. The first of these was the era of classical anarchism, a movement inspired by the thought of Pierre-Joseph Proudhon, Mikhail Bakunin, and Peter Kropotkin, which arose out of the rebellions of 1848 and came to position itself as the most militant wing of the international workers movement. The orientation of classical anarchism towards proletarian socialism was appropriate given that the "labor question" was the dominant political struggle of the time. This embryonic era of anarchist history lasted for nearly a century before meeting its end after the defeat of the anarchists at Kronstadt and in the Spanish Civil War, the achievement of hegemony by Communism on the Left, the massive strengthening of states during the "managerial revolution" of the mid-twentieth century, and the unrivaled levels of militarist bloodshed and statist repression perpetrated by the rival imperialist powers during the two world wars.

The second phase of modern anarchism, what might be termed "neo-anarchism," had its roots in the student rebellions of the late 1960s. Neo-anarchism reflected the general trend within the New Left milieu in which it was born by shifting its focus away from workers' struggles and the proletarian class towards an agglomeration of both privileged class youth and members of traditional social and cultural outgroups, such as racial minorities, feminist women, homosexuals, immigrants, and the like, all the while becoming intertwined with the growing ecological consciousness, pop psychology, and therapeutic culture of the time. This ideological formula continues to dominate anarchist movements at the present juncture nearly a half century after it emerged.

The proletarian socialist orientation of classical anarchism may continue to possess considerable value in those nations and regions where the level of economic and technological development continues to approximate that of the West during the classical anarchist era. Likewise, the orientation of neo-anarchism towards social justice for racial minorities, women, gays, and other outgroups, preservation of the natural environment, and critiquing cultural barriers to self-actualization may retain its relevance in those regions where the cultural revolution of the 1960s and 1970s has not taken root or become particularly entrenched. However, both the orientation of the classical anarchist movement towards the proletarian class and the orientation of neo-anarchism towards the cultural margins have become anachronistic in the modern Western nations where the working class has become integrated into the political mainstream, where labor unions have become respectable public institutions, and where criticism of cultural or demographic sectors regarded as traditionally excluded or disadvantaged has become a taboo subject to severe social opprobrium and, in some cases, legal repression.

If anarchism is to regain the political status that it held in the late nineteenth century, that of the premier revolutionary movement in the West that simultaneously arose on the periphery as the vanguard of anti-colonialist struggles, it will be necessary to construct a theoretical paradigm, ideological formulation, and strategic orientation for twenty-first-century anarchist movements that possesses a contemporary analysis and factual understanding of the nature of the institutions that actually dominate modern societies. If the orientation of previous anarchist movements towards proletarian socialism or cultural radicalism is inappropriate in societies where the state reflects both social democratic and multicultural values, then the question arises of what the primary focus of contemporary anarchist movements should actually be.

The Nature of Contemporary Imperialism

Anarchist anti-imperialism of the classical era had its roots in resistance to the European colonial empires that were in turn outgrowths of the conquests that followed the meeting of European civilization and the societies of Asia, Africa, and the Americas during the Age of Discovery, the commercial revolution, and the development of capitalism as the dominant mode of production. European colonialism reached its zenith at the end of the nineteenth century but went into decline following the decimation of the European nations by the two world wars and the overthrow of the traditional monarchies and aristocracies in these nations by the rising liberal, democratic, and socialist movements of the early twentieth century.[1]

The decimation of the European and Asian continents by war and the resulting destruction of the traditional colonial empires created the international geopolitical conditions for the achievement of American hegemony as the United States had been the only major power that had not experienced the two world wars within its internal boundaries and had therefore avoided the destruction inflicted on the European and Asian powers. For the first four decades following the conclusion of the Second World War, the "First World" hegemony of the United States and its Western European allies and protectorates was countered with a limited degree of effectiveness by the regional imperialism of the "Second World" Soviet Union and its modest efforts to aid anti-colonial struggles in the pre-industrial "Third World." However, the collapse of the Eurasian empire of the Soviet Union in the late 1980s and early 1990s allowed for the full achievement of global American hegemony.[2]

1   William S. Lind, "That Old Romanov Feeling," *The American Conservative*, April 9, 2012.

2   Noam Chomsky, *Deterring Democracy* (New York: Hill and Wang, 1992).

The American model of imperialism during the postwar era was not the traditional model of formal acquisition of colonies through direct military conquest. Rather, the form the American empire began to assume in the mid-twentieth century was one largely predicated on the informal domination of other nations by means of economic hegemony, the cultivation of local elites as clients, cultural imperialism exercised by the increasingly dominant American mass media, destabilization and counter-insurgency campaigns fought with local forces but financed and given diplomatic cover by the American state, proxy wars fought by mercenary armies, and small scale military interventions often conducted under the guise of "police actions." Large-scale warfare was utilized only in extraordinary circumstances, such as American intervention on the Korean peninsula, in the former French colonies of Indochina, and in the Persian Gulf. Though the degree of overt militarism displayed by the American state has escalated since the historic events of September 11, 2001, the general structure of mid to late twentieth-century American imperialism outlined above largely continues as the *modus operandi* of the American empire and the client states and network of international institutions through which its hegemony is maintained.[3]

Our Enemies: Marxism and Totalitarian Humanism

Any serious analysis of anti-imperialist resistance movements during the twentieth century must necessarily seek to address the unquestionable fact that Marxism eventually eclipsed anarchism as the prevailing ideology of those with a radically anti-imperialist perspective. Why was this so? Surely, it was not due to the ability of Marxism to provide a more comprehensive theoretical critique of imperialism than anarchism. The actual historical contrasts between the perspectives of classical

---

3   William Blum, *Killing Hope: U.S. Military and CIA Interventions Since World War II* (Monroe, ME: Common Courage Press, 2003); James A. Lucas, "Deaths in Other Nations Since WWII Due to U.S. Interventions," Countercurrents.Org, April 24, 2007, http://www.countercurrents.org/lucas240407.htm (accessed September 23, 2012).

anarchism and Marxism regarding imperialism have been aptly summarized by Michael Schmidt:

> It cannot be overemphasised how for the first 50 years of its existence as a proletarian mass movement since its origin in the First International, the anarchist movement often entrenched itself far more deeply in the colonies of the imperialist powers and in those parts of the world still shackled by post-colonial regimes than in its better-known Western heartlands like France or Spain. Until Lenin, Marxism had almost nothing to offer on the national question in the colonies, and until Mao, who had been an anarchist in his youth, neither did Marxism have anything to offer the peasantry in such regions—regions that Marx and Engels, speaking as de facto German supremacists from the high tower of German capitalism, dismissed in their *Communist Manifesto* (1848) as the "barbarian and semi-barbarian countries." Instead, Marxism stressed the virtues of capitalism (and even imperialism) as an onerous, yet necessary stepping stone to socialism. Engels summed up their devastating position in an article entitled "Democratic Pan-Slavism" in their *Neue Rheinische Zeitung* of 14 February 1849: the United States' annexation of Texas in 1845 and invasion of Mexico in 1846 in which Mexico lost 40% of its territory were applauded as they had been "waged wholly and solely in the interest of civilisation," as "splendid California has been taken away from the lazy Mexicans, who could not do anything with it" by "the energetic Yankees" who would "for the first time really open the Pacific Ocean to civilization . . ."

So, "the 'independence' of a few Spanish Californians and Texans may suffer because of it, in some places 'justice' and other moral principles may be violated; but what does that matter to such facts of world-historic significance?" By this racial argument of the "iron reality" of inherent national virility giving rise to laudable capitalist overmastery,

Engels said the failure of the Slavic nations during the 1848 Pan-European Revolt to throw off their Ottoman, Austro-Hungarian and Russian yokes, demonstrated not only their ethnic unfitness for independence, but that they were in fact "counter-revolutionary" nations deserving of "the most determined use of terror" to suppress them.

It reads chillingly like a foreshadowing of the Nazis' racial nationalist arguments for the use of terror against the Slavs during their East European conquest. Engels' abysmal article had been written in response to Mikhail Bakunin's *Appeal to the Slavs by a Russian Patriot* in which he—at that stage not yet an anarchist—had by stark contrast argued that the revolutionary and counter-revolutionary camps were divided not by nationality or stage of capitalist development, but by class.[4]

Clearly, Marxism possessed no greater intellectual force in its critique of imperialism than anarchism. Indeed, Marx and Engels were demonstrably pro-imperialist in their geopolitical outlook. It is also abundantly clear from the pervasiveness of anarchist tendencies throughout the world during the classical anarchist era that Marxism traveled with no greater ease than anarchism. Schmidt goes on to describe the vastness of the anarchist presence throughout the colonized world:

By 1873, when Bakunin, now unashamedly anarchist, threw down the gauntlet to imperialism, writing that "Two-thirds of humanity, 800 million Asiatics, asleep in their servitude, will necessarily awaken and begin to move," the newly-minted anarchist movement was engaging directly and repeatedly with the challenges of imperialism, colonialism, national liberation movements, and post-colonial regimes. So it was that staunchly anti-imperialist anarchism and its emergent revolutionary unionist strategy,

---

4   Michael Schmidt, "South Asian Anarchism: Paths to Practice," Anarkismo.net, July, 27, 2012, http://www.anarkismo.net/article/23404 (accessed September 23, 2012).

syndicalism—and not pro-imperialist Marxism—that rose to often hegemonic dominance of the union centres of Argentina, Brazil, Chile, Colombia, Cuba, Mexico, Paraguay, Peru and Uruguay in the early 1900s, almost every significant economy and population concentration in post-colonial Latin America. In six of these countries, anarchists mounted attempts at revolution; in Cuba and Mexico, they played a key role in the successful overthrow of reactionary regimes; while in Mexico and Nicaragua they deeply influenced significant experiments in large-scale revolutionary agrarian social construction.

The anarchist movement also established smaller syndicalist unions in colonial and semi-colonial territories as diverse as Algeria, Bulgaria, China, Ecuador, Egypt, Korea, Malaya (Malaysia), New Zealand, North and South Rhodesia (Zambia and Zimbabwe, respectively), the Philippines, Poland, Puerto Rico, South Africa, South-West Africa (Namibia), and Venezuela—and built crucial radical networks in the colonial and post-colonial world: East Africa, Eastern Europe, the Middle East, Central Asia, Central America, the Caribbean, South-East Asia, and Ramnath's chosen terrain, the South Asian sub-continent.[5]

So why did Marxism or Marxist-inspired movements come to achieve hegemony in the great majority of anti-imperialist struggles during the mid to late twentieth century, in nations throughout Asia, Africa, and Latin America? Two primary explanations for this phenomenon would seem to be the most plausible.

The first is the international prestige of the Soviet Union following the Bolshevik coup of 1917 and the subsequent achievement of a position of dominance on the international Left by Communism, a position that was strengthened by the key role played by the Soviets as a member of the Allied coalition during the Second

5   Ibid.

World War. As mentioned, the regional empire extending across the Eurasian landmass established by the Soviet Union at the conclusion of the war became the principal source of opposition to the international hegemony achieved by the United States as the neo-colonialism of the latter eclipsed and essentially replaced the traditional colonial empires previously maintained by Great Britain and the continental European nations. As part of its geopolitical strategy during the Cold War, the Soviet Union would aid anti-American resistance forces throughout the Third World with the hope of cultivating future revolutionary regimes in these countries as client states (ambition that was of course actually achieved in some instances, for example, in Cuba).

The Soviet efforts at cultivating Third World revolutionary movements as the foundation for future client states in the Cold War with America fit well with the opportunistic ambitions of the leadership of Third World anti-colonial movements, which typically consisted of alienated intellectuals drawn from the ranks of the middle classes and who considered their ambitions to be frustrated by the static, traditional feudal regimes which dominated their own countries. Marxism had the same appeal to late nineteenth- and twentieth-century alienated middle class intellectuals as liberalism and Jacobinism had in the eighteenth century, and the statism of Marxism had a greater appeal to these ambitious opportunists drawn from the privileged classes than the decentralist and libertarian ideals of anarchism.[6]

The second major reason for the eclipsing of anarchism by Marxism during the twentieth century must be understood within the context of what James Burnham described as the "managerial revolution" that occurred during the same era. Burnham observed that all of the industrialized societies of the time, whether capitalist America, socialist Russia, or fascist Italy and Germany, were undergoing a transformation towards a new form of bureaucratic rule that transcended their respective

---

6   Eric von Kuehnelt-Leddihn, *Leftism Revisited: From de Sade and Marx to Hitler and Pol Pot* (Washington, DC: Regnery Gateway, 1990).

ideological differences and defied categorization as far as traditional labels of "capitalist" or "socialist" were concerned. The trend of the time was towards ever-greater centralization, statism, and bureaucracy, meaning that the anarchists were swimming against the tides of the era. Marxism, with its orientation towards state-managed command economies, appeared to be progressive and forward-looking while anarchism took on the appearance of an archaic romanticism.[7]

The defeat of the fascist powers in the Second World War along with the collapse of the Soviet Union and the discrediting of Communism at the end of the Cold War meant that only the form of the managerial revolution that had emerged in the capitalist countries continued to give the appearance of legitimacy or viability. Indeed, the Western model of the managerial revolution (so-called "democratic capitalism") was even touted by some, most notably Francis Fukuyama, as representing the final stage in human political evolution. The disappearance of any effective opposition to the American empire following the demise of the Soviet Union allowed the American state and its international junior partners to arrogantly assert the universality of their own claims to legitimacy. Hence, the post-Cold War acts of military aggression taken by the United States and its allies in the name of democratization and the universal imposition of Western ideological conceptions of "human rights."[8]

This geopolitical framework of "human rights imperialism" provides the foreign policy component of the wider ideological foundations of the contemporary Western ruling classes, the core elements of which also include the previously discussed bureaucratic managerialism, plutocratic liberalism, and welfare capitalism in the economic realm. In the social and cultural arena, the contemporary ruling class ideology exhibits such characteristics as multiculturalism, a general social egalitarianism

7   James Burnham, *The Managerial Revolution: What Is Happening in the World* (New York: John Day, 1941).

8   Francis Fukuyama, *The End of History and the Last Man* (New York: Free Press, 1992).

(feminism, gay rights, "anti-ablism," etc.) which is regarded as necessary for a larger, better integrated, and better trained labor force, therapeutic statism (for example, the obsessive fixation on health represented by neo-puritan campaigns against smoking, fatty food, sugar-laden beverages, and the ongoing war on drugs), mass democracy (with public elections serving as the ritualistic means of political class self-legitimization), media pre-eminence, and educationism (with the mass media and educational institutions serving as the primary means of inculcating ruling class ideology and training subordinate classes to function in a complex, technologically advanced society), infantilization (for instance, the nanny state's perpetual obsession with "protecting the children"), and the ever-expanding police state. Each of these ideological elements in turn reflects a general world view rooted in notions of universalism, egalitarianism, and a linear-progressive view of history that might be collectively labeled as "totalitarian humanism."[9]

The Decline of the State and the Prospects for an Anarchist Renaissance

A rather fascinating convergence of two historical trends has emerged over the last two decades. The first of these is the previously discussed achievement of global hegemony by the American empire following the end of the Cold War. The second is the decline of the state as an institution, the beginning of which Martin van Creveld traces to the period between the conclusion of the Second World War through the economic downturns and backlash against the Vietnam War during the mid-1970s. The decline of the state is itself the product of a convergence of multiple forces, including the prohibitive cost of mass warfare due to the destructive capabilities of modern weaponry, the failure of the state to fully entrench itself in the lesser developed parts of the world and the subsequent spread of disorder from those regions to the West, a prevailing cultural ethos which deemphasizes or even denigrates martial values, the

---

9   Keith Preston, "The New Totalitarianism," chapter 15 of this volume.

exorbitant costs of modern welfare states and its resulting fiscal difficulties, the growth of the global economy, an increase in the private provision of security, and the inability of contemporary states to inspire or retain the loyalty of their citizens.[10]

This accelerating decline of the state would indicate that conventional nationalism is becoming an anachronism. Classical nineteenth-century nationalism and its later ideological descendents are themselves the ideological and institutional outgrowths of the centralizing tendencies of the French Revolution and the subsequent nation-state system that eventually eclipsed the older royal empires. Indeed, a core insight of fourth generation warfare theory is that the loyalty of populations is being transferred away from conventional nation-states and towards non-state entities and that contemporary warfare is becoming increasingly dominated by non-state actors. Further, the ruling classes and national regimes of most of the world's nations, save a few so-called "rogue" nations (as termed by the overlords of the empire), have positioned themselves as component parts and territorial prefects within the empire's expanse.

Many of the component nation-states within the empire practice their own internal imperialisms. No greater example can be found than that of the "mother country" of the empire itself, the United States, whose domestic, continent-wide, "fifty state" empire includes the captive nations of the former Hawaiian kingdom, the scattered African-American communities, the Alaskan natives, the American Indian nations, the former Mexican territories of the American southwest, Texas, Vermont, and the southeastern territories (so-called "Dixie") that were incorporated into the American empire following the defeat of the Southern independence efforts during the American Civil War. A comparable analysis could be applied to, for example, the nation-states of India, China, the British Isles, or the continental

---

10   Martin van Creveld, *The Rise and Decline of the State* (Cambridge: Cambridge University Press, 1999).

European nations. Clearly, the most appropriate ideological foundation for contemporary anti-imperialist struggles is not a reactionary nation-state-centered nationalism but an orientation towards self-determination for all peoples that only anarchism can provide. It is not sufficient to merely liberate national entities from the wider imperial order but to also liberate regions, provinces, communities, ethnicities, tribes, cultures, linguistic groups, and religions that are often held captive to these nation-state systems. Nor is an authentic anti-imperialist struggle consistent with the mere replacement of the global imperialism of the American empire and international plutocracy with an agglomeration of regional imperialisms of the kind practiced by the United States under the guise of the "Monroe Doctrine" during the nineteenth century.

If conventional nation-state nationalism has become archaic, the anti-Europeanism and racist denigration of white ethnicity exhibited by the Left in its present-day incarnations has likewise become anachronistic. The Left's anti-Europeanism and anti-white racism is a reactionary backlash against past events and past social orders that no longer exist, notably America's historic racial caste system, South African apartheid, Nazism, the Holocaust, and the chauvinistic presumptions utilized as a means of self-legitimization by classical European colonialism. However, the European nations and historic white homelands are today colonies of the international plutocratic order grounded in America's neo-colonial political, military, economic, and cultural hegemony, and the national regimes of the white nations are themselves de facto puppet states of the American empire and global plutocratic oligarchy. The struggle against this empire and oligarchy is likewise a global struggle and one that transcends the boundaries of race, nation, culture, religion, political ideology, and socio-economic class. The overlords of the empire seek the subjugation of all races, all nations, all religions, all philosophies, all cultures, and all classes.

The most appropriate ideological foundation for a twenty-first-century anarchist movement would be one that advances beyond both the class determinism and economism of classical anarchism and the counterculturalism and the racial, class, and gender reductionism of the postwar and late twentieth-century Left that has been incorporated into neo-anarchism. Rather than defining the anarchist struggle in terms of either a class conflict between the international working classes and the capitalist classes within their respective nations, or in terms of traditional outgroups versus traditional ingroups, a contemporary anarchism possessing the most penetrating analysis of imperialism and the global plutocratic order would define the struggle as one pitting all subjugated peoples, regardless of race, class, nation, or culture, against the imperial overlords. Therefore, twenty-first-century anarchists, regardless of their sectarian identity (e.g., syndicalist, anarcho-communist, individualist) should position themselves as the most militant wing of international anti-imperialist struggles just as the classical anarchists were the most militant wing of the historic labor struggles. Likewise, just as the classical anarchists became the leadership of mass syndicalist labor organizations, so should contemporary anarchists aspire to become the leadership of anti-state populist movements whose principal aim is resistance to imperialism, the destruction of the national regimes and ruling classes that are its component parts, and the achievement of self-determination for all peoples exhibiting all forms of cultural identity.

At present, the majority of contemporary anarchist movements maintain an orientation towards the most extreme forms of cultural leftism and counterculturalism. This may be fine by itself when expressed as a form of tribal or particularistic identity, but it becomes extraordinarily self-limiting as far as the ability of anarchist movements to grow beyond the level of existing merely as a type of youth subculture or as a sect within the ranks of the reactionary Left. To truly become the vanguard of anti-imperialist struggles, anarchists will necessarily have to cultivate allies and constituents far beyond those towards which they are presently oriented. Anarchists must out of necessity reach out to people of all cultures, classes, political ideologies, and value systems as part of the project of building the anti-imperialist struggle.

The recognition of these issues additionally requires the rejection of the conventional left/right model of the political spectrum in favor of alternative models that define the anti-imperialist struggle as one pitting not the Left against the Right, but pitting the forces of decentralization against centralism or pitting the periphery against the center in the manner suggested by Alain de Benoist.[11] Anarchists should subsequently strive to become the leadership of movements within their respective nations that seek national independence from the empire and international oligarchy. Such movements would possess three primary ideological elements: anti-statism, populism, and anti-imperialism. This anarchist-led anti-state populism might potentially be organized on the basis of nation-by-nation anarchist federations with a synthesist/pluralist outlook. Such federations might be internally layered and decentralized in such a way that anarchists would constitute an ideological center and leadership corps that emanates outward into the ranks of political and cultural forces from across the spectrum and drawing towards itself equally from the ranks of conservatives, nationalists, liberals, progressives, socialists, libertarians, Christians, Muslims, atheists, environmentalists, and others.

While an anarchist-led anti-state populism would transcend class boundaries, it might also be expected that the "vanguard classes" within each respective nation would be the poorest or most marginalized classes (e.g., the urban lumpenproletariat, rural neo-peasantry, and déclassé sectors, and spreading out into the sinking middle classes). Likewise, it would be expected that the "vanguard nations" would be those nations most under the boot of the international imperial order and the nation-states which are its component parts, such as the native, indigenous,

---

11   Daniel McCarthy, "Left, Right, and Le Pen," LewRockwell.Com, April 30, 2002, http://www.lewrockwell.com/dmccarthy/dmccarthy31.html (accessed September 23, 2012).

or aboriginal peoples within each respective nation-state. With regards to the relationship of the anarchist-led anti-imperialist movements to anti-imperialist so-called "rogue states," the most consistent and farsighted position for anarchists to assume would be one of support for the independence and sovereignty of such states against attacks from the empire while favoring ever-greater decentralization within the rogue states themselves and greater autonomy for their own internal regions, communities, and specific cultural identities.

Postmodernism and Cultural Relativism

A final consideration involves the need to respond to those anarchists who would criticize many of the ideas outlined thus far as not fully representing "true" or "authentic" anarchism, however defined, particularly the rejection of the left/right model of the political spectrum, the rejection of class determinism, and the pluralist and accommodating stance assumed towards cultural conservatives, traditionalists, nationalists, and others with whom anarchists have been in conflict with in the past. Such criticisms are well represented and summarized in Michael Schmidt's comparison of the Sarvodaya movement of Gandhi with classical anarchism. As Schmidt observes:

Gandhian Sarvodaya falls outside of the anarchist current, but initially appears, like anarchism, to be part of the larger libertarian socialist stream within which one finds the likes of council communism. There are some parallels between Gandhi's vision of "a decentralized federation of autonomous village republics" and the anarchist vision of a world of worker and community councils. Yet this should not be overstated. Gandhi's rejection of Western capitalist modernity and industrialism has libertarian elements, but . . . Gandhi's opposition to both British and Indian capital seems simply romantic, anti-modern and anti-industrial, a rejection of the blight on the Indian landscape of what William Blake called the "dark Satanic mills." Absent is a real vision of opposing the exploitative mode of production servicing a parasitic class, of seeing the problem with modern technology as lying not in the technology itself, but in its abuse by that class.

This contradiction is at the very heart of the Gandhian Sarvodaya movement. On the one hand, it has a healthy distrust of the state. On the other, it retains archaic rights and privileges, traditional village hierarchies and paternalistic landlordism—in line with Gandhi's own "refusal to endorse the class war or repudiate the caste system" . . . Gandhi's embrace of caste, landlordism, and opposition to modern technologies that can end hunger and backbreaking labour, is diametrically opposed to anarchist egalitarianism.

Moreover, the mainstream of the anarchist tradition is rationalist, and thus opposed to the state-bulwarking mystification of most organised religion, whereas Gandhian Sarvodaya explicitly promoted Hinduism as part of its uncritical embrace of traditionalism. So what do we make of Gandhi himself? . . . On balance, in his völkisch nationalist decentralism, I would argue for him to be seen as something of a forebearer of "national anarchism," that strange hybrid of recent years. Misdiagnosed by most anarchists as fascist, "national anarchism" fuses radical decentralism, anti-hegemonic anti-statism (and often anti-capitalism), with a strong self-determinist thrust that stresses cultural-ethnic homogeneity with a traditional past justifying a radical future; this is hardly "fascism" or a rebranding of "fascism," for what is fascism without the state, hierarchy and class, authoritarianism, and the führer-principle?[12]

These comments contain far more insight than their author likely recognizes. For while the general thrust of classical anarchism was

---

12   Schmidt, "South Asian Anarchism."

rationalist, modernist, and egalitarian, and Gandhi's philosophical premises were largely oriented towards traditionalism, mysticism, and a romantic anti-modernism not dissimilar to that of Catholic anti-modernists such as Hilaire Belloc and G. K. Chesterton, these dichotomies become problematic only within the context of a universalist framework derived from the liberal-rationalist premises of the latter Enlightenment period. Yet these premises have largely been eclipsed by the critiques of them offered by a diverse array of thinkers including Nietzsche, Weber, Heidegger, the theoreticians of the neo-Marxist Frankfurt School, pioneer postmodernists such Foucault, Lacan, and Derrida, and the intellectuals of the New Right. As the liberal-rationalist principles of the Enlightenment have slowly receded and postmodernism has become the dominant mode of contemporary thought, so has the cultural universalism derived from eighteenth- and nineteenth-century liberalism (which in many ways reflected a kind of Western ethnocentrism in a more secularized and ostensibly progressive form) given way to cultural relativism.[13] Hence, the growing conflict between proponents of "universal human rights" and radical multiculturalists.[14]

As a consequence of this paradigm shift in Western philosophy, the seeming conflict between the rationalist-modernism and egalitarian-universalism of the classical anarchists and the traditionalism, romanticism, anti-modernism, and mysticism of, for instance, Gandhi disappears if each of these are recognized as representing merely the particular values of specific cultural, regional, tribal, or philosophical identities with the claims to "truth" or legitimacy of each being contingent upon and relative to their own unique sets of historical, geographical, tribal, and social-psychological circumstances. A twenty-first-century, postmodern, and culturally relativist anarchism with

---

13   Martin Jay, *The Dialectical Imagination: A History of the Frankfurt School and the Institute of Social Research, 1923–1950* (Berkeley, CA: University of California Press, 1996 [1973]).

14   Johann Hari, "How Multiculturalism Is Betraying Women," *The Independent*, April 30, 2007, http://www.independent.co.uk/voices/commentators/johann-hari/johann-hari-how-multiculturalism-is-betraying-women-446806.html

an orientation towards the particular would be fully capable of incorporating into its political framework elements of each of these seemingly polar opposite perspectives in ways such as that represented by the National-Anarchist tendency described by Schmidt. Indeed, such "strange hybrids" are the likely wave of the future in anarchist thought.

Part 3 - A New Anarchist Perspective

Against the State

Anarchist Meta-Politics and Meta-Strategy in the Twenty-First Century

The State: Its Origins and Purpose

In the several million years that human beings and their ancestral evolutionary prototypes have been in existence, the genus *Homo* functioned socially within the context of stateless nomadic bands of hunters and gatherers. Indeed, at the time of the American and French revolutions of the late eighteenth century, the model of the hunter-gatherer remained the most prevalent form of social organization throughout most of the then-contemporary world. Statelessness continued in many post-hunter-gatherer societies even as larger and more complex forms of tribal organization emerged with pastoralism and horticulture and then agriculture replacing the hunter-gatherer model as the dominant mode of production. It has only been since the advent of the industrial revolution that the hunter-gatherer form of social organization has lost its dominance. Further, it was not until the apex of the era of colonialism in the late nineteenth century that the world came to be fully dominated by states. It is astounding to contemplate that the species of *Homo* has lived under the rule of states for much less than one percent of its history.[1]

---

1   Harold Barclay, *People Without Government: An Anthropology of Anarchism* (London: Kahn and Averill, 1982); Robert L. Carneiro, "Political Expansion as an Expression of the Principle of Competitive Exclusion," in *Origins of the State: The Anthropology of Political Evolution*, ed. Ronald Cohen and Elman R. Service (Philadelphia: Institute for the Study of Human Issues, 1978), 219; Tim Ingold, "On the Social Relations of the

The earliest states emerged concurrent to advancements in agriculture and literacy. The former made possible the development of a leisure class whose existence rose above the ordinary level of subsistence production and the latter allowed for the greater centralization of information. The evolution of these two social phenomena created the possibility for the ever-greater centralization of power. The state had its beginnings in the civilizations of Mesopotamia, ancient Egypt, the Indus Valley, China, and Central and South America. These early states came about through conquest and relied upon religious mythology or tradition (such as the belief in the divinity of the emperor) for their legitimacy.[2] In pre-modern societies political rule and ownership were typically synonymous. Land and resources were acquired through conquest, trade, or marriage, and those in possession of a particular territory exercised personal political authority.[3]

Though it was the Greeks who first began to both develop political philosophy and separate rulership from ownership, it was the increasingly centralized monarchies of the late medieval and early Renaissance eras that truly began laying the foundations for the state in its modern form through the development of bureaucratic administrative infrastructures.[4] These bureaucracies eventually eclipsed the power of the monarchy, the Church, and other rival centers of authority. The taxation and information-gathering powers of the bureaucracies made it possible for the bureaucracy to gain a monopoly over the processes of raising armies and waging war. Eventually the bureaucracy assumed control of police, judicial, and penal systems as well, thereby concentrating all

Hunter-Gatherer Band," in *The Cambridge Encyclopedia of Hunters and Gatherers*, ed. Richard B. Lee and Richard Heywood Daly (Cambridge: Cambridge University Press, 1999).

2 Norman Yoffee, *Myths of the Archaic State: Evolution of the Earliest Cities, States and Civilizations* (Cambridge: Cambridge University Press, 05), 102.

3 Martin van Creveld, *The Rise and Decline of the State* (Cambridge: Cambridge University Press, 1999), 1–58.

4 Ibid., 127–54.

political authority into the hands of the bureaucracy. By the end of the eighteenth century, the state bureaucracy began to assume a legal personhood of its own capable of maintaining a permanent, corporative, institutional life independent of that of its individual personnel.[5] Hence, the beginnings of the modern state.

The Evolution of Anarchist Thought

As a political philosophy, anarchism has as its guiding principle its critique of the state as a uniquely and inherently parasitical institution. The earliest states of ancient times were rooted in conquest, subjugation, and expropriation. The primary characteristic of modern states is their maintenance of a coercive political-bureaucratic apparatus with a centralized monopoly over the use of violence within a particular geographical region. Whether in their traditional personalized form or modern corporative form, states exist primarily to control territory, monopolize resources, protect an artificially privileged ruling class, exploit subjects, and expand their own institutional power and that of their individual members.[6] The historic rise of states has been accompanied by the development and evolution of schools of thought devoted to critiquing the state. Strands of proto-anarchist thinking can be found among the ancient philosophers of both China and the Greco-Roman world, and among dissenting Christian movements of the medieval and early modern era.[7]

---

5   Ibid., 184–88.

6   Benoît Dubreuil, Human Evolution and the Origins of Hierarchies: The State of Nature (Cambridge: Cambridge University Press, 2010), 189; Scott Gordon, Controlling the State: Constitutionalism from Ancient Athens to Today (Cambridge, MA: Harvard University Press, 2002), 4; Colin Hay, "State Theory," in Routledge Encyclopedia of International Political Economy, ed. R. J. Barry Jones (London: Routledge, 2001), 3:1469–75; John Donovan et al., People, Power, and Politics: An Introduction to Political Science (Lanham, MD: Rowman and Littlefield, 1993), 20; Martin Shaw, War and Genocide: Organized Killing in Modern Society (Cambridge: Polity, 2003), 59.

7   Barclay, People Without Government; Peter Kropotkin, "Anarchism," Encyclopaedia Britannica, 1910, http://attackthesystem.com/anarchism/; Homer, Iliad, 2.703; Herodotus, Histories, 9.23; Malcolm Schofield, The Stoic Idea of the City (Cambridge: Cambridge University Press, 1991); Max Nettlau, A Short History of Anarchism

The rise of classical liberalism during the Enlightenment period serves as something of a transitional phase between both traditional forms of political legitimacy and critiques of political authority found in the pre-modern era and the development of modern anarchist thought. In the early eighteenth century, the French explorer Louis Armand observed the social structures of the indigenous people of North America and described such systems as "anarchy." Proto-anarchist thinkers influenced the revolutions of the late eighteenth century, including the Americans Thomas Jefferson and Thomas Paine and the Frenchmen Jean Varlet and Sylvain Maréchal. Influenced by the work of Jean-Jacques Rousseau and Edmund Burke, William Godwin developed the first systematic body of modern anarchist thought.

An anarchist thinking continued to evolve throughout the nineteenth and twentieth centuries, anarchist movements tended to splinter into multiple directions representing different types of focuses or emphasis among anti-state radicals. In some ways anarchism is comparable with Christianity with its historic processes of perpetually dividing and subdividing into an ever-greater number of both major traditions and lesser sects derived from those traditions.[8] François Richard identified three major traditions within anarchism: the leftist-socialist tradition, the extreme individualism of the German thinker Max Stirner which overlaps with the Anglo-American libertarian tradition, and an elitist form of aristocratic-individualism that in French political culture has been called "anarchism of the right." The first of these traditions is represented by Pierre-Joseph Proudhon, Mikhail Bakunin, Peter Kropotkin, Errico Malatesta, and Emma Goldman; the second by Stirner, John Henry Mackay, Josiah

(London: Freedom Press, 1996), 8; Bertrand Russell, History of Western Philosophy (New York: Routledge, 2004), 8; William E. Foster, Town Government in Rhode Island (Baltimore: Johns Hopkins Press, 1886); Murray N. Rothbard, "The Origins of Individualist Anarchism in America," LewRockwell.com, 2006, http://www.lewrockwell.com/1970/01/murray-n-rothbard/real-american-history/ (accessed July 2, 2008); Murray N. Rothbard, "Pennsylvania's Anarchist Experiment: 1681–1690," LewRockwell.com, 2005, http://archive.lewrockwell.com/rothbard/rothbard81.html (accessed July 2, 2008).

8   François Richard, Les anarchistes de droite (Paris: PUF, 1997 [1991]).

Warren, Benjamin Tucker, Karl Hess, and Murray Rothbard; and the third by H. L. Mencken, Louis-Ferdinand Céline, Ernst Jünger, J. R. R. Tolkien, and Salvador Dalí.

Classical socialist-anarchism has as its principal focus an orientation towards social justice and uplifting the downtrodden. The radical individualism of Stirner and the English and American libertarians posits individual liberty as the highest good. The Nietzsche-influenced aristocratic radicalism of the anarchists of the right places its emphasis not only on liberty but on merit, excellence, and the preservation of high culture. It would seem that each of these perspectives has its place within the context of an effective anti-state radicalism. The ideals advanced by each of these strands of anarchist thought—social justice, liberty, meritocracy—would seem to be such that no functional or durable civilization can dispense with.

The Variety and Complexity of Anarchist Movements

The number and variety of anarchist movements or tendencies has grown exponentially over the course of the last century, particularly since the end of the Second World War. The anarchists of the nineteenth and early twentieth centuries were primarily divided into the mutualist, collectivist, communist, syndicalist, and individualist camps with occasional outliers such as the rationalist Christian pacifist anarchism of Leo Tolstoy. The cultural upheavals and radical political movements of the 1960s and 1970s along with broader economic, cultural, technological, and demographic changes in Western societies during the same period brought with them not only a renewed interest in the anarchist movements of the past but an immense diversity of new schools of anarchist or anarchist-influenced thought with their own unique emphasis. These include Green anarchism, primitivism, anarcha-feminism, anarcho-capitalism, market anarchism, agorism, voluntarism, queer anarchism, situationism, national-anarchism, platformism,

Islamic anarchism, indigenous anarchism, black anarchism, post-left anarchism, geo-anarchism, insurrectionary anarchism, and others too numerous to mention.

Given the scattered nature of these various anarchist trends and their widely divergent and sometimes even conflicting goals, the first question any serious student of anarchist movements has to first ask is whether anarchism will ever evolve into a movement that is large enough and well-organized enough to pose a credible threat and alternative to the modern state. Virtually all of the contending schools of anarchism have something of value to add to a wider anti-state movement. Some are oriented towards the achievement of socio-economic justice, others towards preservation of the natural environment, still others towards the defense of individual liberty and economic prosperity. Some are focused on the defense of historic outgroups traditionally subject to persecution, others towards the promotion of alternative lifestyles, others towards the defense of traditional cultures, still others towards the perceived needs of particular cultural, religious, or ethnic identities. Many of these objectives would seem to complement each other and provide balance in areas where others fall short. In many ways, these contending schools of anarchist thought reflect the natural diversity of humanity. Each represents a necessary building block in the wider project of creating a future civilization where anarchism is the prevailing political, economic, and social philosophy.

Indeed, if anarchism were to be compared to Christianity, then it might be said that anarchism and Christianity both represent broad meta-philosophical paradigms. Christianity has three major traditions—Catholicism, Orthodoxy, and Protestantism—with many contending smaller sects or denominations. Likewise, anarchism has three major traditions—socialist-anarchism, liberal-libertarian anarchism, and aristocratic-individualist anarchism. Each of the particular trends within anarchism represents yet another anarchist denomination. The most important question that emerges from this analysis is to ask whether the various schools of anarchism can ever be unified for the purpose of attacking the common enemy in the form of the state.

Towards a New Synthesism

To date, the most successful anarchist movement was that organized by the Spanish anarchists during the early to middle twentieth century and which briefly attempted to create a revolutionary society based on classical anarchist principles during the midst of the Spanish Civil War. The Spanish anarchists have been criticized for varying reasons by subsequent generations of anarchists, but the fact that remains is they were one of the few anarchist movements in history that managed to not only win the support of a significant portion of the population of a major country but also provide a fascinating case study of anarchist participation in an actual revolutionary situation and civil war.

Whatever successes the Spanish anarchists were able to achieve seem rooted in several important factors. First, the role of the Iberian Anarchist Federation in acting as the principled militants leading mass organizations that Bakunin had insisted would be necessary during any actual revolutionary struggle. Second, the ability of the National Confederation of Workers to win the support of substantial sectors of the Spanish working class was particularly important. Third, there was the leading role played by the anarchists in organizing the resistance to the uprising by the army against the Republic. Last, there was the compatibility of anarchism with the traditional communal peasant life of rural Spain.

The question that emerges is how these efforts can be replicated in contemporary nations and under contemporary cultural and economic circumstances. Given the immense variation and complexity of contemporary anarchist thought, and the even greater complexity and diversity of modern societies, it would seem that a theoretical framework identified in the past with such terms as "anarchism without adjectives" or "synthesis anarchism" would be the most appropriate. These represented efforts within classical anarchism to unite all of the contending anarchist factions into a comprehensive alliance and which criticized those anarchists who had adopted a Marxist-like class determinism. Among the prominent supporters of this position were Voltairine de Cleyre, Emma Goldman, Alexander Berkman, Errico Malatesta, Max Nettlau, Sébastien Faure, Mollie Steimer, Gregori Maximoff, and Voline. Some of these issued a statement saying:

> To maintain that anarchism is only a theory of classes is to limit it to a single viewpoint. Anarchism is more complex and pluralistic, like life itself. Its class element is above all its means of fighting for liberation; its humanitarian character is its ethical aspect, the foundation of society; its individualism is the goal of mankind.[9]

The Contributions of National-Anarchism

National-Anarchism is a relatively new tendency within anarchism, yet it has grown rather rapidly in recent years. It also remains one of the most controversial strands within contemporary anarchist thought. However, national-anarchism brings to the table an interesting set of ideas which may be quite helpful in the long-term development of a more effective anarchist movement. The principal weaknesses of the present-day anarchist movement are its scattered and fragmented nature which prevents it from exercising a concentrated assault on the state, its lack of a coherent strategy for achieving revolutionary goals, and its failure to develop a more thorough critique of the state as it actually exists in modern societies. The ideas found within national-anarchism make important contributions towards the creation of a new theoretical model that is fully capable of effectively addressing these questions.

---

9   "Reply by Several Russian Anarchists to the Platform," http://attackthesystem.com/reply-to-the-platform-synthesist/.

At the core of the national-anarchist philosophy is the concept of decentralized particularism. Conceptually, this overlaps very well with the insights of neo-tribalism which postulates that humans are hard-wired by evolutionary biology to exist within tribal forms of social organization as opposed to the mass societies of modernity which are increasingly dominated by omnipresent states.[10] Like neo-tribalism, national-anarchism advocates replacing modern mass societies and their all-encompassing states with autonomous, stateless tribes reflecting an open-ended plethora of cultural orientations as opposed to the model of homogenized universalism endorsed by both the left-wing establishment and the forces of global capitalism. This theoretical framework helps to address certain problems faced by modern anarchist movements in several ways.

First, such a framework provides a comprehensive paradigm that is capable of generating a reconciliation and accommodation between contending anarchist factions. While the many sub-tendencies within modern anarchism in many ways complement each other and even serve as correctives to the other's weaknesses, it is also true that the variations in focus found among the scattered anarchist sects will inevitably be the source of irreconcilable conflicts as well. The national-anarchist concept of the tribe allows for the many diverse tribes within anarchism to achieve sovereignty and autonomy within the context of their own independent communities. The model of decentralized particularism means that within the general context of an anarchist civilization some of the component communities will be anarcho-communist, syndicalist, anarcho-capitalist, primitivist, traditionalist, feminist, queer, vegetarian, Christian, Islamic, pagan, etc., according to the preferences of the local community in question and its inhabitants. The model of a confederation of anarchist tribes with each of these reflecting their own particular values fits well with the need to forge a pan-anarchist front that unites anti-state radicals as the leadership

10   Michel Maffesoli, *The Time of the Tribes: The Decline of Individualism in Mass Society*, trans. Don Smith (London: Sage Publications, 1996).

corps of a larger libertarian-populist movement that creates alternative infrastructure towards the goal of pan-secession as its primary strategic vehicle. Tribal anarchism provides a framework where both contending anarchist tribes and stateless tribes of non-anarchists can peacefully coexist and unite against the state.

Second, this model is one that is capable of addressing and accommodating the very real fault lines found among the general population of any real world society. The early proponents of synthesis anarchism recognized in their 1927 manifesto "the difficulty of getting a large part of the population to accept our ideas. We must take into account existing prejudices, customs, education, the fact that the great mass of people will look for an accommodation rather than radical change." Indeed, anarchists are as aware as anyone of the deep-rooted social conflicts involving class, race, religion, culture, nationality, gender, sexuality, regional identities, occupation, social status, age, and so forth. Some anarchists have misguidedly sought to address such matters by agitating for even greater demographic conflict the result of which is to unfortunately cooperate with the "divide and conquer" strategy typically employed by states as a means of preventing unified resistance to itself on the part of subjects by playing different population groups off against one another.

The neo-tribal position advanced by national-anarchism and its endorsement of self-determination for all is in many ways a necessary corrective to the overdeveloped universalist internationalism derived from liberalism and Marxism typically espoused by many present-day anarchists. Instead, the national-anarchist concept of the tribe creates a framework in which a healthy balance can be achieved between traditionalism and postmodernism, cultural preservation and social progress, endogamy and assimilation, ecumenicalism and fundamentalism, puritanism and hedonism, elitism and egalitarianism, individualism and community. Conflicts of this type will likely always exist and tend to play themselves out in the divisions between rural and urban life, waterway-adjacent communities and landlocked communities, densely and sparsely populated communities.

Third, the neo-tribal model of national-anarchism allows anarchists to become the true champions of and cultivate as allies and constituents the many different subcultures, countercultures, ethno-cultures, religious cultures, drug cultures, sex cultures, gang cultures, lumpenproletarian castes, and other such social undercurrents which currently find themselves under attack by the state. Likewise, the national-anarchist paradigm allows for anarchists to become the champions and allies of subjugated indigenous peoples, outcast communities, and local and regional cultures subsumed by states throughout the world, such as the Basques, San, Hmong, Tibetans, Palestinians, Pashtuns, Tibetans, Dalits, Australian aboriginals, and so many others.

Finally, such an outlook places anarchists in a position on the cultural and ideological spectrum that is the polar opposite of the legitimizing ideology of modern states.

Critiquing the Liberal Democratic State

At several intervals throughout history, the foundations of political legitimacy have been severely challenged and subsequently overturned. In the ancient pagan world, rulers justified their position by claiming divine status. With the advent of Christian and Islamic monotheism, earthly rulers could no longer claim divinity but had to resort to an appeal to the divine right of kings. With the rise of the Enlightenment, theological sources of political legitimacy lost their potency and were replaced by secular doctrines invoking popular sovereignty and the natural rights of man. The anarchist project of delegitimizing the modern liberal democratic state and replacing it with decentralized associational liberty would involve a political, cultural, and intellectual revolution every bit as far reaching as the overthrow of the Greco-Roman civilization by Christianity and the displacement of the monarchy, Church, and aristocracy by the liberal philosophy of the Enlightenment.

Anarchism properly understood is a polar opposite political philosophy to the hegemonic totalitarian humanist ideology of the existing Western ruling classes. The institutional foundations of the modern state are the military and police organizations under the state's control, the legally privileged corporate infrastructure, the managerial bureaucracy, the apparatus of the regulatory/welfare state, the institutional framework of mass democracy and compulsory ethno-cultural integration, the legal caste, the component parts of the therapeutic state, and the ideological superstructure maintained by the mass media and educational institutions. This dominant superstructure of totalitarian humanism legitimates the state by appealing to the state's ostensible role as the enforcer and upholder of progressive values against non-state institutions, regions, and localities, and so-called "rogue states" on the international level.

The Left fails to recognize the degree to which self-proclaimed cultural progressivism has become the basis of a new authoritarianism. Unfortunately, much of the anarchist milieu has fallen into the trap of becoming obsessed with the cultural libertinism of the left wing of the middle class. Yet at some point the endorsement of "cultural libertarianism" has to be balanced with the need to advance the struggle against the state, ruling class, and empire. Likewise, on the question of "hierarchy," a necessary distinction needs to be made between coercive and voluntary hierarchies and between organic and inorganic ones.

The process of overcoming some of these failures within the general anarchist milieu involves transcending to some degree the conventional divide between left and right. This means among other things recognizing the valid claims of the Right in terms of grievances and the valid insights of rightist thought. There is plenty of room for both rightist and leftist anarchists and fair hearing for all points of view. Independence of mind is, or ought to be, a primary anarchist value. The core anarchist values of freedom of opinion and free association must necessarily be upheld as inviolable. The great advantage of anarchism is its ability to accommodate conflicting ways of life and world views without oppression and violence: a system of municipal-town-neighborhood-village-provincial   sovereignty in which communities practice self-determination and unhappy individuals can find a home for themselves.

Why I Am an Anarcho-Pluralist, Part One

Over the last few days, there's been an interesting discussion going on over at the blog of left-libertarian philosopher Charles Johnson (also known as "Rad Geek"). I've avoided posting there, due to the presence of an individual who has declared to be my mortal enemy (a role I'm happy to assume), but the subject matter of the discussion provides a very good illustration of why any sort of libertarian philosophy that demands a rigid universalism cannot work in practice. A poster called "Soviet Onion" remarks:

> It seems that both social anarchism and market libertarianism have respectively come to adopt forms of collectivism typical of either the statist left or right. That's a result of the perceived cultural affinity they have with those larger groups, and partly also a function of the fact that they appeal to people of different backgrounds, priorities and sentiments (and these two factors tend to reinforce each other in a cyclical way, with new recruits further entrenching the internal movement culture and how it will be perceived by the following generation of recruits).

> On the "left" you have generic localists who feel that altruism entails loyalty to the people in immediate proximity (they'll unusually use the term "organic community" to make it seem more natural and thus unquestionably legitimate). Most of them are former Marxists and social democrats, this is simply a way to recast communitarian obligations and tacitly authoritarian sentiments under the aegis of "community" rather than "state." This comes as an obvious

result of classical anarchism being eclipsed as *the* radical socialist alternative by Leninism for most of the twentieth century. Now that it's once again on the rise, it's attracting people who would have otherwise been state-socialists, and who carry that baggage with them when they cross over.

On the "right," it's a little more straightforward. Libertarians have adopted the conservative "State's Rights" kind of localism as a holdover from their alliance with conservatives against Communism, to the point that it doesn't even matter if the quality of freedom under that state is worse than the national average, just so long as it's not the Federal Government. And with this, any claim to moral universality, or the utilitarian case for decentralism go right out the window. Like true parochialism, it hates the foreign and big just because it is foreign and big.

That's also one of the reasons why I think there's a division between "social" and "market" anarchists; they each sense that they come from different political meta-groups and proceed from a different set of priorities; the established gap between right and left feels bigger than the gap between they and statists of their own variety. And the dogmatisms that say "we have to support the welfare state, workplace regulations and environmental laws until capitalism is abolished" or "we should vote Republican to keep taxes down and preserve school choice" are as much after-the-fact rationalizations of this feeling as they are honest attempts at practical assessment.

The problem with left-libertarianism (or with the 21st century rebirth and recasting of 19th century individualism, if you want to imperfectly characterize it that way), is that instead of trying to *transcend* harmful notions of localism, it simply switches federalism for communitarianism. It does this partially as a attempt to ingratiate itself to social anarchists, and partly because, like social anarchists, it recognize that this idea is superficially more compatible with an anti-state position. But it also neglects the social anarchists' cultural sensibilities; hence the more lax attitude toward things like National Anarchism.

These are some very insightful comments. And what do they illustrate? That human beings, even professed "anarchists," are in fact tribal creatures, and by extension follow the norms of either their tribe of origin or their adopted tribe, and generally express more sympathy and feel a stronger sense of identification with others who share their tribal values (racism, anti-racism, feminism, family, homosexuality, homophobia, religion, atheism, middle class values, underclass values, commerce, socialism) than they do with those with whom they share mere abstractions ("anarchy," "liberty," "freedom").

Last year, a survey of world opinion indicated that it is the Chinese who hold their particular society in the highest regard, with 86 percent of Chinese expressing satisfaction with their country. Russians expressed a 54 percent satisfaction rate, and Americans only 23 percent. Observing these numbers, Pat Buchanan remarked:

> Yet, China has a regime that punishes dissent, severely restricts freedom, persecutes Christians and all faiths that call for worship of a God higher than the state, brutally represses Tibetans and Uighurs, swamps their native lands with Han Chinese to bury their cultures and threatens Taiwan.

> Of the largest nations on earth, the two that today most satisfy the desires of their peoples are the most authoritarian.

What are we to make of this? That human beings value security, order, sustenance, prosperity, collective identity, tribal values, and national power much more frequently and on a deeper level than they value liberty. Of course, some libertarians will likely drag out hoary Marxist concepts like "false consciousness" or psychobabble like "Stockholm syndrome" to explain this, but it would be more helpful to simply face the truth: That liberty is something most people simply don't give a damn about.

The evidence is overwhelming that most people by nature are inclined to be submissive to authority. The exceptions are when the hunger pains start catching up with them and their physical survival is threatened, or when they perceive their immediate reference groups (family, religion, culture, tribe) as being under attack by authority. We see this in the political expressions of America's contemporary "culture wars." During the Clinton era, many social or cultural conservatives and religious traditionalists regarded the US regime as a tyranny that merited armed revolt. During the Bush era such rhetoric disappeared from the Right, even though Bush expanded rather than rolled back the police state. Meanwhile, liberals who would denounce Bush as a fascist express polar opposite sentiments towards the Obama regime, even though policies established by Bush administration have largely continued. So how do we respond to this? Soviet Onion offers some suggestions:

> The proper position for us, and what could really set us apart from everyone and make us a more unique and consistent voice for individualism in the global Agora, is to recognize all cultures as nothing more than memetic prisons and always champion the unique and nonconforming against the arbitrary limitations that surround them, recognizing their destruction as barriers in the sense of being normative. And to that end there's the instrumental insight that the free trade, competition, open movement and open communication are forces that pry open closed societies, not by force, but by giving those who chafe under them so many options to run to that they make control obsolete, and thus weaken control's tenability as a foundation on which societies can reasonably base themselves. Think of it as "cultural Friedmanism": the tenet that open economies

dissolve social authority the same way they render political authority untenable.

That's what left-libertarianism needs to be about, *not* some half-baked federation of autarkic Southern towns filled with organic farms and worker co-operatives. It can still favor these things, but with a deeper grounding. It doesn't ignore patriarchy, racism, heterosexism, but opposes them with a different and more consistent understanding of what liberation means.

But how far should our *always* championing of the "unique and nonconforming" go? If, for instance, a group of renegades happen to show up at the workers' cooperative one day and commandeer the place, should we simply say, "Hell, yeah, way to go, nonconformists"? As for the question of the "Big Three" among left-wing sins ("racism, sexism, and homophobia"), are we to demand that every last person on earth adopt the orthodox liberal position on these issues as defined by the intellectual classes in post-1968 American and Western Europe? Why stop at "patriarchy, racism, and heterosexism"? Soviet Onion points out that many "left-wing" anarchists do not stop at that point:

> I used to be an anarcho-communist. Actually, I started out as someone who was vaguely sympathetic to mainstream libertarianism but could never fully embrace it due to the perceived economic implications. I eventually drifted to social anarchism thanks to someone whose name I won't mention, because it's too embarrassing.

> After hanging around them for a while I realized that, for all their pretenses, most of them were really just state-socialists who wanted to abolish the State by making it smaller and calling it something else. After about a year of hanging around Libcom and the livejournal anarchist community, I encountered people who, under the aegis of "community self-management," supported:

- smoking and alcohol bans
- bans on currently illicit drugs
- bans on caffeinated substances (all drugs are really just preventing you from dealing with problems, you see)
- censorship of pornography (on feminist grounds)
- sexual practices like BDSM (same grounds, no matter the gender of the participants or who was in what role)
- bans on prostitution (same grounds)
- bans on religion or public religious expression (this included atheist religions like Buddhism, which were the same thing because they were "irrational")
- bans on advertisement (which in this context meant any free speech with a commercial twist)
- bans on eating meat
- gun control (except for members of the official community-approved militia, which is in no way the same thing as a local police department)
- mandatory work assignments (i.e. slavery)
- the blatant statement, in these exact words, that "Anarchism is not individualist" on no less than twelve separate occasions over the course of seven months. Not everybody in those communities actively agreed with them, but nobody got up and seriously disputed it.
- that if you don't like any of these rules, you're not free to just quit the community, draw a line around your house and choose not to obey while forfeiting any benefits. No, as long as you're in what they say are the boundaries (borders?) of "the community," you're bound to follow the rules, otherwise you have to move some place else ("love it or leave it," as the conservative mantra goes). You'd think for a moment that this conflicts with [anarcho-communist] property conceptions because they're effectively exercising power over land that they do not occupy, implying that they own it and making "the community" into One Big Landlord à la Hoppean feudalism.

So I decided that we really didn't want the same things, and that what they wanted was really some kind of Maoist concentration commune where we all sit in a circle and publicly harass the people who aren't conforming hard enough. No thanks, comrade.

These left-wing anarchists sound an awful lot like right-wing Christian fundamentalists or Islamic theocrats. Nick Manley adds:

I have encountered an "anarchist" proponent of the draft on a directly democratic communal level.

Of course, we also have to consider all of the many other issues that anarchists and libertarians disagree about: abortion, immigration, property theory, economic arrangements, children's rights, animal rights, environmentalism, just war theory, and much, much else. We also have to consider that anarchists and libertarians collectively are a very small percentage of humanity. Nick Manley says:

I spend more time around libertarians than left-anarchists—although, I briefly entered "their" world and sort of know some of them around here. I was a left-anarchist at one time, but I no longer feel comfortable with the hardcore communalism associated with the ideology. I don't really want to go to endless neighborhood meetings where majorities impose their will on minorities. I also would agree with Adam Reed that it's naive to imagine such communes being free places in today's world—perhaps, this is less true of New Zealand.

The list of things supported by anarcho-communists posted by Soviet Onion confirms my fears about village fascism posturing as "anti-statism." I frankly do just want to be left alone in my metaphorical "castle"—I say metaphorical, because I am not an atomist and don't live

Why I Am an Anarcho-Pluralist, Part One

as such. I will engage in social activities, but I will not allow someone to garner my support through the use of force or do so to others. Like Charles, I have a strong emotional and intellectually principled revulsion to aiding the cause of statism in any way whatsoever. I'd be much happier being at some risk of death from handguns then in enforcing laws that harm entirely well intentioned peaceful people. This is not a mere political issue for me. I know more than a few people with guns who deserve no prison time whatsoever—one of them has guns affected by the assault weapons ban.

I honestly see a lot of principled parallels between conservative lifestyle tribalism and left-liberal lifestyle tribalism. Oh yes: there are contextual inductive distinctions to be made. A gun is not the same as homosexuality. The collectivist dynamic is still the same. Gun owners become no longer human in sense of rational beings. All of contemporary politics seems to be one thinly veiled civil war between fearful tribalists.

It would appear that tribalism is all that we have. I have been through a long journey on this question. I was a child of the Christian Right, drifted to the radical Left as a young man, then towards mainstream libertarianism, then the militia movement and the populist right, along the way developing the view that the only workable kind of libertarianism would be some kind of pluralistic but anti-universalist, decentralized particularism. Rival tribes who are simply incompatible with one another should simply have their own separatist enclaves. Unlike the other kinds of libertarianism, there is actually some precedent for what I'm describing to be found in past cultures. As Thomas Naylor remarks:

> Conservatives don't want anyone messing with the distribution of income and wealth. They like things the way they are. Liberals want the government to decide what is

fair. Liberals believe in multiculturalism, affirmative action, and minority rights. Conservatives favor states' rights over minority rights.

What liberals and conservatives have in common is that they are both into having—owning, possessing, controlling, and manipulating money, power, people, material wealth, and things. Having is one of the ways Americans deal with the human condition—separation, meaninglessness, powerlessness, and death. To illustrate how irrelevant the terms "liberal" and "conservative" have become, consider the case of Sweden and Switzerland, two of the most prosperous countries in the world.

Sweden is the stereotypical democratic socialist state with a strong central government, relatively high taxes, a broad social welfare net financed by the State, and a strong social conscience. Switzerland is the most free market country in the world, with the weakest central government, and the most decentralized social welfare system. Both are affluent, clean, green, healthy, well-educated, democratic, nonviolent, politically neutral, and among the most sustainable nations in all of history. By U.S. standards, they are both tiny.

Switzerland and Sweden work, not because of political ideology, but rather because the politics of human scale always trumps the politics of the left and the politics of the right. Under the politics of human scale, a politics that trumps our now-outdated and useless "liberal-versus-conservative" dualistic mindset, there would be but one fundamental question: "Is it too big?"

It would seem that contemporary America is precisely the place to build a movement for this kind of decentralized particularism, a huge continent-wide nation which has many different cultures, religions, subcultures, and ethnic groups, which is growing more diverse all the time, where political and economic polarization is the highest it has been in over a century, and where dissatisfaction with the status quo is almost universal.

My challenge to anarchists, libertarians, communitarians, conservatives, radicals, and progressives alike would be to ask yourself what kind of community you would actually want to live in, and where and how you would go about obtaining it. For instance, the geography of the culture war typically breaks down on the basis of counties, towns, precincts, municipalities, and congressional districts rather than states or large regions. So why not envision forming a community for yourself and others in some particular locality that is consistent with your own cultural, economic, or ideological orientation? The Free State Project, Christian Exodus, Second Vermont Republic, Green Panthers, and Twin Oaks Commune are already doing this.

Political victory in the United States is achieved through the assembling of coalitions of narrow interest groups who often have little in common with one another (gun-toting rednecks and country club Republicans, homosexuals and traditional working class union Democrats). Imagine if a third force emerged in US politics with only one unifying principle: a common desire to remove one's self and one's community from the system. The only thing anyone has to give up is the desire to tell other communities what to do.

Why I Am an Anarcho-Pluralist, Part Two

Imagine, for one horribly unpleasant moment, that the anarchist movement (movements?) in North America, in their present form, were to carry out an actual revolution. What kind of social or political system would be the result? The Wikipedia entry on anarchism in the United States lists a number of individuals who represent North American anarchism in different ways. These include Michael Albert (Chomskyite proponent of participatory economics or "parecon"), Ashanti Alston (black power anarchist), Hakim Bey (lifestyle anarchist), Bob Black (nihilist and reputed psychopath), Kevin Carson (Proudhonian mutualist), Noam Chomsky (Marxo-syndicalist-anarcho-social democrat), Peter Coyote (love generation), Howard Ehrlich (social anarchist), David Friedman (anarcho-capitalist), David Graeber (anarcho-anthropologist), Hans-Hermann Hoppe (anarcho-monarchist), Derrick Jensen (primitivist), Jeff Luers (eco-anarchist prisoner), Judith Malina (anarcho-pacifist actress), the late James J. Martin (individualist anarchist and Holocaust revisionist), Wendy McElroy (Rothbardian anarcho-feminist individualist), Jason McQuinn (post-left anarchist), Cindy Milstein (Bookchinite), Chuck Munson (anarchist without adjectives), Joe Peacott (individualist-anarchist), Sharon Presley (left-libertarian feminist), Keith Preston (synthesist anarchist, anarchist without adjectives, anarcho-pluralist), Lew Rockwell (Rothbardian paleolibertarian), Jeremy Sapienza (market anarchist), Crispin Sartwell (individualist-anarchist), Rebecca Solnit (environmentalist), Starhawk (neo-pagan eco-feminist), Warcry (eco-anarchist), Dana Ward (anarcho-archivist), David Watson (primitivist), Mike Webb (murder victim), Fred Woodworth (atheist anarchist), John Zerzan (primitivist), and Howard Zinn (New Left anarcho-Marxist).

This list does not even begin to mention all of the ideological tendencies to be found among anarchists, e.g., indigenous anarchism, anarcho-communism, national-anarchism, insurrectionary anarchism, Christian anarchism, and many others. Even so, anarchists collectively probably do not comprise even one percent of the population at large. Imagine if the anarchist milieu were to grow to include tens of millions of people. Most likely all of these specific tendencies would grow exponentially, and some new ones no one has heard of yet would probably appear. How would anarchists go about organizing society if indeed anarchism was to become a mass movement and the state in its present form was to disappear? More specifically, how would we reconcile the differences between all of these different tendencies, and how would anarchists coexist with persons of other belief systems? Unless we want to start sending people to re-education camps, or placing them in gulags, or engaging in summary or mass executions we had better start thinking some of this out.

There are really only three ways. One would be anarcho-totalitarianism, where whatever anarchist faction or group of factions that happens to have the most power simply represses their rivals, anarchists and non-anarchists alike. Another would be anarcho-mass democracy, where we have an anarchist parliament consisting of the Syndicalist Party, Primitivist Party, Libertarian Party, Ecology Party, Feminist Party, et al., perhaps presided over by, say, Prime Minister Chuck Munson. While this might be an interesting situation, it ultimately wouldn't be much different than the kinds of states we have today.

The only other alternative is the dispersion of power to local units. These could be localities where everything is completely privatized (Hoppe) or everything is completely collectivized (anarcho-communism), or some point in between. The specific anarchist tendencies these communities represented would be determined according to prevailing ideological currents at the local level. One contemporary anarchist observes:

The superficial story is that the primmies control the NW, the SW desert and the Appalachians, while the Reds control the entire NE bloc and have a mild advantage everywhere else.

So "after the revolution" the "primmies" would be dominant in their regions and the "reds" in theirs, and presumably the Free Staters in theirs, and the queer anarchists in theirs, and so forth. It's also interesting to observe how radically different the value systems and definitions of "freedom" employed by different kinds of anarchists are. One anarchist has noted that some anarchists wish to bar alcohol, drugs, tobacco, meat, porn, S&M, and prostitution from their communities. This should go a long way with those libertarian-libertine anarchists for whom anarchy is synonymous with all sorts of legalized vice. Then there's the conflict between the ethno-preservationist national-anarchists and the anti-racist left-anarchists, and between the proprietarian anarchists and the communal anarchists. I've even come across an anarchist proponent of the draft. Of course, the different kinds of anarchists will insist that others are not *true* anarchists, but that's beside the point. Each of the different anarchist factions considers *themselves* to be the true anarchists, and that's not going to change.

The adherents of many of these philosophies act as though the fate of the world depends on their every move, when in reality each of these tendencies will often have no more than a few thousand, maybe a few hundred, maybe even just a few dozen sympathizers (or even fewer than that). Rarely is any attention given to the question of how anarchists will ever achieve any of their stated goals, to the degree that anarchists have any common goals, or any goals at all.

If anarchists want to have any impact on the wider society whatsoever, I believe there is only one way. Anarchists need to band together in large enough numbers to become single-issue political pressure group. This would be a pressure group just like those in the mainstream: pro-choice, pro-life, pro-gun, anti-gun, pro-gay marriage, anti-gay marriage, marijuana decriminalization, etc. The purpose of this pressure group would be to reduce political authority down to lowest unit possible, which I believe is the local community, i.e., cities, towns, villages, districts, neighborhoods, etc. I recognize some anarchists wish to reduce politics down to the individual level. I'm a little more skeptical of that. For instance, I'm not so sure competing criminal codes could exist in the same territorial jurisdiction, but I'm willing to agree to disagree on that. I say let's work to reduce things down to the city-state, county, or village level, and then debate how much further to go from there. Such a pressure group could include not only anarchists of every kind, but also left-green decentralists, conservative local sovereignty groups, regionalist or secessionist tendencies, or even good old fashioned Jeffersonian states' rightsers.

This idea does not mean that every locality would need to be an independent nation unto itself. They could be sovereign entities within broader territorial confederations, so long as they retained their right of withdrawal or to veto policies favored by the larger bodies. This way, even communities with radically different cultural values or economic arrangements could collaborate on projects of mutual interest such as maintenance of transportation systems, firefighting, or common defense.

Meanwhile, outside the context of this single-issue movement for radical decentralization, the different anarchist factions could continue their other interests in different contexts. Libertarians could continue to push for private money or competing currencies. Syndicalists could continue to push for anarcho-syndicalist unions. Primitivists could set up tech-free communes or villages. Anti-racists could protest Klan marches, and national-anarchists could set up ethnic separatist intentional communities. Pro-lifers could agitate against abortion and feminists could agitate against pro-lifers. Gun nuts could belong to the NRA and pacifists could belong to the Catholic Workers. Anarcho-communists could organize Israeli-style kibbutzim and anarcho-capitalists could set up their preferred private defense agencies.

Additionally, different factions with different beliefs could target certain geographical areas for colonization as the Free Staters are doing in New Hampshire, the Christian Exodus is doing in South Carolina, the Native Americans are doing in the Lakota Republic, or the Ron Paulites are doing in the Liberty Districts. Indeed, Bill Bishop's interesting book *The Big Sort* describes how Americans are in the process of self-separation along the lines of culture, religion, ideology, political affiliation, sexuality, age, income, occupation, and every conceivable other issue. Colonization can then become a movement for full-blown local secession. The values and ideals of those whom you disagree with are not as personally threatening if you do not have to live under the same political roof, and the worse someone's ideas, the better that they be separate from everyone else.

This does not mean that sovereign communities cannot have institutionalized protections for individual liberties, minority rights, or popular rule. Some state constitutions or municipal charters already have protections of this type in some instances, and sometimes on a more expansive level than what is found in the US Constitution. Individual sovereign communities could make such protections as extensive as they wanted. Nor does this mean that libertarian anti-statism is the "only" value. There are some values in life that transcend politics, and one can also be committed to other issues while also being committed to political decentralization and local sovereignty. For instance, I am also interested in prisoners' rights, legal, judicial, penal and police reform, ending the war on drugs, repealing consensual crime laws, abolishing compulsory school attendance laws, opposing zoning ordinances, eminent domain, the overregulation of land and housing markets, sex worker rights, the right to bear arms, self-defense rights, the rights of students, the homeless, the handicapped, medical patients and psychiatric inmates, freedom of speech and the press, labor organizing, worker cooperatives, mutual aid associations, home schools and alternative education, credit unions and mutual banks, LETS, land reform, indigenous peoples' rights, alternative media, non-state social services, and many other topics. My primary area of interest is foreign policy. In fact, foreign policy was the reason I became an anarchist and have remained one, in spite of being continually underwhelmed by the organized anarchist movement. I think the American empire and its effects on peoples throughout the world is an abomination, and I want to see it ended. Yet, I think at the same time an agglomeration of anarchist communities in North America would need some kind of "national defense" system, given that Europe and Asia may not "go anarchist" at the same moment, which is why I am interested in the paleoconservatives with their traditional American isolationist views.

At the same time, there are some topics that many anarchists are committed to that don't particularly interest me. Environmentalism is one of these. Like all reasonable people, I think we need clean air and water, and it's not cool to build a toxic waste dump in a residential area. Yet, the eco-doomsday ideologies associated with ideas like global warming and peak oil are not things I'm sold on as of yet. I also really just don't see what the big deal about endangered species is. The overwhelming majority of species that have existed thus far have already gone extinct, so what's a few more? Still, if this is an issue others care passionately about, by all means engaged in direct action on behalf of sea turtles or spotted owls or against urban sprawl. Don't let me get in your way. Gay marriage is another topic I really just don't give a fuck about, not because I'm anti-gay but because I view marriage as an archaic religious and statist institution that anarchists or libertarians or radicals of any stripe should not be promoting. But that's just me. As an atheist, I also don't care much for the militant politicized atheism found in some circles. I agree that compulsory religious instruction and practice should not exist in state-run schools, but I think extending this idea to things like prayers at city council meetings or football games, or extracurricular religious clubs in state institutions, is taking things a bit far. It is this sort of thing that alienates the usually religious poor and working class from radicalism.

Lastly, we need to consider how to appeal to all those ordinary folks out there whose assistance we might need in order to achieve these kinds of goals. An anarchist-led, libertarian-populist, radical decentralist, pan-secessionist movement that appeals to the tradition and ideals of the American Revolution is the only possible avenue. What I have outlined here is essentially the same set of views promoted by Voltairine de Cleyre in her essays "Anarchism without Adjectives" and "Anarchism and American Traditions." If you don't like my views, then come up with a plan of your own and let the rest of us hear about it.

Anarcho-Pluralism and Pan-Secessionism:

What They Are and What They Are Not

A close colleague recently put a question to me that I regard as important enough to be well worth discussing publicly. I was asked if whether or not my own assumption of controversial stances on a variety of issues might have the effect of weakening my wider advocacy of an "anarcho-pluralist" political framework and a "pan-secessionist" strategy for achieving it. For instance, by attacking political correctness, am I not alienating many people with PC views on many issues who might otherwise be sympathetic to my wider outlook? By challenging the "open borders" preferences of mainstream libertarians, am I not pushing away anti-statists and decentralists who might also hold pro-immigration views? Indeed, might not even illegal immigrants themselves be viable allies within a pan-secessionist or anarcho-pluralist meta-political framework given that, at least on some levels, they are in conflict with the existing state?

Clearly, a number of important distinctions need to be made regarding such questions. The most significant of these distinctions involves defining what "anarcho-pluralism" and "pan-secessionism" actually are. "Anarcho-pluralism," as I conceive of it at least, is a brand of anti-state radicalism that has "anti-universalism" and what might be called "radical localism" as it core defining characteristics. It is "anti-universalist" because it rejects the view that there is one "correct" system of politics, economics, or culture that is applicable, much less obligatory, for all people at all times and in all places.

Russell Kirk observed: "There exists no single best form of government for the happiness of all mankind. The most suitable form of government necessarily depends upon the historic experience, the customs, the beliefs, the state of culture, the ancient laws, and the material circumstances of a people."

Anarcho-pluralism advocates "radical localism" as the best possible method of avoiding the tyrannies and abuses of overarching Leviathan states, and accommodating the irreconcilable differences concerning any number of matters that all societies inevitably contain.

"Pan-secessionism" is the strategy for achieving anarcho-pluralism. Given that most modern societies are under the rule of overarching states possessing expansive bureaucratic tentacles and police powers, the simple territorial withdrawal of regions and localities and renunciation of the central state by the secessionists would seem to be the most practical and comprehensible method of resistance. These few simple ideas are all that anarcho-pluralism and pan-secessionism really amount to. Theoretically, one could hold to just about any other set of beliefs or values and operate within the framework of anarcho-pluralism and pan-secessionism. In its essence, the anarcho-pluralist/pan-secessionist program does nothing more than work to abolish the central state and give every political interest group its own territory to create whatever kind of society it wishes, with ultimate success or failure being the sole responsibility of the local organizers, residents, or participants.

With regards to political correctness, it is certainly possible for persons holding stereotypical PC views to operate within a wider anarcho-pluralist/pan-secessionist framework or to join an alliance for the organization of such. For instance, the late, great, feminist extremist Andrea Dworkin was actually a proponent of "lesbian separatism" and apparently favored the creation of communities for those with views like hers complete with "land and guns" of their own. Some in the left-wing anarchist milieu favor an idea called "libertarian municipalism," a perspective advanced by the late anarchist-ecologist Murray Bookchin which basically involves creating independent city-state-like municipalities organized on the New England town meeting model, presumably espousing the usual communitarian-green-feminist-rainbow values of the far Left. It is theoretically possible that if and when the day comes that a pan-secessionist movement that is actually large enough and well-organized enough to mount a credible challenge to the authority of the US regime and ruling class emerges, a majority or even a super-majority of the individuals, organizations, and communities participating in such an effort could potentially reflect the kinds of "far Left" values and positions on issues of the kinds that most current left-anarchists espouse.

A similar theoretical formulation could be applied to the immigration question. It is entirely possible that many if not most participants in a pan-secessionist action could indeed be persons or groups favoring a completely "open borders" policy for their respective post-secession communities. Indeed, it is even possible that many participants in a pan-secessionist movement or action could be immigrants, even those who immigrated illegally according to present US law, or the immediate descendants of such.

Yet a number of obvious and vital questions remain. The most immediate of these would be: what is the purpose of anarcho-pluralism/pan-secessionism in the first place, its core principles aside? Anarcho-pluralism/pan-secessionism is an outlook that myself and some colleagues developed in the late 1990s in response to certain problems that we perceived in the mainstream of the anarchist milieu. From my earliest involvement in the anarchist movement, I noticed that quite frequently anarchists seemed to be, among other things, much more interested in promoting the standard laundry list of liberal or left-wing causes, or simply engaging in countercultural lifestyle practices, rather than advancing the struggle against the state. Opposition to the state as an institution is the very essence of any anarchist ideology worthy of the name. Anarchism differs from classical liberalism, which views the state as a neutral agent whose purpose is to uphold and protect abstract "rights." The anarchist view regards the state as a self-interested entity claiming monopoly privileges for its members. Anarchism also differs from leftism in that it regards the state as a parasite and usurper rather than as a reflection of some mythical "general will" (the democratist view) or as an agent of class rule (the Marxist view). The traditional anarchist critique of capitalism regards plutocracy as the result of state-imposed privilege for private interests allied with the state (see Proudhon), and the traditional anarchist opposition to war, militarism, and imperialism results from the anarchist view of these things as simple acts of aggression and plunder by states, no different in kind from ordinary criminality.

An additional factor that shaped my own view was the recognition that many thinkers and activists outside the anarchist milieu possess cogent criticisms of the state, plutocracy, empire, and imperialism. Indeed, many of these thinkers originate from outside the subculture of the "far Left" where most anarchists tend to function. Further, I found some "far Right" criticisms of the existing world order overlapped quite well with the traditional anarchist critique. While studying the works of leading commentators and theorists from these schools of thought more carefully, I came to the conclusion that a good number of entirely valid and legitimate issues and questions were being raised by many in these camps. Initially, I began pushing for greater collaboration between anarchists and the libertarian-left and paleoconservatives, the militia-patriot-constitutionalist milieu, right-libertarians and anarcho-capitalists, the populist-right, and so forth. I then discovered the neo-secessionist tendencies that were starting to organize at the time, and around ten years ago I encountered for the first time the national-anarchist tendency that had recently emerged. This in turn introduced me to the world of "third-position" ideologies, to the French New Right of Alain de Benoist, and so forth. I began to understand that quite often the only key differences between many of these "right-wing" perspectives and traditional anarchism are matters of culture, and in some instances mere aesthetics or individual tastes. I wrote a letter to a left-anarchist journal in 1999 where I outlined these views, and I later reworked the letter into an article expounding upon these ideas further.

Anarcho-pluralism/pan-secessionism was created as a tendency whose specific purpose was to reorient the focus of modern anarchism away from liberal and leftist social causes and countercultural lifestyles, and towards a more concentrated attack on the state, the empire, and the plutocracy. A related purpose is to form tactical alliances towards this end with many others sharing overlapping critiques or concerns, including some from the "far Right" or other points on the political spectrum apart from the radical Left milieu. Additionally, strategic and organizational issues are to be placed at the forefront of our ongoing efforts and expressed concerns. In other words, anarcho-pluralism/pan-secessionism differs sharply from the mainstream anarchist movement by:

1. Shifting focus away from left-wing social causes and countercultural lifestyles towards attacking the state, empire, and plutocracy as the primary values or objectives.

2. Working for the construction of an anti-state, anti-plutocratic, and anti-imperialist political alliance comprised of opposition forces from across the political spectrum.

3. Developing or promoting regional and local secessionist movements as the strategic and organizational vehicle for the political advancement of such a tactical alliance.

4. Rejecting the universalistic claim that all participants in the anarcho-pluralistic/pan-secessionist project must hold to "ultra-liberal," "far Left," or countercultural lifestyle

views on such matters as abortion, gay rights, feminism, transgendered rights, environmentalism, animal rights, "anti-racism," "anti-fascism," immigrants' rights, "open borders," veganism/vegetarianism, economic preferences, nuclear power, capital punishment, religion, drugs, family organization, squatting, dumpster diving, punk rock music, and many other things. This is not to say that participants in such a project *cannot* hold "ultra-liberal" or countercultural views on such matters, but that such an outlook, while acceptable, is not mandatory.

5. Recognizing that a post-state, post-plutocratic, and post-empire nation or civilization where anarchists are politically dominant would contain a genuine diversity of forms of political, cultural, and economic organization, and not just the kinds favored by the "far Left." Consequently, a post-revolutionary political order would likely include communities and institutions of a conservative, religious, ethnocentric, traditionalist, patriarchal, or just plain old middle-of-the-road, moderate nature as well as those of a leftist or countercultural nature.

The Necessity of Confronting Totalitarian Humanism

Once upon a time, I generally agreed with the standard leftist view that much of the conservative critique of "political correctness" amounts to little more than sour grapes on the part of right-wingers who are on the losing end of history and political struggles. However, upon further experience and reflection, I found it necessary to alter my view. When I first began promoting the ideas outlined above in the anarchist milieu, I knew it would be controversial and that many would object. However, I was somewhat surprised by the level of vociferous hostility and threats of violence I received from the critics. Now, on one hand, if some anarchists regard immigrants' rights, gay rights, transsexual rights, animal rights, or the most extreme forms of "anti-racism" to be the most important issues, then they are still perfectly within their rights to feel this way. If they prefer to tolerate or endure the present system rather than cede any ground, politically or geographically, to the Right, or to have any sort of association with cultural conservatives, then they likewise have the right to make this value judgment for themselves. However, the fact that they cannot accept that some of us would choose a different way, and that they cannot coexist with our own tendency without making threats of violence and assuming a generally obscurantist attitude, indicates that their commitment to such core libertarian values as freedom of speech and thought is rather limited. This essentially cancels their supposed "progressive" credentials and essentially renders them to the status of either a pre-Enlightenment cult movement, or secular theocrats, or a variation of the modern totalitarian movements that have emerged since the French Revolution. As a biographer of the anarchist historian Paul Avrich observed:

Avrich does not shy away from controversy in his books, treating the anarchist acts of violence honestly and in the context of the time. He does not condone the violence of Berkman, but says he still admires his decision, considering how brutal Frick acted toward striking workers. But Avrich does not have the same patience for some contemporary anarchists, who choose to destroy property and who, he says, come mainly from educated and middle-class backgrounds. "I'm not so crazy about anarchists these days," he says. "Anarchism means that you leave other people alone and you don't force people to do anything." He says he is sad that the old-timers are not around to guide the resurgent movement. "They were nicer people—much nicer people."

Of course, the anarcho-leftoids, antifa, and other related groups are merely a symptom of the growing totalitarian movement of which Political Correctness is a manifestation. I have written about this third totalitarianism before, and will continue to do so in the future. For now, it is simply enough to say that Political

Correctness must be confronted by serious anarchists in the same way that it was necessary for perceptive anarchists to confront Communism as Proudhon, Bakunin, and Kropotkin did in the days when it was the emerging totalitarian movement of the nineteenth century. This is simply a matter of self-defense, as the left-wing enemy has declared war on us. Given the rabid hatred expressed by PC Left (including its "anarchist" and "libertarian" contingents) towards anyone with political, social, or cultural values that conflict with hard-left orthodoxy, it is unlikely that these elements will ever be able to peacefully coexist with those who are different from themselves. The PC Left contains within itself the Lenins, Stalins, Maos, Castros, and Pol Pots of the future.

This is not to say that one cannot theoretically be a cultural leftist and simultaneously oppose Totalitarian Humanism. One can be a worker, a political leftist, or even a socialist, and oppose Marxism. One can be black, Jewish, or Hispanic and oppose totalitarian multiculturalism. Many do. One can be a woman and oppose the feminazis. There are many of these. One can certainly be gay and oppose the "homo-totalitarians." Plenty of examples of this exist. Many of my own views on various issues are well to the left of the Democratic Party, if not the Green Party. Yet Totalitarian Humanism needs to be recognized for what it is, the third triplet after Communism and Fascism.

The Necessity of Strategic and Organizational Thinking

A criticism that has been issued against my outlook in the past is that it is overly concerned with pragmatic or strategic considerations and not rooted strongly enough in matters of abstract principle. But ideas are worthless (Stirnerite "spooks") if they cannot be translated into real world action. If we wanted, we could simply form a monastery where we sit around and debate whether drunk driving interferes with anyone's property rights or whether non-coercive ageism or transphobia conflicts with the natural rights of man, but for what purpose other than intellectual masturbation? If that is what some wish to do, so be it, but for those of us who want an anti-state movement that is a real world contender, matters of strategy and organization are indispensable. Therefore, considerations of what kinds of demographic groups, sub-tendencies, organizational methods, and tactical efforts are most conducive to the success of the objectives outlined above, and considerations of time frame, are essential to our wider theoretical framework.

The Necessity of High Intellectual Standards and Political Foresight

While considerations of strategy and action are important to the formulation of theory, this does not mean that we should not aspire to high intellectual standards. For one thing, the purpose of ARV/ATS is not to simply be popular and attract sympathizers, but to cultivate an elite leadership corps who will be the revolutionary elite of a future anarcho-pluralist/pan-secessionist populist movement. A competent leadership corps has to first possess not only high intellectual standards but a capacity for serious political foresight. These considerations are relevant to many different questions. For now, we can reflect a bit on the relevance of these to the immigration question, given that immigration is at present a prominent and controversial public issue.

With the exception of the paleolibertarians, national-anarchists, and perhaps some Green-anarchists, most present-day anti-state radicals generally advocate "open borders," meaning that the existing states should simply order their border and coast guards to stand down and allow entry into their respective countries by anyone who wishes to enter for whatever reason. If that's how many if not most libertarians or anarchists feel at present, then that's their prerogative. Yet the popularity of a position should not be a barrier to its challenge. After all, if the goal were to simply be popular in the anarchist milieu, our own tendencies would not even exist in the first place.

I criticize the "open borders" beliefs of many anarchists for a variety of reasons. First, I regard mass immigration as a phenomenon that is actually generated by the forces of State, Capital, and Empire, and serves the interests of present-day political elites and ruling classes. Second, I am skeptical as to whether a civilization of anarchic communities would actually have "open borders" as many anarchists conceive of such. "Open borders" simply invites the existing state to impose a uniform immigration standard on all communities and institutions within the wider society. There is likely to be a considerably greater degree of variation with regards to matters of immigration and citizenship in the absence of an overarching statist system. Third, it is doubtful that the cultural and social ultra-liberalism promoted by many anarchists and libertarians is compatible with the importation of unlimited numbers of persons from profoundly illiberal cultural environments. Fourth, the history of efforts by genuinely multi-ethnic and multicultural societies to maintain civil peace is not a particularly happy one or a cause for optimism. Fifth, there are the practical costs of mass immigration. For instance, do we really want North America to become as populous as China or India? Lastly, I am skeptical as to whether anarchists who champion "open borders" the most fervently are motivated primarily by anti-statist or civil libertarian concerns.

For instance, many anarchists have not devoted nearly as much effort, or no effort at all, to opposing statist legislation that is far more onerous or draconian in content and effect than the recently enacted Arizona immigration law. So are these anarchists motivated by anti-statism and civil libertarianism, or are they motivated more by universalism, e.g., the view that immigration is a good unto itself regardless of the state's role in fostering or prohibiting it? What sort of concerns do they express? What sort of criticisms do they raise? Do they say, "Requiring travelers to display passports is a statist interference with freedom to travel"? Perhaps they do at times, but there are plenty of laws on the books of a comparable nature that they rarely if ever discuss, for instance, those requiring motorists to obtain and carry a driver's license. Are they not more likely to say, "Restricting immigration is racist and xenophobic"? It is fairly clear that for many of the "open borders" anarchists and libertarians, universalism rather than anti-statism is the guiding value.

Now, to be fair, it should be pointed out that those anti-statists with anti-immigration views are often likewise motivated by values beyond those of mere concern with the role of the state in promoting or sponsoring immigration. The same could be said of libertarians holding opposing views on other controversial matters like abortion or capital punishment. Yet, anti-statists who are anti-immigration are typically much more likely to demonstrate anti-universalism. For instance, Hans-Herman Hoppe is a leading paleolibertarian critic of "open borders" libertarians, yet he recognizes the degree of discrimination or non-discrimination, inclusion or exclusion, homogeneity or heterogeneity, will inevitably vary from community to community and institution to institution minus a system of uniformity imposed by the central state. Likewise, the national-anarchists typically recognize that the internal norms and standards of differing "tribes" or communities will vary greatly in the absence of the state, and typically understand that without the state homogeneous communities will coexist with multicultural ones. Neither paleos nor national-anarchists typically engage in slander, vilification, threats, or violence towards those who do not share their views. Therefore, their claims of authenticity are at present the most valid and compelling.

The Necessity of Theoretical and Tactical Flexibility

The matter of immigration raises a few other issues that are relevant to the anarcho-pluralist/pan-secessionist paradigm. For instance, I have had some no doubt sincere and well-intentioned people ask questions such as these:

1. How can it be argued that the state promotes immigration

and immigrants benefit from statism when illegal immigrants are subject to arrest by the ICE or other police agencies?

2. Is not criticizing immigration promoting division among enemies of the state, thereby weakening the anti-state cause?

3. Is not criticizing immigration actually strengthening pro-state elements on the Right, who are after all motivated not by anti-statism but by statist nationalism?

4. Would not it be strategically more feasible to ally with immigrants against overarching common enemies, such as the global plutocracy?

Here are some short answers to these questions:

1. The state is not a monolithic conspiracy. Many anarchists and libertarians seem to regard "the state" the same way Marxists regard "the capitalists" or Nazis regard "the Jews." The state is a collection of certainly overlapping and interconnected interests, but one that also contains within itself plenty of contradictions and conflicts. Yes, certain elements within the state (for instance, the ICE or Joe Arpaio) might well have self-interest in enforcing immigration law. But plenty of other interests within the state actually benefit from immigration. These have been widely documented by immigration critics. Further, simply being a lawbreaker does not necessarily make one an enemy of the state *per se*, much less an anarchist revolutionary. If mere law-breaking were to be our standard of anarchist authenticity, then we would have to say that dirty cops are among the most anarchistic of all. After all, dirty cops commit perjury, plant evidence, engage in police brutality, confiscate drugs and then use them or sell them, steal from evidence lockers, accept bribes, participate in illegal searches and seizures, solicit sexual favors from suspects or prisoners, or even engage in outright common crimes such as robbery, rape, kidnapping, and murder. There

are certainly plenty of laws prohibiting these things, but are we prepared to argue that such cops measure up to anarchist standards?

2. For reasons that are widely known, it is doubtful whether immigrants, or even illegal immigrants, can be classified as enemies of the state on any kind of consistent level. Andrew Yeoman succinctly put it:

> . . . the ideal is to decentralize political power and increase the power of local institutions outside state control. This does not mean supporting illegal immigrants, who aren't outside the state—to the contrary. Illegals represent a minority that is trying to impose its will on the majority by fully integrating itself within the state. Illegals oppose state power just as much as they oppose capitalism, which is to say, not at all—they are here to make money and eager to take advantage of all the benefits of the welfare system. They are also seeking race replacement.

3. It is undoubtedly true that many on the anti-immigration Right are motivated less by an opposition to the imposition of a uniform and universalist immigration policy by the central state, and more by a desire for a xenophobic brand of statist nationalism? But to what degree are these elements reflective of ruling class values or elite consensus, or even the mainstream of public opinion? For instance, the *New York Times* (which Abbie Hoffman used to refer to as "the voice of the ruling class") has consistently taken an "open borders" stance, as has the *Wall Street Journal* (which might be called "the voice of the global plutocracy"). The evidence is overwhelming that while elites and the radical Left share the common goal of total or near-total abolition of immigration controls, hard-core "xenophobes" are a fairly marginal, fringe movement. Research indicates that the average American of all races or colors generally has a tolerant view of legal immigrants, while regarding present immigration rates as

too high and believing that illegal immigration should be barred. This is hardly an indication of imminent genocide as "immigrants' rights" hysterics would have us believe.

4. All of these issues aside, are there indeed areas or situations where illegal immigrants might well be potential allies? Aside from my strenuously un-PC views on certain questions, one of the areas of my own thinking that often raises the most eyebrows is my position that outlaw organizations might well be valuable allies against the state in certain instances. For instance, motorcycle gangs, survivalist militias, common street gangs, exotic cults, and the like. There are a number of reasons why I hold to this view. One is the obvious. Many of these groups view themselves as a nation of their own that is at war with the government, therefore in a situation of direct conflict with the state, they may be viable military allies against a common enemy. Second, many of these groups have a history of being in direct conflict and combat with the repressive apparatus of the state, e.g., the BATF, FBI, DEA, or state and local SWAT teams or paramilitary police. Thirdly, by recruiting them as allies or mercenaries for "our side" we prevent our various enemies from doing so. There are other, less significant reasons why I take this position as well.

This brings us to the final question of on what issues might it be appropriate to take a pro-immigration stance or to ally ourselves with illegal immigrants. As mentioned, individual participants in the anarcho-pluralist/pan-secessionist project can have any other views they wish. By extension, they can advocate for their own tribe, community, or territory whatever political values they wish. For instance, if some left-anarchists, left-libertarians, Hispanic ethno-nationalists, or liberal multiculturalists decide to organize a Miami secessionist movement (the "Republic of Miami") and decide they wish for an independent Miami to have completely open borders, so be it. If most people in a liberal metropolis like New York City or San Francisco prefer that these regions be "sanctuary cities," then that's how it will be. Likewise, while I would defend Arizona's sovereignty against the feds regarding the controversial immigration law, if one of Arizona's cities or counties, say, Tucson or Flagstaff, decided to secede from Arizona in protest of the immigration law, I would defend their right to do so as well. Nor does this mean that any policy of any seceded polity is necessarily "written in stone." For instance, in an independent Arizona, pro-immigration advocates could certainly agitate for less restrictive immigration policies, and I would defend their free speech rights to do so. In an independent "Republic of Miami" with open borders, immigration restrictionists could push for more limits on immigration, and I would likewise defend their free speech rights as well.

An analogy could be made to class issues. Any interest of mine is organizing secessionist efforts by large cites with an emphasis on class issues. While I am a Southerner, neo-Confederate ideology or Dixieland revivalism doesn't really interest me much. Instead, I would prefer to develop secession movements on the part of the large metro areas like Richmond, Nashville, Memphis, Atlanta, New Orleans, Chattanooga, Charleston, and so forth. The focus would be on achieving economic self-sufficiency and self-determination for the lower classes, and on repealing policies that generate much of the violent crime in these urban areas, particularly drug prohibition. Consequently, if we were to organize a general strike or mass walkout by workers in fast food chains, superstore chains, meatpacking plants, crony-capitalist real estate developments, or agribusiness plantations, I would very much advocate labor solidarity among all the workers, even though many of these places employ illegal immigrants.

At the same time, as part of the process of developing a pan-secessionist movement, I am certainly open to class collaboration on certain issues. While my personal focus would be on the urban lower classes, in many of the counties surrounding my own city there are affluent, upper-middle class communities with strong conservative leanings. If indeed a secessionist movement motivated by a desire to simply not pay taxes to Washington, D.C., or the state government were to emerge among such people, I would certainly back their efforts. Likewise, even though I am a pro-abortion atheist who thinks the cause of gay marriage is more silly than offensive, if a rural county or small town comprised of evangelical Christians or other religious conservatives were to secede rather than recognize *Roe v. Wade* or gay rights/gay marriage laws, I would support their efforts as well.

In a similar vein, given the reality that the future of the American Southwest likely belongs to Aztlán, it may well be likely that tactical collaboration with Hispanic ethno-nationalist secessionists in the Southwest, including many illegal immigrants or their immediate descendants, will be strategically feasible or even necessary at some point in the future.

Part 4 - Strategic Formulations

Liberty and Populism:

Building an Effective Resistance Movement in North America

A smell of *fin du régime* hangs over Washington, just as it did over the last days of decaying Soviet empire when an out of touch leader presided over a lost foreign war, and a swamp of influence peddling and bribery, as the secret police struggled to keep a lid on growing dissent.

—Eric Margolis

Half a century after the end of World War II, and in places as far apart as the US, Europe and Japan, so little inclined are people to trust the state or risk their lives for it that even the death of a few soldiers is likely to result in an outcry and lead to campaigns being abandoned. In all these countries more and more the media tend to present the state as corrupt, inefficient and wasteful; not so much an aid to justice and social peace, as an obstacle on the way to obtaining them . . . [W]hat is going to take the place of the state? . . . If implosion is one result that may follow from the weakening of the state, integration may be another. From ASEAN through the EU and NAFTA and MERCOSUR, technological and economic changes are forcing states to cooperate with each other, not seldom at the expense of at least some parts of their sovereignty . . . individual states are being taken over by a larger organization. At present this new organization already makes law, exercises justice and makes money, though it does not yet either declare war or levy taxes. Above all, it is not sovereign and does not represent a state; that is why it is called a Union or a Community . . .

As states integrate into a larger organization that encompasses them, they are often made to devolve some of their internal powers to regions, districts and communities . . . While many states are either imploding or coming together, all of them face increasing competition from other forms of organization. Some of those organizations are private, others are public . . . Playing an independent role, they will exercise growing power over members and non-members; e.g. by making their own laws, exercising their own justice, levying their own taxes, and even manufacturing their own money in the form—as is often done at present—of stock-options. Depending on the issue and on the moment, they may cooperate with governments, exercise pressure on governments, oppose governments, and even wage war on governments.

— Martin van Creveld

If the observations of Eric Margolis and Martin van Creveld in the above quotations are indeed rooted in an accurate perception of present trends, then some major, major political changes are on the horizon. If the United States is now in a condition parallel to that of the Soviet Union in its geriatric years, then it stands to reason that the United States is headed for a major collapse and perhaps complete disintegration. If van Creveld's analysis is correct, the downfall of the United States would itself be only a signaling event in the emergence of an age whereby political institutions as we have traditionally thought of them are disappearing in favor of something almost entirely new. The world order towards which the twenty-first century will take us will be one that combines greater decentralization with a greater role for transnational institutions, at the expense of the nation-state, with both kinds of political arrangements submerged in a global market economy. Additionally, we may well be witnessing the beginning of the age of decline of traditional state militaries as these are proving to be more and more ineffective against so-called "fourth generation" insurgent forces such as non-state guerrilla armies. The disappearance of nation-states and national military forces would mark a political transformation comparable to the decline of feudalism and the rise of industrial society.

1. The Ideological Foundations of Twenty-First-Century Political Struggles

What will be the consequences of these developments for political struggles in the twenty-first century? In the realm of political economy, we are seeing the rise of a transnational corporate-mercantilism and a global supra-national political order where the sovereignty of traditional states has been eradicated but a global state is far from being fully consolidated at the expense of local autonomy. The ideological conflict likely to emerge from this arrangement will pit the forces of increased centralization and corporatism against the forces of decentralization and populism. All of the modern countries are now under the ideological domination of one or another form of neo-Marxism, whether the Marcusean cultural Marxist revisionism of the European ruling class and the left wing of the US ruling class, the Shachtmanite right-wing Trotskyism of the US Republicans, or the post-Maoism of the Chinese Communist Party. It stands to reason that the foundations of political struggle in the coming century will essentially be a continuation of the oldest and most historic divide of the traditional Left, that between the Marxists and the Anarchists. This development in turn marks the fulfillment of William Graham Sumner's prediction from a century ago that one day men would be divided into only two political camps, those of the Anarchists and the Socialists.

The crumbling of the US regime within a global framework of greater leanings towards (partial) decentralization and polycentrism will provide libertarian radicals in North America with unprecedented opportunities. It would be a foolish error of a truly historic magnitude if we were to let these opportunities go to waste. In developing a new North American radicalism, we must first consider the nature of the enemy. The US ruling class continually drifted leftward over the last century to the point where the "Old Left," the Marxist/Trotskyist/New Deal intellectual Left of the 1930s, are now the ostensible conservative Republicans while the Marcusean cultural Marxists of the 1960s "New Left" are now the liberal Democrats. If this historical pattern continues, then an ongoing leftward drift will mean that within a couple of decades the ostensible "conservatives" or "right-wing" will be the present-day reactionary liberalism of Dianne Feinstein, Charles Schumer, Ted Kennedy, Jimmy Carter, Bill and Hillary Clinton, Albert Gore, John Kerry, Michael Moore, and Morris Dees. We can easily envision an ideologically and intellectually decrepit lot such as these presiding over the final days of the crumbling US empire.

In formulating a new American radicalism, we have the relevant historical precedents to draw upon, including the aristocratic populism of Thomas Jefferson, the anti-slavery movement of William Lloyd Garrison and the abolitionists, the classical farm and labor populist movements, and, to a lesser degree, the upheavals of the 1960s. From anarchist history, there is the precedent of the anarchist mass movements of Spain, France, and other Latin countries in the decades leading up to the Second World War. In the realm of strategy, I have to confess to being a fairly orthodox Bakuninist. This perspective emphasizes the necessity of a militant vanguard and conspiratorial secret societies composed of radical intellectuals and activists acting as a leadership corps of a larger populist movement of which the lumpenproletariat and the rural population are the class vanguard. This is the strategy that was utilized by history's most successful anarchist movement, that of the Spanish anarchists. Indeed, it was Bakunin's emissary Giuseppe Fanelli who first planted the seeds of what was to become classical Spanish anarchism. As

I will attempt to demonstrate, this approach might be quite feasible for modern North America as well.

At present, the primary intellectual framework of a new American radicalism is pretty well complete. We have the contributions to economics provided by Kevin Carson, a historical narrative provided by Jack Ross, and a geopolitical approach to foreign policy provided by Troy Southgate and other European New Rightists (which makes an excellent supplement to both Noam Chomsky's anti-American, pro-Third World, New Left approach and the traditional isolationist approach of the paleo-right). There is also the approach to cultural conflict provided by the national-anarchists and certain paleo-anarchists, Thomas Woods' paleo critique of the modern liberal account of US history, and Hans-Hermann Hoppe's critiques of centralized mass democracy and the national security state. Matthew Raphael Johnson's work on Russian history makes an excellent effort at debunking the conventional Marxist approach to that nation's history, just as the works of Ross and Woods make similar contributions to the study of US history. Lastly, there are the efforts of Larry Gambone and myself to address the question of anarchist strategy.

2. Assembling the Vanguard

The next step is the assembling of the "principled militants" whom Bakunin recognized as the intellectual and activist vanguard of the insurgency. This is not to be confused with the Marxist-Leninist concept of the "vanguard" whose only purpose is the achievement of military dictatorship for the sake of managing a centrally planned economy. We are now in need of an organizational framework that can play the same role as that of the Iberian Anarchist Federation (FAI) in the development of Spanish anarchism. Translated into modern American terms, such an organization would be a combination of a think tank and activist and propaganda front, sort of an anarchist alternative to ruling class entities of a similar nature such as the American

Enterprise Institute or Democratic Leadership Council. Perhaps a better model might be Marcus Raskin's Institute for Policy Studies or some of the radical libertarian think tanks like the Ludwig von Mises Institute or the Independent Institute. To play its proper role, such an organization would have to not only issue position papers and conduct conferences but also involve itself in day-to-day activist efforts of the type the Stalinists coordinate with their International ANSWER and maintain a presence within larger, more mainstream political organizations such as the ACLU, NRA, labor unions, single-issue pressure groups, territorial secession movements, grassroots community action groups, or the minor political parties. Obviously, the only kind of ideological framework suitable for such an effort would be something akin to Voltairine de Cleyre's "anarchism without adjectives," i.e., a non-sectarian, non-purist, tendency open to anarchists of all hyphenated tendencies as well as their fellow travelers. When I met Abbie Hoffman in 1987, I asked him what he thought the most common mistake made by radical activists was and he quickly replied that the main problem was that too many radicals waste time arguing over secondary issues like this or that "ism" rather than focusing on more immediate problems. We would do well to heed his advice. Larry Gambone describes the problem with doing otherwise:

> Read even the most superficial book on anarchism and you will discover that many forms of anarchism exist— anarchist-communism, individualist-anarchism, anarcho-syndicalism, free-market anarchism, anarcho-feminism and green-anarchism. This division results from people taking their favorite economic system or extrapolating from what they see as the most important social struggle and linking this to anarchism. . . . The hyphenation presents a danger. Like it or not, everyone, without exception, compromises, modifies or softens their beliefs at some point. Where they compromise is what is important. Do they give up on the anarchism of the other aspect? You can be sure that most hyphenated anarchists will prefer to drop the libertarian

side of the hyphen. There are plenty examples of this occurring.

In other words, our core creed must be "Anarchy First!" applied within context of decentralism, populism, and libertarianism. Here is a set of potential "first principles" for an anarchist-led libertarian-populism:

1. Minimal and decentralized government organized on the basis of community sovereignty and federalism.

2. A worker-based, cooperative economy functioning independently of the state, the corporate infrastructure, and central banking.

3. A radically civil libertarian legal system ordered on the basis of individual sovereignty, individual rights, and restorative justice.

4. A neutralist, non-interventionist foreign policy and a military defense system composed of decentralized, voluntary militia confederations.

5. A system of cultural pluralism organized on the basis of voluntary association, civil society, localism, regionalism, decentralism, and mutual aid.

6. The achievement of the above through an all-fronts strategy of grassroots local organizing, local electoral action, secession, civil disobedience, militant strikes and boycotts, organized tax resistance, alternative infrastructure, and armed struggle.

This is a generalized program that anti-state radicals of virtually any ideological stripe ought to be able to agree upon. I suspect that those who do not agree might be inclined towards an excess of purism, sectarianism, or utopianism. Unfortunately, those with such an outlook will simply have to fall by the wayside. Principled realism should be our primary analytical and strategic tool. The first order of business in developing a strategic paradigm is to give due consideration to the actual structure of the United States, politically, economically, and culturally. I also include Canada and Mexico within a program for a new North American radicalism, but there are differences in those countries that might require a somewhat varying approach from those of radicals in the United States. For ideas on a building on libertarian radicalism in Canada, I would highly recommend the works of Larry Gambone. For Mexico, we might of course wish to look to the EZLN for leadership.

3. Left/Right and the "Culture Wars"

A principal issue for American radicals is overcoming the conventional Left/Right divide. An understanding of the distribution of the US population, geographically and ideologically, might be of some help in dealing with this problem. The majority of the US population lives in 75 large metropolitan areas. These are also the areas that tend to be the most culturally mixed, the most leftward leaning politically and with the greatest numbers of minorities, whether ethnic and religious minorities or feminists and homosexuals. Whenever a national election is held, much is made over the blue-state/red-state divide, but this is not an adequate description of the political distribution of the US population. The actual divide is much more decentralized, with big cities, university towns, environmentalist havens, and coastal and border areas constituting the "blue" and landlocked areas, smaller towns, and rural counties representing the "red." When the entire US population is broken down on purely ideological lines, about half of the US public votes "blue" and the other half votes "red." In fact, it is only because the US Electoral College system allows influence for the "reds" beyond their actual population numbers that the "blues" are not completely dominant as they would be in a completely majoritarian system (in my view, this is a good thing).

Breaking down the "red/blue" divide on stricter ideological grounds, it is important to realize that rank and file Democratic voters are typically far more reasonable people than the cultural Marxists or shyster politicians who comprise their leadership. Similarly, most rank and file Republican voters are not radical theocrats or crypto-Nazis as the reactionary Left hysterically proclaims. Indeed, most Republican voters are political moderates, "small c" conservatives in the Goldwater tradition, libertarians, Second Amendment advocates, or simply taxpayers or business interests "voting with their pocketbooks." Even many on the "religious right" are single-issue voters opposed to abortion and perceived, and often genuine, attacks on their culture or religious liberty by militantly secular liberal elites. And the hardcore racist right wing exemplified by the Klan, Nazis, skinheads, etc., has no sympathy in mainstream American society. A conventional politician who received the endorsement of David Duke or the National Alliance would regard such an endorsement as a liability. Unpleasant though it may be for persons with a generally cosmopolitan cultural outlook to consider, like the "religious right," the "white right" is not without legitimate grievances against mainstream society. A "white nationalist" website lists some of these:

> It is a long list. Burdensome racial preference schemes in hiring, racial preference schemes in university admissions, racial preference schemes in government contracting and small business loans. Beyond quotas there is the denial of rights of free speech and of due process to Whites who are critical of these governmental policies. We have special punishments for assaults committed by Whites if the motives might be racial. In addition, Whites pay a proportion of the costs of the welfare state that is disproportionate to what they receive in benefits. But the most exploitative aspect of the situation is that neither the racial quotas, the business preferences, the loss of freedom of speech, nor the disproportionate contributions to the welfare state have managed to sate the appetites of non-

Whites living in the United States. The more Whites sacrifice, the more non-Whites demand. Many Whites are beginning to believe that no amount of tribute, other than mass suicide, would satisfy the non-White demands. If our presence stirs up that much hatred in the hearts of non-Whites, then the only sensible course of action is to separate ourselves from them.

Anyone familiar with the totalitarian speech codes of the US university system, the "anti-whiteness" theory of the type subscribed to by the crazier sectors of the reactionary Left, or the increasingly repressive policies concerning free speech in the European Union countries (for example, the David Irving case) that will eventually be imported into the United States as the cultural Marxists come to power with their Marcusean ideology of "repressive tolerance" will understand that the complaints of the white nationalists are not exactly without merit.

As I mentioned earlier, the real political battle of the future is not between the Left and Right but an intra-Left civil war between the liberal-Marxist-statist-totalitarian Left and the libertarian-populist-decentralist-anarchistic Left. An authentic Right of the Burke-Metternich-Maistre variety does not exist in the United States (it never really did) and the closest things to it (the "religious right" and the "white right") represent points of view that were dominant in America long ago but have been losing power consistently for decades upon decades and are trying to "go down fighting." If our principal enemies of the future are going to be the cultural Marxists of the type that now dominate the EU, then we must prepare ourselves for the day when the Clinton-Gore-Kerry types are the conservative Republicans. This process is developing very rapidly. The present neocons were to the left of the liberal Democrats of the 1960s. Now they are the establishment Right. The New Left of the 1960s is now in the on-deck circle and will soon be up to bat. Any viable strategy for the libertarian-left must be prepared to meet this challenge head-on.

The strategy that I am going to recommend is tripartite, multi-tiered, and "all-fronts" oriented in nature. The "tripartite" aspect of it involves building a radical movement that draws from the Left, Right, and Center alike against the neoconservative/cultural Marxist ruling class. The "left" element involves assuming certain positions and undertaking actions that are actually to the left of the 1960s-style "New Left." The first matter is to adopt an attitude of complete rejection of the state. While 1960s radicalism had an anarchistic strand to it, the mainstream of the New Left's view of the state was standard left-liberal, social-democratic New Class welfarism. Few enthusiasms from that era have proven to be a greater failure. This does not in any way mean that we adopt the "neoliberal" economic outlook of the corporate right. Far from it. We need an authentic libertarian-populist approach to economic radicalism that regards "big government" and "big business" as two sides of the same enemy coin. This is obviously a complicated matter and I will address the issue in more detail below. Second, we need to abandon the bourgeois identity politics that have grown out of the New Left. The legacy of this has been to create a constituency for the left wing of capital among elite members of traditional minority groups, including educated professionals among blacks, feminists, and homosexuals, middle-class ecology enthusiasts, animal-lovers, and so on. The best approach here would be to attempt to pull the rank-and-file elements of the traditional minorities out from under their bourgeois leadership. This means that anarchist revolutionaries such as ourselves would need to seek out common ground with nationalist and separatist elements among the non-white ethnic groups against the black bourgeoisie of the NAACP, poor and working class women against the upper-middle class feminist groups like NOW, and the gay counterculture (complete with its transsexual, hermaphrodite, and transgendered elements) against the more establishment-friendly gay middle-class.

Indeed, we have not even begun to touch on the possibilities for building a radical movement rooted in part in marginalized social groups ignored, despised, or persecuted by the establishment.

These elements include the handicapped, the mentally ill, students, youth, prostitutes and other sex workers, prisoners, prisoner's rights activists, advocates for the rights of the criminally accused, the homeless and homeless activists, anti-police activists, advocates of alternative medicine, drug users, the families of drug war prisoners, immigrants, lumpen economic elements (jitney cab drivers, peddlers, street vendors), gang members, and many others too numerous to name. On these and other similar issues, our positions should be to the left of the ACLU. Adopting this approach will bring with it the opportunity to politically penetrate the rather large lumpenproletarian class that exists in the United States with little or no political representation. At the same time, the last thing we should wish to do is emulate the mistakes of the New Left by adopting an ideology of victimology and positioning ourselves as antagonists of the broader working masses. Nothing could be more self-defeating. The defense of marginal populations way beyond any efforts in this area offered by the left establishment should be part of our program, but only part. Our main focus should be on the working class itself, the kinds of folks who work in the vast array of service industries that comprise the bulk of the US economy.

This is the "center" part of our strategy. I am not advocating a return to old-fashioned labor unionism of the type championed by the classical anarcho-syndicalists. I believe the decline of unions is permanent in nature and while traditional labor unions might still have a role in play in a twenty-first-century class struggle, it will only be on the margins. Instead, the economic foundation of class struggle in the future will be alternative economic enterprises and service delivery arrangements operating independently of state and corporate structures. Foremost among them will be worker-owned and operated enterprises and non-state social or health services originating from what is called the "independent sector." This is an article on political strategy and not economics so I will not go into a great deal of detail here except to say that the main political implication of this is that organizations formed for the defense of such economic institutions against state repression or state-imposed monopolies will be vital part of any future radical coalition.

As for the broader question of the relationship between the state and the economy, we need a populist economic program that favors elimination of state intervention into the economy on behalf of privileged interests and the reduction of taxes starting from the bottom up. This is an issue that dissidents from across the spectrum ought to be able agree on, from socialists to libertarians to paleoconservatives to Greens. Kevin Carson's "A 'Political' Program for Anarchists" provides a good overview of how to approach this. As anti-state radicals, we should take a position of rejecting the welfare state as a means of poverty relief, while at the same time rejecting the scapegoating of the poor common to the talk radio right wing. We should instead be quite outspoken about the damage to done to poor communities (particularly rural farmers and inner-city minorities) by state interventions such as agricultural policy and urban renewal. As an intermediate stage to full abolition of the welfare state, we might consider the "negative income tax" suggested by Milton Friedman back during the Nixon era, whereby the costs of welfare management could be cut back drastically by distributing cash payments or vouchers directly to the poor and eliminating the bureaucratic middlemen that absorb most of the welfare budget. With this approach, it might even be possible to increase subsistence payments to the poor while simultaneously cutting back significantly on both bureaucracy and taxes. The writings of Murray Rothbard, Karl Hess, Hans-Hermann Hoppe, Kevin Carson, and Larry Gambone also contain some interesting ideas on how to go about "de-statizing" those industries and services presently operated by the state.

It is of the utmost importance that the working masses view us as the champions of their economic interests. Nothing less will be sufficient. Our populist coalition must include rank and file blue-collar workers, working class taxpayers, union members, small businessmen, farmers, the self-employed, the urban poor, single moms, and the homeless. We do this not by promising entitlement rights to all, but by eliminating state-imposed obstacles to economic self-determination and self-sufficiency, placing state or state-corporate industries and services directly into the hands of the workers and consumers, developing alternative economic arrangements independently of the state, eliminating taxes from the bottom up, and gradually phasing out archaic state-assistance programs, with poverty relief and social security programs being the last to go once the corporate state has been fully dismantled. This is precisely the opposite of the "cut taxes and regulations at the top, eliminate subsidies to the bottom" approach favored by the right-wing corporatists. Our approach should be "cut taxes and regulations at the bottom, eliminate subsidies to the top." On these matters, authentic fiscal conservatives and authentic class war militants should be able to agree. We should describe our economic program as neither "conservative" nor "socialist" but as simple "economic justice."

If we appeal to the Left with a defense of marginalized or scapegoat population groups and to the Center with an emphasis on economic justice, then how will we appeal to the Right? This is likely to be the most controversial aspect of our program. There are indeed many areas where the radical Left and the radical Right have much in common. One obvious area of possible collaboration would be opposition to imperialist warfare and military interventionism on behalf of ruling class interests. Another is on libertarian-populist economic issues of the type mentioned above. There is certainly no reason why the libertarian-left cannot endorse the civil liberties issues of the right, such as freedom of religious practice, the right to home school, Second Amendment rights against the gun-grabbers, personal property rights against eminent domain and asset forfeiture laws, opposition to the use of anti-racketeering laws to harass anti-abortion activists, abusively anti-male "child support" and other divorce-related laws, speech codes, self-defense rights, tax resistance, intrusive zoning, licensing, or environmental laws, and so on. If militiamen or right-wing patriot types wish to drive without licenses or tags, so be it. Common law rules of tort and liability would still apply.

4. Left/Right and Radical Decentralization

The main obstacle to alliances between left-wing and right-wing populists and decentralists are cultural in nature. A substantial sector of the radical right views itself as being under attack by an elite that is hell-bent on imposing militant secularism, totalitarian multiculturalism, homosexual radicalism, extremist feminism, and other manifestations of cultural Marxism on the broader society, and doing so in a way that displays total disregard for the traditional American liberties of free speech, freedom of association, economic or religious liberty, and Second Amendment rights. One need not share the cultural outlook of the socially conservative right wing to recognize that there is much truth to their complaints against the cosmopolitan liberal establishment. On this question, the radical left typically puts the cart before the horse. It is well and good to defend unpopular minorities against genuine oppression and to agitate for the ongoing expansion of civil liberties. But it is strategically foolish to adopt an antagonistic stance towards the traditional and majoritarian culture of the working masses by attempting to pit varying demographic groups against one another in the form of blacks against whites, women against men, gays against straights, immigrants against natives, tree-huggers against loggers, animal lovers against meat-eaters, eco-freaks against small property owners, peace creeps against veterans, hippies against blue-collar workers, poor Appalachian whites against Jewish bankers, or whatever. A grievous strategic error undertaken by the left during the 1960s and 1970s was its abandonment of the class struggle orientation of the historic left and reinventing itself as what the Nixonites would sneeringly refer to as "the party of amnesty, acid, and abortion." Paul Craig Roberts describes the consequences of this:

> President Bush has used "signing statements" hundreds of times to vitiate the meaning of statutes passed by Congress. In effect, Bush is vetoing the bills he signs into law by asserting unilateral authority as commander-in-chief to bypass or set

aside the laws he signs. For example, Bush has asserted that he has the power to ignore the McCain amendment against torture, to ignore the law that requires a warrant to spy on Americans, to ignore the prohibition against indefinite detention without charges or trial, and to ignore the Geneva Conventions to which the US is signatory.

In effect, Bush is asserting the powers that accrued to Hitler in 1933. His Federalist Society apologists and Department of Justice appointees claim that President Bush has the same power to interpret the Constitution as the Supreme Court. An Alito Court is likely to agree with this false claim. This is the great issue that is before the country. But it is pushed into the background by political battles over abortion and homosexual rights. Many people fighting to strengthen the executive think they are fighting against legitimizing sodomy and murder in the womb. They are unaware that the real issue is that America is on the verge of elevating its president above the law.

Bush Justice Department official and Berkeley law professor John Yoo argues that no law can restrict the president in his role as commander-in-chief. Thus, once the president is at war—even a vague open-ended "war on terror"—Bush's Justice Department says the president is free to undertake any action in pursuit of war, including the torture of children and indefinite detention of American citizens. The commander-in-chief role is probably sufficiently elastic to expand to any crisis, whether real or fabricated. Thus has the US arrived at the verge of dictatorship.

The "red-state fascists" who constitute Bush's most enthusiastic grassroots supporters may not care if Bush and his cronies were to create an executive dictatorship for themselves, but they should consider the future consequences for their own interests when such powers subsequently fall into the hands of President Hillary Clinton. A preview of this was granted during the Bill

Clinton/Janet Reno era. As the 1960s generation becomes the elderly generation, the cultural Marxists of the New Left will be the unquestioned status quo. As mentioned, the likes of Charles Schumer and Dianne Feinstein will be the "conservatives." The goal of this crowd is the creation of a pseudo-Stalinist state where "freedom," "democracy," "human rights," and other shallow pieties amount to extravagant affirmative action, unlimited abortion, gay marriage, and little else within the context of a Mussolini-like corporatist economy and an overtly fascistic police state. The old-style civil libertarian left of Nat Hentoff or the libertine "sex, drugs, and rock 'n' roll" left of Abbie Hoffman and Jerry Rubin is long dead. The establishment left of today is the left of Morris Dees, Catharine MacKinnon, and Michael Moore.

I believe the best way to approach the possibility of a rapproche-ment between the radical libertarian-left and the populist radical-right is to convince both sides that their cultural interests are best defended within the context of a radically decentralized political order. Much of the right should be open to this idea as respect for venerable American traditions such as "states' rights" and "local sovereignty" is common on the right. Indeed, cultural conservatives frequently lament the alleged "judicial activism" of federal courts that have legalized abortion, pornography, and homosexuality nationwide, mandated racial desegregation, expanded criminal rights, and removed religious instruction from public schools. This is an exaggeration. The rulings of the federal courts on these matters, particularly those of the Warren and Burger Supreme Courts, only reflected prevailing trends of the times. Most of the individual states were already starting to adopt a more liberal approach in these areas when the courts stepped in and speeded up the process a bit. For example, when the Supreme Court struck down state anti-sodomy laws in 2003, only thirteen of the fifty states still retained such laws. Social conservatives, cultural, religious, racial, or otherwise, are losing the so-called "culture wars" on all fronts. The more perceptive and intelligent persons within those milieus recognize this. For example, Paul Weyrich, a founder of the religious right, has called for "cultural secession" by conservatives, recognizing that the cultural left has largely won the war. A territorial secession movement of this type, the Christian Exodus Project, has emerged. And no serious person among the white nationalists believes there will ever be a neo-Nazi regime in the United States or that the old Southern racial caste system will ever be reinstated. Instead, these forces have adopted a purely defensive position. For the cultural right, the choice is clear enough: Either adopt an outlook of separatism and decentralism, or prepare to be ruled by the cultural Marxists. The right should have no problem choosing the former over the latter.

For the libertarian-left, the question is a little more problematical. The left tends to associate slogans like "states' rights" or "local sovereignty" with apologies for slavery and white supremacism. And much of the left ignorantly believes that in a decentralized system the entire American heartland would fall under the rule of Christian Talibanists or the American Nazi Party. This perspective reeks of elitist paranoia and bigotry. It is necessary to demonstrate to the left that their interests are also best advanced through decentralization and local sovereignty. As mentioned, the majority of the US population resides in 75 major metropolitan areas. It is in these areas where ethnic, religious, and sexual minorities, the urban poor, the youth countercultures, the homeless, marginal populations, and other groups championed by the left tend to be concentrated. If these areas were independent city-states, it would be much easier to advance to interests of these populations politically. Here's an interesting case in point: In my own state of Virginia, there have been debates in the legislature about how to go about changing the state's sodomy laws now that the Supreme Court has declared them unconstitutional. Generally speaking, the "pro-sodomy" delegates tend to originate from the Washington, D.C. suburbs in northern Virginia, the heavily populated Atlantic coast region, and the metropolitan area around the capital city of Richmond. The "anti-sodomy" delegates tend to originate from the conservative, rural areas in the western part of the state. Obviously, it would be more advantageous for the "pro-sodomy" crowd if the more liberal, densely populated areas could simply legalize sodomy on their own and by-pass the state legislature.

Such a political framework would be very advantageous in ending the drug war. The large urban areas in the United States, where most drug addicts as well as most prohibition-related crime is located (and where most drug war prisoners come from), could simply end the drug war à la Amsterdam on their own with conservative, rural areas, and smaller towns maintaining prohibition on the "dry county" model. Leftists often argue that in such a decentralized system abortion rights would disappear, but this perception is inadequate. Abortion rights advocates will point out that roughly 85 percent of American localities (cities, towns, and counties) do not have any abortion services available due to poverty, local taboos, or whatever. In other words, decades after abortion was legalized nationwide, it is still de facto prohibited in most American communities through sheer unavailability, legal or not. Meanwhile, if *Roe v. Wade* were to be overturned, state governments would be authorized to prohibit abortion even in metropolitan areas where "pro-choice" sentiment is quite strong and urban abortion rights activists would be at the mercy of state legislators from counties with strong religious fundamentalist leanings. Of course, we could reverse this and apply the same analysis to Second Amendment rights. If the Supreme Court were to rule that the Second Amendment protects only state militias and not an individual's right to bear arms, then rural gun owners would be at the mercy of suburban and urban state legislators representing vociferously anti-gun constituencies. So it works both ways.

5. Black/White and Radical Decentralization

A libertarian-populist insurgency will out of strategic necessity need to divide and disrupt the popular coalitions that comprise the grassroots support base of the left and right wings of the ruling class. We can draw from the right in the ways already mentioned, i.e., defending both the economic interests and the cultural liberties of the conventional working class. Our ability to draw from the left will be dependent on our aptitude for pulling the rank and file members of the traditional minority groups out from under their bourgeois leadership and cultivating not-so-traditional minorities as constituent groups. Of all the issues raised by this question, none are quite as inflammatory as the matter of race. Ruling classes have maintained a "divide and conquer" stratagem for the subjugation of their populations since time immemorial. In the interest of frankness, here's how I interpret America's present racial situation: Cultural openings and cultural conflicts of the past fifty years have created a situation where a multi-ethnic ruling class attempts to micromanage social conflict and expand the reaches of the state with the ideology of totalitarian multiculturalism. The US ruling class is still primarily European in its ancestry, but is increasingly accepting of members of other ethnic groups into its ranks. Contrary to the imaginings of professional anti-Semites, "the Jews" do not rule America but organized Jewish ethnic interests do play the role of junior partners to the broader plutocracy. We might say that the Jewish elite play the role of Tony Blair with the mainstream white ruling class assuming the role of George W. Bush. Meanwhile, the loyalty of the elite members of the African population is maintained through an elaborate racial spoils system operating at the expense of the white working class majority. This in turn creates resentment on the part of whites which the elites channel into the scapegoating of poor, urban minorities who are the most subject to attack under the cover of public hysteria concerning drugs, guns, and crime, and whose plight their ethnic leadership ignores or helps perpetuate by acting as a buffer between the ruling class and an authentic black insurgency.

What I am really saying here is that the socially or even racially conservative white working class shares a common enemy with the black urban lumpenproletarian class. Political leaders who are able to build bridges across the divide between these two classes will possess a mighty weapon to be used against the ruling class enemy. How can this be accomplished? Rather than emulating the conventional liberal "strategy" of promoting some sort of utopian ideal of endless brotherly love where the lion and the lamb lie down together, it might be best to adopt an approach more consistent with the principles of realpolitik. We need to create a political program where both poor blacks and the white working class have more to gain from aligning themselves with each other than either does by aligning themselves with the ruling class against the other. The best approach would probably be one of sovereignty, reparations, and amnesty to advance the interests of blacks, and the elimination of race-based favoritism, affirmative action, antidiscrimination laws, etc., to advance the interests of whites. The black bourgeoisie would not find this to be an acceptable trade-off but many nationalist, separatist, or urban "underclass" blacks might. The white liberal bourgeoisie would be appalled by such a suggestion but the white working class would probably approve. Therefore, the anti-ruling class black factions and the anti-ruling white factions would find themselves on the same side of the fence against the common class enemy. This is how it should be.

The matter of implementing such a settlement to America's historic ethnic divides brings with it certain complications. The "pro-white" aspects of the settlement proposed above would be simple enough to enact. It is merely a matter of repealing particular laws (like antidiscrimination statutes) and policies (like affirmative action) and ending subsidies to particular interests (like "minority set-asides"). The "pro-black" aspects of the settlement are a little more difficult. On the question of sovereignty, various black nationalist factions have proposed widely divergent ideas. It would seem that the best approach would be one that involved the least amount of disruption possible. Some years ago, the Peoples' Democratic Uhuru Movement proposed that the majority black section of St. Petersburg, Florida, be separated from the rest of the city into a sovereign municipality. There is no reason why such an arrangement could not be put into place in all American cities with sizable black sections. The only serious criticism of this approach is that the disconnected black communities might degenerate into Bantustans of the type the former South Africa was famous for. At least a partial solution to this problem would be for sovereign black municipalities and their satellite towns and villages to be federated into larger "black nationalist" states on a national or regional basis. There is certainly sufficient precedent for such a territorially disconnected nation. One need only think of the United Kingdom at its height with its scattered island states and protectorates. On the question of reparations, it is obviously best to avoid an approach that requires administration by a large, obtrusive state bureaucracy. Instead, we might consider the suggestions of Kevin Carson:

> In frontier areas like America, the ruling classes feared the economic independence that open land would give laborers, and relied on the state to restrict access to unclaimed land. Even when land was opened to settlement, as in the much-vaunted Homestead Act, the state gave wealthy land speculators preference over ordinary settlers. Most of the white laborers who settled America, through the early nineteenth century, were indentured servants or convicts. Considering the harshness of punishment under the indenture system, and the number of minor infractions for which the term of indenture could be extended for years, it is likely that most indentured laborers died in service. We are today forced to sell our labor on the bosses' terms, because in the past we were robbed. "Forty acres and a mule"—for all of us—ain't just a cliché. It's JUSTICE.

> Which brings me to the point of this article—reparations. The furor over reparations must really be a hoot for the ruling class. It's the oldest trick in the book: keep the producing classes fighting each other so they'll be too busy to fight the bosses. For example, for most of the

seventeenth century in Virginia, there was little legal distinction between black and white servants. Servants of both races often intermarried, and began to develop a common class consciousness. The servant class, black and white, fought the planters in Bacon's Rebellion. Clearly, this wouldn't do. The Slave Codes, "white skin privilege," and racist ideology on a large scale, were the ruling class response to this crisis. And it worked pretty well, didn't it?

The same is true of the reparations movement. Like "affirmative action" for professional jobs ("black faces in high places"), it is more about the interests of the black bourgeoisie than those of working people. Cabinets, legislatures, and boardrooms that "look like America" just mean everyone can have the pleasure of being screwed by people of the same skin color. Likewise, although I've seen a few people on the libertarian left, like Lorenzo Komboa Ervin, who genuinely intend to use the proceeds of reparations for grassroots empowerment, it's a fair guess that most of the civil rights establishment view it as a cash cow for themselves. For Jesse Jackson, it's probably just another shakedown like the Anheuser-Busch distributorship.

At the same time, reparations will not hurt the plutocracy. So long as the statist roots of class privilege are left untouched, the usurers, profiteers and landlords will manage to adapt any "reform" to their own benefit. Monopoly capitalism will just pass the increased cost of reparations along to consumers, as it does all other forms of "progressive" taxation. Which means that the descendants of convict laborers and indentured servants will effectively be taxed to pay reparations, which in turn will almost certainly be skimmed off by people like Jackson. Just another example of how identity politics is being used to disrupt solidarity between working people of all races.

So as an alternative to reparations for slavery, how about

reparations for primitive accumulation instead? Let's make a united front in the class war, instead of letting class be hidden behind race relations. The way I see it (I'm a Proudhonian mutualist, by the way, not a Marxist), all tenants paying rent on apartments, urban tenements, public housing, etc., should stop. Those of us working for manufacturers and other large employers should "fire the boss," as the Wobblies put it, and keep the fruit of our own labor. Agricultural wage laborers should dispossess the agribusiness companies and rich landlords whose plantations they work. Possession, for groups and individuals, should be the basis of ownership. The land to the cultivator, the shop to the worker, free and equitable exchange.

In other words, it is only possible to achieve racial "justice" if the broader demand for economic "justice" or class "justice" is satisfied. Any such settlement to race and class based conflict must necessarily include amnesty. It is well-known that the United States maintains the world's largest prison population. More than one-quarter of all the world's prisoners reside in US prisons. A grossly disproportionate number of these are blacks or other minorities. A comprehensive amnesty program is essential to any serious effort to dismantle the US Leviathan state. As a model for amnesty, we might look to that implemented by Saddam Hussein, President of Iraq, prior to the commencement of the current war. Most prisoners were given full amnesty, foreign spies excepted. Thieves were pardoned on the condition of victim restitution. Even violent criminals had their sentences commuted if the victim or the victim's mother agreed to a pardon. If this was good enough for Saddam Hussein, it ought to be good enough for anti-state radicals in North America. Under such a general amnesty, the only remaining prisoners would be those who refused to compensate victims or whose crimes were serious enough to discourage the victim from granting a pardon. The rest of the prison population, from tax evaders to drug vendors to owners of "illegal" firearms to those convicted of violations of arcane regulatory statutes, would simply be cleared out. Likewise, those imprisoned for self-defense, whether against common criminals or the government (for example, Leonard Peltier, the surviving Branch Davidians, or those resisting "no-knock" raids) should also be granted amnesty. Additionally, panels of legal experts should be commissioned to review the cases of those convicted of even the most serious crimes. Given the notorious incompetence of the US legal system, it is likely a significant number of these are innocent.

Two extremely controversial issues that will naturally arise out of discussions of these types are those of crime and immigration. Thus far, much of the anti-state movement has failed to work out a consistent position on these questions. On crime, I propose the following approach: We should be tough on crime, but equally tough on cops, courts, and laws. On the issues of legal restrictions on the investigative and arrest powers of the police, the powers of the courts to prosecute the accused and impose sentences, and the powers of penal institutions to hold incarcerated persons and the conditions they are held under, we should take positions as "liberal" as those of the ACLU, the National Lawyers Guild, and beyond. However, when it comes to the right of private citizens to keep and bear arms, to use them in defense against criminals and to form private organizations (neighborhood watches, militias, posses, private security guard services, vigilance committees, and common law courts) for the purpose of mutual self-protection against crime (including government crime), we should take positions as "conservative" as the Gun Owners of America, the Michigan Militia, and beyond.

As a trivial but pertinent example of how such a policy might be implemented on a practical level, many people in large urban centers are persistently annoyed by the presence of aggressive bums demanding handouts from passers-by and issuing threats when refused. Now, we would not want to interfere with general free speech rights by prohibiting panhandling. Nor would we want to interfere with genuinely poor or disabled people, runaway kids, or others who wish to be peaceful beggars. Nor do we want to kowtow to bourgeois elements who object to the presence of such lumpen elements as an "eyesore," "blight," or, more specifically, a perceived threat to real estate values. We certainly do not want to turn public streets into "Official Police Property." What, then, should be done about annoying or threatening panhandlers? A simple common law rule that states that if an aggressive panhandler continues to annoy a pedestrian after being refused twice before, the person being subjected to the annoyance may, in the presence of at least one witness, physically strike the annoyer once with a hand, foot, fist, or non-lethal object, and in a non-lethal way, should be efficient. Such would be a common sense conservative policy whereby government gets out of the way in favor of individual responsibility, initiative, and self-sufficiency.

On immigration, it is clear enough that the only viable solution is one of local sovereignty. Obviously, we should not wish to strengthen our great common enemy, the US federal government, by militarizing the borders and building a Berlin Wall along the Rio Grande. Instead, the Swiss model can be applied to immigration policy and individual communities can decide whether to be pro-immigrant "sanctuary" communities, anti-immigrant communities with the Minutemen stationed at the county line, or somewhere in between. The great Israeli dissident Israel Shamir discussed the value of the localist approach in his debate with Noam Chomsky:

> Does this critique mean that the no-state idea should be discarded? Not at all. But instead of non-territorial millets, we may support small semi-independent territorial communes, as envisaged by Marx in his *Civil War in France* and by Lenin in his *The State and Revolution*, or indeed by Plato in his *Republic*. Such a solution is extremely suitable for Palestine and for the US, and for the rest of the world.

> In the US, it would solve many problems; people would be able to choose whether to live in a mixed or a separated

community, a liberal or conservative one, with or without abortions and gay marriages, and would not be imposing their social vision upon others. The federative framework consisting of independent units would not be an aggressive state prone to send troops to Iraq, but it would be able to organise its mutual self-defence. It would mean undoing the lifework of a Bismarck or Garibaldi, and good riddance, too! Full autonomy for every commune would slow down if not eliminate migration flow and would help people to regain their roots. Indeed, let the people of Boston or Atlanta decide whether they want to accept immigration from Ghana or Sweden, instead of having this question decided for them by the New York-based media and Washington lobbies. This was the rule in Switzerland: Alexander Herzen, a Russian noble and dissident of the 19th century, discovered that the Swiss federal government had no power to grant citizenship or even rights of residence to a stranger; it was a prerogative of a local commune. This wise rule can be implemented today everywhere.

6. Resistance on All Fronts

In formulating a strategy for resistance to the US regime and ruling class, it might be best to observe the efforts of successful resistance movements from other nations and to also take a look at the lessons from the past. Most successful or semi-successful resistance forces, whether the IRA/Sinn Fein in Northern Ireland, Hezbollah in Lebanon, Hamas in Palestine, the Vietcong, or the present-day insurgency in Iraq have followed rather consistent patterns in terms of their strategic approach. Each of these have applied an underground/overground strategy that included a wide range of actions such as electoral politics, grassroots community organizing, international propaganda campaigns, cultivating "friends in high places," maintaining alternative institutional infrastructure, and armed struggle. Obviously, some of these are more suitable for present-day North America than others. As anarchist radicals in the United States, there are two historical precedents we might wish to draw on, one from anarchist history and the other from American history. The Spanish anarchist movement of the 1930s had as its militant leadership corps the Iberian Anarchist Federation (FAI), a strongly Bakuninist but relatively non-sectarian outfit. The FAI comprised the political leadership of the much larger National Confederation of Workers (CNT), an anarcho-syndicalist labor union federation. When the Spanish Civil War began in 1936, the anarchists put together an even larger militia confederation drawn from the ranks of anti-fascist, anti-Soviet, and anti-capitalist forces of all ideological stripes, ranging from non-Stalinist Marxists to non-fascist nationalists. The French anarchists of the same era maintained a similar arrangement. The French counterpart to the FAI, the Union Anarchiste, organized a "Revolutionary Front" alliance of the same kinds of anti-fascist, anti-Stalinist, and anti-capitalist forces that made up the militias of Spain.

This was the only time in history when anarchists achieved even the most meager amounts of success. The question is how to replicate this in twenty-first-century North America. An obscure but interesting part of American history might provide us with a clue. There was a long-forgotten antislavery party, the Liberty Party, which competed in US national elections during the 1840s. Its electoral performance was comparable to that of today's Libertarians, Greens, or Constitutionalists. The party leadership made a strategic decision to orient the party towards the primary goal of blocking the furtherance of slavery into the western territories. Towards this end, they aligned themselves with the "know-nothings," a virulently racist party that also opposed the westward expansion of slavery, but for ideologically opposite reasons. The antislavery activists knew they were aligning themselves with persons whose values they would find extremely distasteful, but they also knew that the political victory of this alliance would be the death knell for slavery itself. The alliance of the Liberty Party, the "know-nothing" American Party and, later, the Free Soilers and the anti-Southern Constitutional Union with the left wing of the remnants of the Whig Party once that party could no longer sustain itself became the basis for the founding of the Republican Party of Abraham Lincoln. This is not to say that Republican ideology and ambitions, then or later, were benign or salutary. It does, however, demonstrate how a small, radical party with militantly libertarian ideals managed to advance itself beyond its wildest dreams in less than two decades.

I propose that anti-state radicals in the United States work towards the goal of recreating the general framework of the Spanish and French anarchist movements in America using the strategy and methodology employed by the Liberty Party. What would this mean? As mentioned, we need a militant anarchist vanguard organization comparable to the FAI or the Union Anarchiste that would in turn serve as the leadership corps, brains trust, primary intellectual and activist base, principal strategists, propaganda front, and mediating coordinators of a much larger populist movement utilizing some of the concepts I have already outlined. The only organizational vehicles that ever brought the classical anarchists any success were the mass anarcho-syndicalist labor federations of the early twentieth century. Now, the time of organized labor as a mass movement seems to have passed and an attempt to revive such a movement would probably be to take an archaic and reactionary position. Instead, a comparable organizational structure that is relevant to North American political culture would be a political party but a very unique type of political party. Such a party would be organized internally as a federation of local and regional parties, with these in turn having economic, institutional, and military arms of their own. At the national level, the party would deal only with a handful of the most pressing matters that dissidents of virtually all stripes agree upon such as opposition to US imperialism, the corporate state, and the federal police state. All other matters, whether specific ideological tendencies, specific political, economic, or cultural arrangements or controversial social issues (abortion, the death penalty, gay marriage, stem cell research, immigration, school prayer) would be dealt with on a local basis. Therefore, the party platforms of the Idaho or

Texas branches of the party might be similar to those of the present-day Constitution, American Independent, or America First parties. The platforms of the Vermont or Oregon parties might resemble those of the Libertarian or Green parties and the programs of the most reliably centrist regions might be similar to the Reform or Independence parties. The South Carolina party might reflect the ideals of the Christian Exodus Project while the northern California party might reflect the values of the Republic of Ganjastan.

Such a party could have its own economic arm in the form of dissident labor unions (a foreshadowing of this might be seen in the recent AFL-CIO split), an assortment of alternative economic enterprises, its own internal social service and health care delivery system (Hezbollah and Hamas might be models to emulate here), a system of alternative media (we can learn from both talk radio and the religious right on this one), legal defense organizations (modeled on the ACLU and NRA), fundraising organizations, single-issue oriented organizing projects, and a vast network of community and support organizations. We might commence our drive towards the realization of this ambition through the practice of entryism into one of the present minor parties (I would suggest either the Libertarians or the Greens, or both simultaneously) with the goal of achieving leadership positions, particularly in the realm of strategic formulation. From where will our ideological support base come from? Point Four of the American Revolutionary Vanguard Twenty-Five Point Program states:

> American Revolutionary Vanguard seeks to network with and form alliances with all groups and individuals engaged in active resistance including decentralists, non-supremacist separatists, constitutionalists, autonomists, patriots, populists, anti-corporate libertarians, anarchists, sovereigns, common law advocates, regionalists, anti-state conservatives, non-statist nationalists, agorists, mutualists, syndicalists, individualists, guild socialists, council communists,

individualist anarchists, collectivist anarchists, national anarchists, municipalists, Georgists, farmer liberationists, agrarians, radical traditionalists, micronationalists, Luddites, radical environmentalists, deep ecologists, non-reactionary third postionists, geonomists, geolibertarians, libertarian socialists, non-racist militias, anarcha-feminists, libertarian feminists, queer activists, anti-globalists and non-statist class struggle advocates of every kind.

It is also important to remember that most of American politics is driven by individual issues rather than by ideology. Our party must be a "coalition of coalitions" organized around such issues. Here they are:

- authentic fiscal conservatives vs. corporate plutocrats
- welfare recipients vs. New Class social service bureaucrats
- students/parents vs. educrats unions
- black nationalists, separatists, and the urban "underclass" vs. the black bourgeoisie, civil rights industry
- white working class vs. white liberal elite
- non-Zionist Jews/anti-Zionist Jews vs. Israel Firsters
- labor militants vs. corporate stooge labor bosses
- authentic class war militants vs. social democratic politicians
- gay counterculture vs. gay middle class
- prisoners, prisoners' advocates and families vs. prison-industrial complex
- soldiers, veterans vs. foreign policy elite, military-industrial complex
- antiwar activists vs. "humanitarian" interventionists, revolutionary democratists
- rank and file evangelical Christians vs. televangelist charlatans

- drug users, medical marijuana advocates vs. DEA, narcotics police, drug war profiteers
- American Indian tribes vs. Bureau of Indian Affairs
- gun owners vs. gun grabbers, BATF
- lumpenproletariat vs. urban bourgeoisie
- taxpayers, tax resisters vs. IRS
- anti-Zionists vs. Israeli lobby
- small property holders vs. regulators, land grabbers
- environmentalists, land rights advocates vs. state-corporate monopolists
- farmers vs. agribusiness
- alternative medicine advocates vs. medical-industrial complex
- mental patients vs. psychiatric industry
- civil libertarians vs. police state
- parents' rights advocates vs. Child Protective Services, social service bureaucrats
- fathers' rights advocates vs. family courts, feminist lobby
- libertarian-individualist feminists, poor and working women vs. bourgeois gender feminists
- consumer advocates vs. corporate lobbies
- common law advocates vs. legal industry
- young people vs. selective service, drinking ages, curfews, music censorship, truant officers, schools
- sex workers vs. vice police
- small broadcasters, alternative media vs. FCC
- "hate" groups vs. "anti-hate" professionals
- "cults" vs. religious bigots
- immigrants vs. INS
- anti-immigration activists vs. antidiscrimination laws, entitlements for non-citizens

- gang members vs. gang-enforcement units
- Third Worldists vs. US imperialism
- Muslims, Arab-Americans vs. Zionists, imperialists
- smokers vs. health Nazis
- free speech vs. political correctness
- isolationists vs. imperialists
- paleoconservatives vs. neoconservatives
- populists vs. professional politicians
- conspiracy theorists vs. NWO, CFR, TLC elites
- ethnic preservationists vs. totalitarian multiculturalists
- nationalists vs. internationalists
- states' righters, localists vs. centralists
- hunters vs. middle class animal lovers
- animals vs. factory farming industry
- economic scapegoats (money launderers, bookies, loan sharks) vs. federal, state prosecutors
- anti-abortion protestors vs. Department of Justice, RICO statute.

If indeed an insurgent libertarian-populist movement were able to put together a "coalition of coalitions" such as this, then we would de facto have the majority of the US population in our camp. Such a coalition would also splinter and neutralize the existing grassroots support coalitions maintained by the two rival wings of the ruling class, the neoconservatives and the cultural Marxists. In other words, victory would be ours. How will we get there from here? The present efforts by Kevin Zeese are an excellent model to draw on. Mr. Zeese is currently seeking the nomination of the Green, Libertarian, and Populist parties simultaneously in his bid for the Senate in Maryland. Zeese is running on a straightforward program of opposition to the Iraq war, salvaging the economy from ultimate ruin, opposing the PATRIOT Act, and ending the drug war. This might be a prototype for a radical future. Ultimately, we may at some point be able to combine the Green, Libertarian,

Populist, Constitution, Natural Law, and other minor parties into a single party, organized in the manner I have thus far outlined. I would suggest calling such a party the "Federalist Party" for several reasons. First, there is a precedent for this from American history. Second, it accurately describes what the internal structure of the party should be. Third, it provides a model for the general types of institutional arrangements we should seek to develop. Perhaps our party flag could be an anarchist black flag with the snake from the "don't tread on me" Gadsen battle flag embroidered on it.

It is of the utmost importance that our rhetoric and propaganda resonate well with American history and political culture. We should not publicly call ourselves "anarchists," "radicals," or "revolutionaries." Instead, we are "federalists," "localists," "constitutionalists," "states' righters," "decentralists," "libertarians," "populists," "Jeffersonians," "democrats," "patriots." We advocate "economic justice," "freedom," "democracy," "liberty," "constitutional rights," "decentralization," "human rights," "social justice," "American ideals," "self-reliance," "the pioneer spirit." Our icons are Thomas Jefferson, Paul Revere, Edmund Burke, Davy Crockett, Frederick Douglass, Robert La Follette, Jane Addams, Mark Twain, Charles Lindbergh, Samuel Gompers, Dorothy Day, Robert Taft, Barry Goldwater, Malcolm X, and Eugene McCarthy. It would be best if those of us who are to be the intellectual leadership of the insurgency remain in the background and attempt to avoid becoming public figures (if you are reading this, you are probably included in this category). We should avoid the "public eye" and calling unnecessary attention to ourselves. We need the freedom to be able to speak and write whatever we need to communicate without too much attention from the press or our enemies. We should seek to be Machiavelli rather than Lorenzo de' Medici, Rasputin rather than Tsar Nicholas II, the privy counsel rather than the king. From our enemies' perspective, we should be the subversives who whisper poison into the ears of princes.

7. The Face of the Insurgency

Thus far, much of what I have outlined follows a fairly conventional model of American political organization. Some anarchists will no doubt object that my approach reeks far too much of a reformist/electoralist outlook. While I certainly respect this point of view, I believe it is unnecessarily sectarian and archaic. The classical anarchists often advocated boycotting elections and for good reason. In most of the countries where the classical anarchist movement existed on a scale of any significance, the "right to vote" was either non-existent or the franchise was very limited. Even in nominal democracies like Switzerland and America, women and other large population groups were denied the vote. Even at that, many Spanish villages elected anarchist mayors and village councils in the years leading up to the civil war. I believe modern anarchists need to develop an approach to this question that is relevant to the nature of modern states and modern societies. The approach I favor is one of cold realism and pragmatism. It is indeed possible for ordinary people with conventional levels of resources to be elected to local and state offices in many parts of the United States. Persons who achieve some level of success in this area are then in a position to influence appointments to other positions of influence. This can be very important as a means of keeping the worst elements away from seats of power.

The worst mistake that virtually all of the minor parties currently make is to waste millions of dollars in resources and thousands upon thousand of hours of labor on symbolic but utterly futile Presidential campaigns. If a coalition of minor parties could be united in the kind of confederation I have outlined, it would be best to develop a strategy of campaigning for positions that can actually be won and boycotting those where the odds are flagrantly stacked in favor of the establishment. A large minor party that campaigned, often successfully, for positions like city councils and county boards of supervisors, school boards, state representatives, local sheriffs, planning commissions, and (where feasible) governors and attorney generals, but openly boycotted presidential and senatorial elections and denounced them as fraudulent would have a propaganda field day. Meanwhile, we could gradually build up our influence at the local and regional levels, make common cause with local and regional secessionist movements, and work to pull the rug out from underneath the feds. I would suggest that the public faces of our movement should be familiar community activists, issue-oriented dissidents, or sympathetic celebrity candidates. We need plenty of Jesse Venturas of our own. An eighteen-year-old kid was elected mayor of a Minnesota town. Anti-police militant Tom Alciere was elected as a stealth candidate to the New Hampshire state legislature. A Republican delegate to the Arizona state legislature introduced a bill calling for secession by Arizona in the event of gun confiscation or the imposition of martial law. As mentioned, the intellectual leadership of the movement should remain in the background, primarily as strategists, advisors, and formulators of policy proposals.

The achievement of victory by the kind of "coalition of coalitions" organized around anti-state, pro-class struggle issues of the type previously mentioned would mean the de facto abolition of the state. It is important to remember that all political systems contain a mixture of ideological currents and institutional models. All revolutions inevitably bring with them remnants of the previous system. It may well be that the victory of the anarchist movement in North America will take place inside the shell of the traditional constitutional system. That system has remained in place on the formal level for over two centuries even though the internal *modus operandi* has been altered radically a number of times. The US Presidency may continue to exist in the same manner as the British monarchy. Congress may well continue to exist on much weaker basis, akin to that of the European Parliament. Another possibility might be that the United States will split apart into a collection of smaller countries à la the former Soviet Union or the Ottoman Empire. We should be more concerned with substance than with form. Much more thought needs to be given to the kind of institutional framework that will be utilized following the victory of the anti-state movement. Examining the views of many of the anarchist sects on this question, I find many of their ideas and suggestions to be less than sufficient.

The primary forms of political organization favored by most anarchists are either the New England town meeting "direct democracy" model of the Bookchinites, the "private defense agency" model of the Rothbardians or the industrial union model favored by most traditional anarcho-syndicalists. Each of these perspectives might have something to offer. "Direct democracy" is probably as good a model for the management of individual neighborhoods or county villages as any other. Private defense agencies could certainly be one method of crime control along with neighborhood watches, militias, posses, elected local constables, etc. The syndicalist model might be one means of industrial organization. However, each of these presents dangers of their own. The actual history of regimes organized on the "direct democracy" model is not exactly a happy one. It was this kind of system that executed Socrates and instigated the Salem witch trials. Likewise, "private defense agencies" often sound remarkably similar to traditional feudatories or warlord systems when described by their anarcho-capitalist proponents. Workers' syndicates also bring with them the dangers of new kinds of monopolies and bureaucracies.

One of the most important insights of the Machiavellians is that all human organizations of any size are oligarchies. There is no other. So the question is not whether or not there will be elites but rather what kind elites we will have. There seems to be two basic choices, either plutocracy ("rule of money") or meritocracy ("rule of merit"). We should endorse the latter rather than the former. In the spirit of what Jack Ross calls the "Virginia radicals" of the Revolutionary War period, we should seek to cultivate an aristocratic populism that recognizes that the liberty of the leadership of the insurgent forces is dependent on that of the lowest commoners or most marginalized outcasts. Serious cultural, ethnic, or religious conflicts can be handled through decentralism, separatism, and mutual self-segregation. Aristotle noted that the Greek cities contained among themselves at least 158 separate and distinct constitutions. The Holy Roman Empire existed for centuries as a rather stable confederation of hundreds of largely sovereign kingdoms intermixed with thousands of independent territories or free cities. Likewise, the Swiss confederation has also existed for centuries with comparatively high levels of liberty, prosperity, and peace. Even today, there are political oddities around the world that might be prototypes for future anarchist institutional arrangements. The Israeli kibbutzim might be a model for anarcho-communists or, alternately, anarcho-racialists, Somalian kritarchy for anarcho-capitalists, the Mondragon worker cooperatives for anarcho-syndicalists, Liechtenstein for anarcho-monarchists, Amsterdam for anarcho-stoners, and Malta for anarcho-papists.

As the nation-state system declines and the welfare-warfare states that have emerged over the past century are discredited, the core political task of the next wave of radical intellectuals will be the establishment of political arrangements that eventually replace the state as it is now understood. The dangers of concentrated power are now well-known and recognized. The inability of the plutocratic democracies that have come to dominate modern societies to effectively control power will be fully understood soon enough. The Greek cities, the Holy Roman Empire, traditional Swiss political culture, and contemporary micronations are all models to draw upon. We might first consider how the United States managed to begin as a federation of thirteen largely sovereign colonies along the Atlantic Coast and subsequently degenerate to the present level in barely two centuries. The Holy Roman Empire, the Icelandic Kingdom, and other pre-modern societies managed to maintain much higher levels of stability and consistency (not to mention limited government) over a longer period of time than that. The Swiss confederation has existed for seven centuries. Where did America get off track?

I believe that the rapid degeneration of America since its founding is traceable to a number of sources. Some of these include obvious things like the unfortunate by-products of population growth, technological expansion, and general intellectual trends. However, there are two historically unique features of the American system that have led to its downfall. The first of these was America's making her merchant class into the ruling class at the time of the founding. Most previous societies had been organized on the model of the Old Order, with the merchant class being subordinate to the landed aristocracy, the monarchy, and the Church. A look at the powers delegated to Congress by the US Constitution reveals that the American constitutional system was originally designed as a state-capitalist class dictatorship. These powers included those necessary for the advancement of the interests of capital, such as central banking, uniform bankruptcy laws, transportation subsidies, a large free trade area, and so on. Such a framework could only lead to the entrenchment of the plutocratic "monied interests" warned against by Jefferson. The early American leader Samuel Adams warned of the evils of plutocracy:

> If ye love wealth greater than liberty, the tranquility of servitude greater than the animating contest for freedom, go home from us in peace. We seek not your counsel or your arms. Crouch down and lick the hands which feed you. May your chains set lightly upon you, and may posterity forget that ye were our countrymen.

If "capitalism" (or rule by the mercantile bourgeoisie) is one head of the dragon of Leviathan, then "democracy" is another. Originally, the United States was designed as an aristocratic republic on the model of Republican Rome. Neither the President nor the Senate were elected by popular vote and what little voting there was had been limited to a small portion of the general population. It was during the Jacksonian era of the early nineteenth century that Jacobin notions of "democracy" began to be imported into the United States from France. Indeed, the classical liberal Frenchman Alexis de Tocqueville was alarmed by this trend and wrote about it in his classic *Democracy in America*. Specifically, Tocqueville warned about the dangers of the Provider State, a kind of soft totalitarianism that he could only speculate about in his time and one that Aldous Huxley would discuss much more thoroughly a century later. Even at the time of the American founding, Jefferson had warned of this danger:

> I predict future happiness for Americans if they can prevent the government from wasting the labors of the people under the pretense of taking care of them.

The problem with mass democracy is this: Politicians must obviously appeal to more and more constituent groups the more universal the franchise becomes. This in turn requires the radical expansion of the state in order to satisfy the demands for state assistance from all of these groups and the creation of massive bureaucracies in order to manage the distribution of state favors. In other words, mass democracy must by nature be totalitarian and, indeed, even the most "liberal" democracies of today are totalitarian by historic standards.

There is an even greater danger than the bureaucratic regimentation of daily life inherent in the nature of modern capitalist democracies. The core values of these states are those of egalitarianism, consumerism, and therapeutism (as opposed to merit, frugality, and responsibility). It is considered the sacred duty of the state to provide everyone with "equal rights" and not only the pursuit of happiness but happiness itself. Theoretically, this is to be done through a generalized ethos of materialism and consumption to the point of gluttony, endless psychological conditioning techniques, and a Nanny State resolved to protect everyone from falling into "unhappiness" as a result of poverty, illness, racism, sexism, or drug addiction. In other words, modern "democratic capitalism" is nothing more than the Provider State warned against by Tocqueville or, more specifically, Huxley's

"Brave New World." Even prior to the Second World War, perceptive thinkers like Huxley and George Orwell understood the menacing nature of the culture of materialism and false egalitarianism then developing in America. Martin Heidegger argued that the universal triumph of such a system would be the "night of the world" or a new dark ages. Erik von Kuehnelt-Leddihn warned that egalitarianism can only breed mediocrity for egalitarianism does not raise the inferior to the level of the superior but only reduces the superior to the level of the inferior. Herbert Spencer understood that "to shield people from their own folly," the central purpose of the Nanny State, "is to populate the world with fools." Nietzsche insisted that a civilization whose principle purpose was the pursuit of comfort and the avoidance of danger would that of the "Last Man," a prelude to complete barbarism generated by decay and mediocrity. As I have said elsewhere:

> The nations of the West are driven by an almost as fanatical devotion to Mammon, that is, to wealth, luxury, power, pleasure and privilege. Further, the culture of the West combines this unabashedly materialist ethos with rejection of strength and discipline in favor of a maternalistic emphasis on health, safety, "sensitivity," "self-esteem," "potential," "personal growth," "getting in touch with one's inner child," "feelings" and other concepts common to pop culture psychobabble. Of course, the socio-cultural ramifications of this are to create a society of weaklings, mediocrities and crybabies.

Indeed, it is in those nations where this kind of system is the most well-established and long-established that the process of decay is the most advanced. And yet it is precisely this kind of system that America wishes to export to the rest of the world. Fortunately, this will prove to be a failed ambition. An empire whose ideology is a combination of advertising slogans, psychobabble, and silly pseudo-humanitarian platitudes (presumably enforced by tanks and air strikes), and whose subjects pledge allegiance to nothing other than their credit cards, convenience, "sensitivity" (for themselves but not for anyone else), the latest celebrity gossip, and the latest model cell phone, is not really an empire that is suited for world domination for very long. The ancient cultures of Asia and the Near East are once again asserting themselves. Nietzsche insisted that the warrior ethos was essential to the survival of civilization. I was in Europe when the present war in Iraq began in March of 2003. Watching coverage of the war on International CNN in the lounge of my Amsterdam hotel, I observed the militancy and zealotry of the Iraqi militiamen and contrasted their warrior spirit with that of the American soldiers being transported into battle. Most of the Americans looked like what they were: a bunch of scared shitless, barely-out-of-high-school kids wondering, "How the fuck did I get here?" There was no doubt in my mind who would win this war.

Back to the question of what we will replace the present welfare-warfare state with once it has finished running itself down, an event that is likely to occur soon enough. We should aspire to establish the foundations for a civilization that can endure and be preserved not merely for decades or even centuries, but for millennia. The Icelandic Kingdom survived as quasi-anarchy for three centuries and even then fell under the rule of only the Norwegian monarchy. The Holy Roman Empire endured for nine centuries before the rise of the absolute monarchs and the god-awful nation-state system during the sixteenth century. And the traditional civilizations of Russia and China enjoyed a similar lifespan. Indeed, Matthew Raphael Johnson reveals an astonishing truth about Russia prior to the coup d'état of Lenin and Trotsky in 1917:

. . . there were 5,000 full time policemen in the entire empire of 180 million souls, which would make Russia one very poor example of a police state. In fact, the total number of government workers, including the *zemstvo* employees, policemen and employees at all levels never exceeded 330,000. By contrast, much smaller France, in

1906, had budgeted for 500,000 employees.

How can we replicate this on an even greater level? The primary dangers to any political order are plutocracy, bureaucracy, and mobocracy. Plutocracy can be avoided by the establishment of a cultural foundation that devalues material pursuits and glorifies learning, knowledge, and wisdom in the ideological realm, and the decentralized control over resources by individuals, families, workers, and community groups in the structural realm. Bureaucracy can be avoided through decentralized political systems involving small states governing small populations with limited amounts of resources and an expansive voluntary sector. Mobocracy can be avoided in part by the principle of radical decentralization so that "voting with your feet" actually becomes feasible.

If any society is to advance itself, it must make a painstaking effort to insure that its heretics are safe from persecution, whether by greedy plutocrats, power hungry bureaucrats, or ignorant mobs. Those who are familiar with the internal operations of modern democratic regimes know well that legislation is typically for sale to the highest bidder. In other words, democratic governments constitute a type of marketplace for coercion, a shopping mall of political repression and plundering. Those who wish to order government on the market seem to forget that there exists a market for coercive violence. And if the proprietors of interest group democracy are not constrained by the Bill of Rights or the constitutional separation of powers, there is little reason to believe that the proprietors of quasi-feudal insurance agencies will be constrained by Murray Rothbard's "Libertarian Law Code."

"Participatory democracy" (or "direct democracy" as it is sometimes called) brings with it the flaws endemic to all democratic orders. If Plato's warnings about the susceptibility of the masses to the demagogue and Thomas Aquinas' fears of mobocracy apply to modern parliamentary states, would they not apply much more to unbridled popular democracy? The historical track record of these kinds of regimes is not a particularly appealing one. As previously mentioned, it was popular democracy that killed Socrates and initiated the Salem witch trials, and some of the more appealing aspects of the traditional US constitutional system are those existing outside the reach of majority rule, such as the Bill of Rights. Personally, I am more into the idea of limited government than popular government. We should consider the words of Proudhon on this question:

> . . . because of this ignorance of the primitiveness of their instincts, of the urgency of their needs, of the impatience of their desires, the people show a preference toward summary forms of authority. The thing they are looking for is not legal guarantees, of which they do not have any idea and whose power they do not understand, they do not care for intricate mechanisms or for checks and balances for which, on their own account, they have no use, it is a boss in whose word they confide, a leader whose intentions are known to the people and who devotes himself to its interests, that they are seeking. This chief they provided with limitless authority and irresistible power. Inclined toward suspicion and calumny, but incapable of methodical discussion, they believe in nothing definite save the human will.
>
> Left to themselves or led by their tribunes the masses never established anything. They have their face turned backwards; no tradition is formed among them; no orderly spirit, no idea which acquires the force of law. Of politics they understand nothing except the element of intrigue; of the art of governing, nothing except prodigality and force; of justice nothing but mere indictment; of liberty, nothing but the ability to set up idols which are smashed the next morning. The advent of democracy starts an era of retrogression which will ensure the death of the nation . . .

If we reject both plutocracy and mobocracy when searching for the most optimal system of social management, we might wish to consult the "wisdom of the ancients" on the matter. It was

Socrates who was among the first to postulate the concept of consent as the foundation of political legitimacy. For Socrates, the rules of the *polis* were "just" if they were predicated on the right of emigration, whereby the dissenting citizen could leave the city with his family and property. It is essential to recognize Socratic notions of consent as explicit and conventional in nature, as oppose to the implicit or metaphysical conceptions of "consent" later found in the works of liberal thinkers like John Locke. Explicit consent as the foundation of legitimacy necessitates that political units be highly localized and autonomous in nature, a fact recognized by Aristotle. Such arrangements allowed for a wide plurality of political or cultural identities.

The notion of explicit consent continued into the medieval era, when "no taxation without consent" would often be the battle cry of subjects in revolt against their exploitative lords. Explicit or direct consent is to be differentiated from the conception of "no taxation without representation" found in early liberal theory, whereby the process of "consent" is removed from the individual subject to political functionaries claiming to speak for entire communities. Obviously, "consent" of this type is bogus and impossible. Indeed, it was in response to the failure of liberal regimes to curb the usurpations of the state that classical anarchism arose as a revolutionary force in the nineteenth century. So for consent theory to maintain legitimacy, it should be obvious enough that the highest and primary unit of social organization should be the sovereign local community, the *polis* of Aristotle. The implementation of the Socratic-Aristotelian-Jeffersonian-Proudhonian ideal would require the dismantling of conventional nation-states into autonomous provinces, and the subsequent decentralization of the provinces into confederations of free cities, supreme counties, townships, and village communities, with each of these in turn organized as an aggregate of sovereign citizens (indeed, a conceptually interesting "sovereign citizen movement" has taken root among elements of the American "far right" in recent years).

From American history, we see the Puritan founding of Massachusetts, the Anglicans in Virginia, the Quakers in Pennsylvania, Mormons in Utah, and so on. Norman Mailer offered a similar vision in his campaign for the independence and decentralization of New York City:

> I ran for mayor of New York in the hope that a Left-Right coalition could be formed and this Left-Right pincers could make a dent in the entrenched power in the center. The best to be said for that campaign is that it had its charm. I am not so certain, however, that this idea must remain eternally without wings. It may yet take an alchemy of the Left and Right to confound the corporate center. Our notion was built on the premise that we did not really know the elements of a good, viable society. We all had our differing ideals, morals, and political ethics, but rarely found a way to practice them directly. So, we called for Power to the Neighborhoods. We suggested that New York City become a state itself, the fifty-first. Its citizens would then have the power to create a variety of new neighborhoods, new townships, all built on separate concepts, core neighborhoods founded on one or another of our cherished notions from the Left or the Right. One could have egalitarian towns and privileged places, or, for those who did not wish to be bothered with living in so detailed (and demanding) a society, there would be the more familiar and old way of doing things—the City of the State of New York—a government for those who did not care—just like old times.

In addressing this question of how to best avoid the combined dangers of plutocracy and mobocracy, I can only roll out a few meager suggestions. As Erik von Kuehnelt-Leddihn said of the political outlook of Plato:

> According to Plato, there can be no good government unless the philosophers are kings and the kings philosophers,

by which he does not mean Ph.D.s and crowned heads. What he does mean is the rule of those well-informed and knowledgeable. But do not forget there are two aspects to this: There is knowledge, and there is experience, and they have to go together. Knowledge alone is insufficient; practice alone is insufficient. To be a good ruler, one needs the combination of knowledge and practice.

Kuehnelt-Leddihn contrasted the Platonic view with that of modern plutocratic democracies:

> In the United States illiterates are now admitted to the polls. Sometime in the coming century, people will rack their brains pondering how nations with tremendous scientific and intellectual achievements could have given uninstructed and untrained men and women the right to vote equally uninstructed and untrained people into responsible positions.

If anarcho-capitalism brings with it the danger of plutocracy and if "participatory democracy" of the type favored by most left-anarchists brings the danger of mobocracy, perhaps a third alternative would be something akin to the classical Chinese civil service examination system. In that system, a citizen typically studied for decades in order to pass the most rigorous of examinations in order to be allowed admittance into political management. The examination system was rather egalitarian in nature, allowing entry by qualified persons from all social classes. Its main weakness was the fact that the scholarly elite were still subject to the dictates of the Emperor and his broader system of nepotism and patronage, so the scholars ended up being little more than court intellectuals for the ruling class. However, a way to reverse this would be to make the highest body of government into a type of monastery of scholars, where only the most demonstrably brilliant minds were admitted into positions of leadership. Even then, there is the danger of a new caste system developing whereby the scholarly caste simply becomes the new priesthood or the new Brahmins.

The best check on this problem might be to make the policies and plans formulated by the scholarly elite subject to public accountability by means of public assemblies, public juries, and popular referendums. For example, a federation of anarchies might conduct foreign policy through a "council on national defense" composed of the most experienced and best trained minds in the fields of history, military science, international relations, cultural studies, social psychology, diplomatic history, political economy, and so forth, with the general council then being assisted by sub-councils of an even more specialized nature. However, the "council on national defense" could not simply decide to make war on its own initiative. A proposal for war would have to be approved by a super-majority vote of the entire affected population. Matters of supreme importance (like war and peace) might be subject to approval by general referendum, while matters of lesser importance (like a treaty establishing an agreement to share a particular seaport with another country) might need to be approved only by a popular assembly composed of recallable delegates sent by local community or occupational committees. Similarly, any law enacted (whether by legislation or by judicial precedent) would be subject to ongoing approval by popular juries and competing private judges or judicial panels enjoying the full legal right of nullification.

Let us now summarize what I regard as the core propositions we must postulate. First, we need a "vanguard" of radically anti-state and anti-ruling class activists and intellectuals to come together as the brains trust and leadership corps of a broad anti-establishment populist movement. The most optimal method of pursuing this objective in modern America would be the creation of a coalition of minor political parties and activist organizations and the consolidation of these into a larger party, organized as a federation of local parties. The national party would deal only with pressing national matters on which there is common agreement among all of the radical camps, with matters of specific economic, political, or cultural arrangements, or matters of religious, ethnic, and social conflict, being left to the local parties. The principal purpose of the party would be the creation of a "coalition of coalitions" organized around anti-state and anti-ruling class issues, with the programs of the local party units orienting themselves towards local political culture. In the electoral arena, we would boycott major national elections on the ground that these are fraudulent, and instead seek local and regional positions which might be more reasonably attainable. It is essential that the electoral organizations be both assisted and policed by networks of grassroots activist organizations as well as anarcho-Machiavellian advisors who are largely directing things from behind the scenes. Electoral action would be regarded not as an end but as a means to an end, along with militant strikes, boycotts, civil disobedience, riots, the creation of alternative infrastructure, tax resistance, and other subversive actions.

In breaking down the state, we should seek to bolster local and regional secessionists and other separatist movements. We should also work to create a plurality of power structures that can effectively challenge the state. This has sometimes been referred to as "building the new society within the shell of the old." We can agitate for an end to the states' monopolistic courts system in favor of competing private, common law, merchant, or customary courts, systems of negotiation, mediation, or arbitration, and an end to the bureaucratic police forces maintained by the state in favor of citizen posses, militias, and so forth. We can also form popular assemblies that run parallel to the state's legislatures and demand the legal empowerment of these. We can agitate for the decentralization of state governments to the municipal or county level and the subsequent decentralization of the county and city governments to the neighborhood or village level. Another effort might be a push for the closing of the federal and state prison systems and the relocation of prisoners to penal colonies with more normalized living conditions. We can demand an end to the use of patronage in political appointments in favor of a system of meritocracy perhaps drawn on the model of the Chinese civil service examination system. This model might be particularly beneficial as a process for the staffing of appeals courts, the supervisory staffs of penal institutions, and, as mentioned, institutions of defense and diplomacy. Localities and regions can begin to assert their traditional Jeffersonian right of nullification of the decrees of objectionable central authorities just as juries can begin to reclaim their traditional Magna Carta right of jury nullification of objectionable prosecutions. On the economic level, we can develop organizations whose purpose is to agitate for the conversion of state or state-corporate industries and services into worker, consumer, or municipal cooperatives. These can be supplemented by independent labor organizations and organizations formed for the defense of alternative economic enterprises.

8. Extremism Without Apologies

Extremism in the defense of liberty is no vice. And let me remind you also that moderation in the pursuit of justice is no virtue.

—Barry Goldwater (speech written by Karl Hess)

The most frequent objections I encounter to my own political outlook and agenda are typically those summarized or accompanied by the labels of "extreme," "inflammatory," "fanatical," or "violent." To these charges, my plea would be one of "guilty, but proud." Those who make these charges are typically middle-class Americans with little or no experience of direct conflict with the System. However, when I test my views on those who know what it means to be on the bottom end looking up, they pick up on what I am saying right away and are frequently in complete sympathy. The classical anarchist Mikhail Bakunin recognized that the class vanguard in the struggle against the state must come from those with the least to lose. I agree. Bakunin's recognition of the necessity of the role of principled militants as the intellectual and activist vanguard of the revolutionary struggle is also consistent with Friedrich von

Hayek's observation that new and revolutionary ideas typically begin with the intellectual and philosophical elite and then "trickle down" into the ranks of the masses, finding their way into the minds of dissident intellectuals, their student radical followers, bohemians, counterculturalists, the lumpenproletariat, the conventional poor, the working classes, the middle classes, and then, finally, the establishment. Over time, all ideas that begin as radical or revolutionary ideas are compromised and moderated as their popularity and acceptance increases. For better or worse, success tends to breed moderation. However, in its initial stages a revolutionary outlook must seek not popularity and passive acceptance but fervent commitment. For this reason, those who would seek to build an authentic insurgent movement against the present American regime and ruling class must be unapologetic extremists.

This does not mean that we do not produce propaganda campaigns oriented towards appealing to the ordinary sensibilities of the commoners. However, it does mean that attitude is just as important as strategy or ideology. Far too many North American radicals are have fallen prey to the delusions of liberalism, democratism, pacifism, humanism, and other "feel good-do good" mentalities. This kind of attitude needs to be abandoned in favor of the Nietzschean warrior spirit. We need to cultivate among ourselves and our sympathizers a mindset that more closely resembles that of the Islamic jihadists or the guerrilla fighters of Latin America. In the nation of Colombia, a substantial portion of the insurgent forces consists of teenage girls. These young women no doubt display a much greater warrior spirit that what is typically found among adult males in the North American radical milieus. A determined resistance force could launch an effective assault on the decadent and decaying US regime and ruling class with relative ease. Kevin Carson aptly describes the crimes of our enemies:

> Capitalism was not, by any means, a "free market" evolving naturally or peacefully from the civilization of the high

Middle Ages. As Oppenheimer argued, capitalism as a system of class exploitation was a direct successor to feudalism, and still displays the birth scars of its origins in late feudalism.

Romantic medievalists like Chesterton and Belloc recounted a process in the high Middle Ages by which serfdom had gradually withered away, and the peasants had transformed themselves into de facto freeholders who paid a nominal quit-rent. The feudal class system was disintegrating and being replaced by a much more libertarian and less exploitative one. Immanuel Wallerstein argued that the likely outcome would have been "a system of relatively equal small-scale producers, further flattening out the aristocracies and decentralizing the political structures" . . .

. . . Although such medievalists no doubt idealized that world considerably, it was still far superior to the world of the sixteenth and seventeenth centuries. Kropotkin described, in terms evocative of William Morris, the rich life of the High Middle Ages, "with its virile affirmation of the individual, and which succeeded in creating a society through the free federation of men, of villages and of towns." "In those cities, sheltered by their conquered liberties, inspired by the spirit of free agreement and of free initiative, a whole new civilization grew up and flourished in a way unparalleled to this day." The free cities were virtually independent; although the crown "granted" them a charter in theory, in reality the charter was typically presented to the king and to the bishop of the surrounding diocese as a fait accompli, when "the inhabitants of a particular borough felt themselves to be sufficiently protected by their walls. . . ."

. . . The technical prerequisites of the industrial revolution had been anticipated by skilled craftsmen in the urban communes, scholars in the universities, and researchers in the monasteries; but the atmosphere of barbarism following the triumph of the centralized state set technical progress back by centuries. The nineteenth century was, in a sense, a technical and industrial "renaissance," built atop the achievements of the High Middle Ages after a prolonged hiatus; but because of the intervening centuries of warfare on society, industrial technology was introduced into a society based on brutal exploitation and privilege, instead of flowering in a society where it might have benefited all . . .

. . . The Renaissance as it happened, G. K. Chesterton argued, was only an anemic ghost of what it might have been had it taken place under a democracy of guilds and peasant proprietors. Had Wat Tyler and John Ball been successful, Chesterton speculated, "our country would probably have had as happy a history as is possible to human nature. The Renascence, when it came, would have come as popular education and not the culture of a club of aesthetics. The New Learning might have been as democratic as the old learning in the old days of mediaeval Paris and Oxford. The exquisite artistry of Cellini might have been but the highest grade of the craft of a guild. The Shakespearean drama might have been acted by workmen on wooden stages set up in the street like Punch and Judy, the finer fulfillment of the miracle play as it was acted by a guild."

The real advancement, the real humanism and progress of the High Middle Ages, has been neglected, and the barbarism and regression of the age of the absolute state disguised as a rebirth of civilization. In short, history has been not only rewritten, but stood on its head by the victors.

Carson then cites Kropotkin's *The State: Its Historic Role*:

How many lies have been accumulated by Statist historians, in the pay of the State, in that period! Indeed have we not all learned at school for instance that the State had performed the great service of creating, out of the ruins of feudal society, national unions which had previously been made impossible by the rivalries between cities? . . .

And yet, now we learn that in spite of all the rivalries, medieval cities had already worked for four centuries toward building those unions, through federation, freely consented, and that they had succeeded.

Matthew Raphael Johnson describes the apparatus of lies used to obscure these crimes:

The purpose of *The Third Rome* is to alter the political universe of those who read it. In other words, it was to challenge the assumptions that underlie the liberal/ conservative consensus in western countries. Such assumptions include the superstitious belief in progress, the linear (i.e. evolutionary) development of history and, importantly, the continued dominance of the idea that western democracies are morally superior to not merely the rest of the globe, but also superior to all systems of rule that have ever existed . . .

. . . For the *exoteria* of western politics, one is routinely treated to myths about the linear development of European history from the "darkness" of the middle ages to the "light" of the Enlightenment, science and its progeny, postmodernism. The "tyranny" of medieval and early modern kings is contrasted to the benevolence of modern republics. The evils of feudalism are contrasted to the capital/state alliance. This makes up every introduction to political science in universities, and it is at the very nature of "civic discourse" as it is contrived in the west. The only difficulty is that it is nonsense . . .

. . . At no time in global history have ruling classes amassed such centralized power: surveillance techniques, media power, armies, advanced weapons, computers and a disciplined bureaucracy that can track each and every citizen with pinpoint accuracy throughout his life form the vulnerable underbelly of the tripe concerning "democracy" and "republicanism" in the west. Tyranny previous to modernity was largely impossible: the technological apparatus needed to create "totalitarianism" simply did not exist. Only modernity can create tyranny . . .

. . . [T]he day to day functioning of royal government, is not contrasted with the actual functioning of republican systems, but rather with idealistic theory of republicanism . . . The peasant commune controlled the social life of the peasant, and was completely independent of the tsar. An "individual," isolated from his commune or region, would, as in all "democracies," be a meaningless legal fiction, easily exploited. This is the *esoteria* of "individualism" in political theory; it is easier for the oligarchy to dominate isolated individuals than to deal with larger and more powerful communal and municipal structures . . .

. . . In liberal democracies, those who have the most ambition to rule are those who run for office. Nicholas showed the opposite that, even when the crown was handed to him, he rejected it in favor of the (formal) heir apparent. Only under pressure did he accept the crown. In democratic thinking, only the ambitious and obnoxious are capable of doing what is necessary to get elected. American politicians are whores. They are forced to alter their views depending on the group with which the politician is meeting with or speaking. He is constantly asking for money with far less grace than a common prostitute . . .

. . . St. Nicholas II was brought to the throne in 1894. He found a Russia far from being "backward," but, in a few years—by the start of World War I—was the envy of the world. She had the lowest taxes in all Europe. Direct taxation per capita amounted to 3.1 rubles per year, versus 13 for Germany, 10 for Austria, 12 in France and 27 in progressive, democratic and capitalist Britain. Indirect taxation was also the lowest in Europe, amounting to 6 rubles per capita for Russia, but 10 for Germany, 11 for Austria, 16 for France and 14 for Britain . . . Russia was just beginning her economic expansion into world markets. There can be no question that the refusal of the Romanovs to set up a central bank under the rule of the global financial elite marked them for extinction. Imperial Russia was the only major European power who refused to set up a Central Bank, though the Bolsheviks, as always, willingly obliged . . .

. . . in 1861, what took the American republic years and hundreds of thousands of American lives to accomplish (in the case of slavery), the Russian Tsar accomplished in one fell swoop, the elimination of serfdom and the liberation of the peasant . . . By 1917, the peasantry controlled the overwhelming majority of farmland—more than three times what was controlled by the nobility. . . . "Free elections" are the easiest way for an oligarchy to enslave a population without them knowing it.

What Erik von Kuehnelt-Leddihn said of Russia might well apply to modern Western civilization as a whole:

Imagine a very popular, intelligent, conscientious, good-looking and responsible young man, obviously destined for a highly successful life. One day, having had a few drinks too many, he runs his car into a tree and ends up a paraplegic. Accidents happen not only in the lives of persons, but also in the lives of nations.

Perhaps a more appropriate analogy might be to compare the Western ruling classes to drunken drivers. Their respective nations might be compared to motor vehicles that have been crashed into a pile-up on the freeway. The producing classes are their casualties who have been maimed and dismembered.

In formulating a culture of resistance, we must not hesitate to pull out all of the stops. By all means, we should attempt to utilize peaceful and legal means of resistance of the type that I have thus far outlined. However, it is foolish to think that this will be enough. The neoconservative/cultural Marxist ruling class will never consent to the handing over of power to the type of libertarian-populist resistance coalition that I have argued for. Are we really going to believe that the ideological descendents of Robespierre, Trotsky, Adorno, Marcuse, and Strauss are simply going to step down without a fight? They would be much more inclined to repeat the Reign of Terror, the Kronstadt massacre, or the treachery of Barcelona. During the Reagan administration, plans were drawn up for the implementation of martial law by executive order. The present neocon regime is creating the pseudo-legal framework whereby the executive branch can simply ignore acts of Congress, court rulings, or international treaties and engage in indefinite detention without trial or access to counsel, conduct searches and seizures without warrant, engage in torture, hold secret tribunals, and, presumably, administrative death sentences and summary executions. The only remaining steps would be to cancel elections and abrogate constitutionally imposed presidential terms limits in favor of absolute despotism. Even if the neocons do not go all the way with this program, the cultural Marxists who succeed them might. Therefore, preparations must be made for such an occurrence.

Whenever I assert that an armed insurgency against the present US regime is not only feasible, but likely to result in the victory of the resistance forces provided they utilize the correct strategy and maintain the proper level of determination, the usual response I get is one of skepticism. I beg to differ. This is a regime that cannot even maintain "law and order" in its capital cities. This is a regime that cannot even maintain order in the event of natural disasters like the New Orleans floods of 2005 or uprisings like the "L.A. Riots" of 1992. In the latter event, the LAPD (the largest and best trained police department in the world) simply turned and ran for cover. The present regime is simply a house of cards that maintains an elaborate smoke and mirrors show as a means of hiding its fundamental weakness and incompetence. If the US military (the largest, most technologically advanced, and best equipped in history) can be defeated by ragtag insurgents in the jungles of Vietnam, the mountains of Afghanistan, or the streets of Baghdad, there is absolutely no military reason why the US regime cannot be defeated in the swamps of the Gulf Coast, the mountains of the Midwest, or the streets of New York, Los Angeles, or Miami. A Vietnam veteran, Bill Bridgewater, describes the possibilities here:

> Is there even a shred of possibility that an armed citizenry could succeed against the strongest military power on Earth today? Perhaps we should review the years 1960–1975 again. The United States blindly stuck its oar in the muddied waters of Viet Nam very shortly after the French got their heads handed to them on a platter and were invited not to be a colonial power in Viet Nam any more.

> Finally, we found ourselves in the position of guaranteeing the survival of an independent South Viet Nam when the Northern part of the country made it clear that they were interested in reuniting the country under their particular brand of socialism. For a decade and a half, we changed the leadership of South Viet Nam quite regularly; increased the pressure on the Johnson thumbscrews; bombed, quit, bombed, quit, ad infinitum; quantified the war; and finally turned it into an electronic war. At home we kept telling the citizens that we were just about to win decisively and elected another president to drive crazy with this goofy little war.

> Finally the president declared that all was over and the troops could come home. But they did not return home

in triumph with the bugles blaring. They came home with their tails between their legs just like every other defeated army in the history of the world. And the reason that they did so, my friends, was that the world's most powerful nation got its backside severely whipped by a small, backward, agrarian nation who started the war against us with an assortment of ancient bolt-action rifles, no lines of support, no manufacturing base, and no infrastructure that the country absolutely depended upon.

It is not a joke that they made sandals from cut-up truck tires—it's the truth. They fought the only kind of war they could hope to fight and win successfully—a guerrilla war. They had two good models: the American colonies against the British in our war for independence, and the American Indian wars, where the value of slash-and-run against a superior foe was escalated to a fine art by the world's finest light cavalry. Twice the North Vietnamese allowed themselves to be suckered into main force set-piece battles, and they got cut into ribbons for doing it. Otherwise, they stuck to General Giap's plan of guerrilla warfare to the finish. The North finally *did* get to mass their troops and tanks during their final sweep to victory into Saigon.

Why did this happen? Why did the world's most powerful nation get its teeth kicked in and sent home in disgrace? Because we forgot our very own origins! We forgot that we were the ones who hid behind logs, berms, and bushes and shot British troops and their mercenaries as *targets of opportunity* while denying our opponents a target of any kind. We used the skills of the mountain and plains Indians against an Army that was trained in only one form of combat. We refused to engage in the British methods of combat until we had superior forces and the odds were highly in our favor. General Vo Nguyen Giap did exactly the same thing against us in the 1960s and 1970s while we used our superior firepower and technology to create ten million deaf monkeys and water buffalo. We defoliated tens of thousands of acres of jungle forest to prove that Giap's troops weren't there. We constructed every kind of trap known to mankind to capture and destroy divisions of enemy troops where there weren't any. We very patiently fought a European theater-type of warfare against a steadfast foe who fought a completely different kind of war that simply made our complex weapons systems useless. By inflexibly insisting on doing it our way, we lost the whole shooting match to a man who played it his way and won . . .

. . . A revolution could be waged against the current American government far easier than you might imagine without careful examination. Consider:

- The sheer numbers of firearms of all kinds in the hands of the American public would have made the American commanders in Viet Nam quake in their boots. We're not talking junk equipment here, either. The average deer hunter with a .270 or .308 could give a platoon of regular troops more grief than they want. There was a special on the tube recently about military armaments on sale in the black market (including Stingers).

- The population base from which revolutionaries could be recruited is *massive*—250 million.

- There are literally millions of well-trained men who served as officers and NCOs who learned face-to-face how guerrilla warfare works. They haven't forgotten it, either.

- There are millions of young men out there with military training and experience with weapons of every conceivable kind, who would make top-quality guerrilla troops.

- Every one of the 100 counties in the state of North Carolina could field at least one full company that would be formidable in capability. If one assumes that North Carolina is no more capable than other states, that could amount to 180 divisions. These potential rebel troops would be fast-moving light infantry, with the capability of melting into the general population when necessary. American military leaders would be in the position of having an inventory of high-tech weapons that they would be dependent upon your son or nephew to use against you. There would be no enemy states in which you could say that any weapon could be used against the rebels. They would be from each and every state and major city.

By the same token, there would be no sanctuary for the federal troops anywhere in the land. No matter where stationed, they would be subject to attack and harassment. The infrastructure on which the federal government depends would be rather easily disrupted by those who live there. Airfields and major lines of communications could be shut down and kept down for days at a time. Disruption of supplies to major bases and to centers of government would be simple. You don't have to cut them off, just keep them hungry. The federal government would be denied the use of all their major weaponry because they would still "own" the cities and villages. How do you justify bombing your own city just because there is a rebel company in it? One bombing would be the biggest recruiting drive ever for the rebel forces. Now just how powerful do those 12 Army divisions and those three Marine divisions really look to you? Just how scary is the Air Force against America? What will the Navy do, shell all coastal cities? I don't think so.

One of these days a truly charismatic individual is going to walk out of the heartland of America and point out that the Declaration of Independence has never been repealed and that it *requires* all citizens to rise up against an oppressive government. With the current attitude toward our government and the people who populate it, a massive groundswell of support for throwing the current crop to the dogs and starting over again might not be so difficult. As for the *ability* of the American citizens to successfully wage a guerrilla war on their own government, the likes of which this world has never seen nor contemplated before, I am absolutely convinced that it could be done, and a lot more swiftly than many might believe possible. How many highly-capable long-range snipers can your county put together?

I have absolutely no doubt that a determined left/right-black/white-libertarian/populist alliance could, if it played its cards right, achieve such a victory. There are over thirty thousand street gangs in America, with their collective membership totaling more than one million people. The nationalist/separatist elements of the various minority groups who would be an essential part of any resistance alliance command the respect of these groups. A nationwide alliance of urban street gangs into a militia/paramilitary force could easily defeat and eliminate municipal police departments loyal to the ruling class. Suburban militias composed of rebellious youth and countercultural radicals organized in a manner similar to Mao's Red Guards or Colombia's FARC could easily defeat the rent-a-cops that comprise suburban police departments. Just as the LAPD turned and ran during the "L.A. Riots" so did the suburban SWAT team at the scene of the Columbine massacre in 1999 hide behind ambulances and fire trucks cowering in fear of two teeny-boppers with ordinary household firearms. The principal problem of many of these wayward youth, urban gang members, and suburban "school shooters" alike, is that they realize instinctively that they are under attack, but are unable to trace these feelings to their proper source, so they simply take it out on the nearest target, their schools, neighborhoods, or each other. What they need is something worthwhile to fight for, like eliminating the present depraved regime and the creation of a superior civilization, one that is liberated from the parasitical albatross of state and capital.

Citizen militias drawn from rural, small town, and heartland communities, including within their ranks many military veterans of the Timothy McVeigh model, could wage an insurgent war against the US regime in the same manner as the present-day insurgents in Iraq. As Tariq Aziz said prior to the US invasion of Iraq:

People say to me, you [i.e., the Iraqis] are not the Vietnamese. You have no jungles and swamps to hide in. I reply, let our cities be our swamps and our buildings our jungles.

Indeed, these militias, mercenaries, guerrillas, gangs, and paramilitaries will be the foundation of the defense forces of our future Jeffersonian-Proudhonian-Bakuninist-Rothbardian federations of anarchies and republics of republics. As Jefferson reminded us:

God forbid we should ever be twenty years without such a rebellion. The people cannot be all, and always, well informed. The part which is wrong will be discontented, in proportion to the importance of the facts they misconceive. If they remain quiet under such misconceptions, it is lethargy, the forerunner of death to the public liberty. . . . And what country can preserve its liberties, if its rulers are not warned from time to time, that this people preserve the spirit of resistance? Let them take arms. The remedy is to set them right as to the facts, pardon and pacify them. What signify a few lives lost in a century or two? The tree of liberty must be refreshed from time to time, with the blood of patriots and tyrants. It is its natural manure.

Let's do Uncle Tom proud!

Smashing the State:

Thoughts on Anarchist Strategy

For nearly two centuries, anarchist thinkers have drawn from the fields of philosophy, economics, history, cultural studies, military science, political science, and many other disciplines to produce a voluminous amount of empirical evidence that destroys the very notion of the legitimacy of the state. Yet the state continues to exist, and in a more potent and destructive form than ever before. Of all of the prevalent myths of the modern age, none are as false and deadly as the idea that the state is somehow a positive expression of human social evolution capable of benevolence and the fostering of progress. Belief in the state is simply the flat earth theory or the geocentric model of the solar system of the present era. The question that remains is the matter of how the idea of the state could be so wrong intellectually yet enjoy near universal acceptance.

Past states of the *ancien régime* variety were typically justified in the name of religion. The emperor was regarded as a descendent of the sun god. The king ruled by divine right as the Creator's appointed earthly steward. Ideas of this type were demolished by the political, scientific, and intellectual revolutions that emerged from the Enlightenment. With all due respect to my religious friends, most intellectuals in the advanced countries, including myself, no longer believe in God or the divine sanctioning of human institutions. Similarly, most variations of the state—fascist, communist, monarchical, theocratic, aristocratic, military—are considered illegitimate as well. Only democratic states, ostensibly justified in the name of popular sovereignty, social contract, and the general will, retain their legitimacy in the eyes of contemporary intellectual elites. For this reason, democracy is the primary enemy of anarchism. The deadliest battles we anarchists will fight in the future will be not with communists and fascists but with democrats. In our fight against the state, we should begin by heaping ridicule and scorn upon the very notion of democracy.[1]

Anarchist thinkers as diverse as Murray Rothbard and Noam Chomsky have recognized that a new class of "court intellectuals" has emerged as apologists for the modern state. These elements, drawn primarily from the realms of media and academia, collectively formulate a type of "secular priesthood" whose political function is the use of their positions of perceived authority and expertise to inculcate in the masses the idea of the benevolence, wisdom, and virtue of the state and those who control it.[2] Consequently, it is a grave strategic error for anarchists to appeal to the intellectual classes as a means of advancing their ideas. Intellectual elites have a vested interest in the preservation of the state, the primary source of their affluence and prestige. For every Noam Chomsky or Gore Vidal, there are a thousand Henry Kissingers, James Carvilles, or David Horowitzes willing to act as a mouthpiece for state power. Instead, anarchists should take their message directly to those most victimized by the state.

Anarchist ideas on strategy for the abolition of the state are thus far grossly underdeveloped. Most of what we have seen in the realm of anarchist or free market strategy so far provides us with little more than some examples of what not to do. For instance, the Cato Institute began as a think tank set up to promote the ideas of Murray Rothbard and subsequently succumbed to the

---

1   Democratist ideology has been thoroughly destroyed by Hans-Hermann Hoppe in *Democracy: The God That Failed* (New Brunswick: Transaction Publishers, 2001). See my "Democracy as Tyranny," http://attackthesystem.com/democracy-as-tyranny/. Similarly, the "social contract" theory behind constitutionalist justifications for the state was demolished by Lysander Spooner's individualist anarchist classic *No Treason: The Constitution of No Authority.*

2   For a general discussion of this, see Kevin Carson, "The New Class' Will to Power: Liberalism and Social Control," http://attackthesystem.com/liberalism-and-social-control-the-new-class-will-to-power/.

lure of corporate money and Beltway access and somewhere along the way developed the idea that kissing Republican ass is the way to advance liberty.[3] The principal strategic contribution of the Ayn "nuke 'em towelheads" Randroids has been to set up a fanatical cult primarily oriented towards the excommunication of heretics. The "conservative libertarian" Foundation for Economic Education featured arch-police statist Rudy Giuliani as the keynote speaker at one of its events. The paleolibertarians, admittedly a much better group than the others, apparently seek to appeal to the remnants of the old WASP culture that has been slowly dying since the 1960s. Last and perhaps least, the leftist-anarchist movement has taken up every crackpot left-reactionary cause yet to be invented and postulated nothing quite so much as an incoherent brand of "anarcho-social democracy." Clearly, the anarchist and libertarian milieus are desperately in need of new ideas on strategy.

One mistake many anarchists make is to employ what I call an "evangelical" approach to the dissemination of their ideas. What I mean is that these anarchists attempt to "convert" others to the anarchist position by means of intellectual argument or moral suasion. Very few people are interested in ideology. Fewer still have much in the way of moral substance beyond that of personal interests and cues taken from peers and leaders.[4] I suspect this is the main reason why the Libertarian Party and other groups heavy on ideological content have not gotten very far. Intellectual or moral arguments may sway a handful of people, but my experience has been that most people simply do not care enough about these matters for this approach to work on any large-scale basis. It seems that a better approach would be to simply appeal to the immediate self-interest of as many different groups and

3   The origins of the Cato Institute are described in Justin Raimondo's biography of Murray Rothbard, *An Enemy of the State: The Life of Murray Rothbard* (Amherst, NY: Prometheus Books, 2000).

4   *Obedience to Authority: An Experimental View* (New York: Harper and Row, 1974) by Stanley Milgram is a classic study of the human psyche's natural relationship to authority. *They Thought They Were Free: The Germans, 1933–45* (Chicago: University of Chicago Press, 1955) by Milton Mayer describes how ordinary Germans during the Hitler era perceived their society.

individuals with a grievance against the state as possible with the broader goal of forming a large enough coalition of disparate interest groups to effectively weaken and destroy the state.

The classical anarchist Bakunin envisioned a cadre of "principled militants" serving as the intellectual and activist leadership corps of a mass movement for the overthrow of the state. The function of such militants would be to inspire the masses by example and simultaneously articulate the political desires of the masses of those exploited by the state.[5] This classical Bakuninist approach, adapted to the modern world and modified to fit the framework imposed by the modern state, may show some promise yet. It is doubtful that anarchists will ever be more than a relatively small number of people. I tend to concur with Emma Goldman that anarchists are born rather than made. At the risk of hubris, we might say that anarchists are the natural aristocracy, a type of natural vanguard, in the historic struggle against the state.

The abolition of the state would, of course, be an event of profound historical significance akin to the Protestant Reformation or the American Revolution. I suspect that the anarchist "movement" is currently in the same stage of its evolution as the classical liberalism that overthrew the *ancien régime* was in the early days of seventeenth-century rationalism. The classical anarchism of the nineteenth and twentieth centuries provides us with a flawed but inspiring prototype that we can use as a foundation on which to build a more perfect body of anarchist thought. Later anarchist thinkers, such as Rothbard and Hoppe, have helped to point us in the right direction. It is up to us to take it from there. Liberal democracy, once a radical and revolutionary doctrine feared by the ruling classes, has now become all but universal. It has taken root even in much of the Third World.[6] The

---

5   It is of course necessary to differentiate between the classical Bakuninist concept of a revolutionary vanguard, based on the concept of natural leadership, and the Marxist-Leninist idea of the "vanguard party," utilizing coercion and treachery as a means of obtaining state power.

6   For example, all of the nations of Latin America, save Cuba, now have elected civilian governments. This exportation of democracy to the Third World has produced even

realization of anarchism necessarily involves the overthrow of liberal democracy in the same manner as the gradual elimination of traditional monarchies in earlier times.

It should go without saying that anyone attempting foment revolution against the existing political order ought to, when considering questions of strategy, attempt to appeal to the indigenous culture of the common people and the cultural history of the country in question. This is one of the reasons why the contemporary leftist-anarchist movement, with its fanatical hostility to all things "American," hatred of authentic working class culture, and adoption of a Euro-leftist cultural stance, is doomed to failure. Fortunately, we Americans enjoy cultural traditions of rebellion against tyrannical government as expansive as those of any nation. These traditions, symbolized by such historical phenomena as the Boston Tea Party, Whiskey Rebellion, Underground Railroad, the Southern War of Independence, the Haymarket martyrs, labor uprisings, the civil rights movement, etc., provide us with a broad cultural history that we can play to and build upon.

Much can be said for the philosophy of "Keep It Simple, Stupid." When attempting to communicate with the broader public, anarchists should avoid reference to arcane ideological abstractions. Instead, it is best to remain focused on a handful of issues that are the most serious and most immediate. At present, such issues would be the coming war with Iraq, and its role as a component in a larger program of globalist imperialism, and the ongoing assaults on civil liberties under the guise of the wars on terrorism, drugs,

sorrier results than those to be found in the wealthy, technologically advanced nations. "Democratic" Mexico is so economically depressed that its southern region wants out of the country and millions of its citizens pour across its northern border annually in search of economic refuge. Likewise, "democratic" Argentina is in the midst of a depression after a succession of elected governments ran its economy into the ground. "Democratic" Columbia is a death-squad regime that has lost forty percent of its territory to Marxist insurgents. "Democratic" India elected a fascist government that sanctions mob violence against its Muslim and Christian minorities. South African "democracy" has resulted in little more than the replacement of a tyrannical white fascist regime with a tyrannical black communist one. As for "democratic" Israel, the less said the better.

crime, etc., and the role of these as means to the consolidation of state power into a totalitarian state apparatus. Already, a number of local communities have issued resolutions opposing both the Iraq war and the Orwellian USA PATRIOT Act. This phenomenon of grassroots, popular-based local revolt against central tyranny provides us with some clues as to how we might proceed in our efforts to advance the broader anarchist cause.

Local rebellion against the state has its roots in the best elements of American political and cultural history, whether we are considering the original secession of the thirteen colonies from the Crown or the Confederate secession from the Lincoln regime. More recently, the "county rights" movement in the West has resulted in formal refusal by localities to comply with directives issued by federal bureaucracies. Similarly, during the Persian Gulf War, the city of Madison, Wisconsin, declared that it would grant safe haven to draft resisters in the event of imposition of military conscription. The proliferation of localized resistance movements of this type seems to be the best bet for effectively engaging Leviathan. Towards this end, anarchists should seek to become influential in grassroots opposition activities of the type previously described.

Anarchists should seek to become leaders within their own communities. This might involve joining community organizations, neighborhood associations, pressure groups, or other intermediary institutions involved with local issues and using one's influence to advance the anarchist agenda. A similar tactic might be employed on a national level. Anarchists should join single-issue pressure groups and seek leadership positions. Clusters of anarchists on the boards of directors of the National Rifle Association or the American Civil Liberties Union would probably be much more useful than a motley crew of tofu-munching ne'er-do-wells carrying tacky hand-lettered signs outside the latest convention of the International Monetary Fund or some other globalist entity. Furthermore, anarchist involvement in local and regional secessionist activities could expand our influence enormously. Anarchists should make common cause with groups like the Free State Project, the League of the South, and the Republic of Texas. Think of the advantages of a large regional secession movement whose leaders and hard-core activists included a substantial minority of anarchists.

I cannot overemphasize the importance of anti-state coalition building. If we look at the mainstream political system, we see that all effective political coalitions involve seemingly incongruous alignments of divergent groups. What do country club Republicans have in common with the "religious right"? What do labor unions have in common with the gay lobby? Yet these types of coalitions provide the major voting blocs for the Republicans and Democrats alike. A similar strategy employed by the anti-state movement might yield significant dividends, particularly if it had the effect of successfully disrupting and neutralizing the grassroots coalitions maintained by the ruling class. For example, if gun rights supporters or ethnic minorities were to defect en masse from the Republican and Democratic parties respectively, the "big tents" relied upon by these interests might begin to implode. Once anarchists began to establish themselves as effective and influential community leaders and grassroots activists, they could begin to draw others to them by means of coalitions organized around common issues. For example, opposition to zoning ordinances could draw support from poor people victimized by such intrusions along with conservative defenders of property rights. Opposition to the public schools could draw support from both religious fundamentalists and countercultural youth. It would then be the responsibility of leaders within various movements to combine their forces into a broader popular front against the state in its entirety.

Secessionist efforts could be a central rallying point for many single-issue groups. Imagine, for instance, a California independence movement with anarchists heavily represented among its leadership and including among its grassroots support base elements as diverse as advocates of medical marijuana, homeschoolers, property rights advocates, AIDS activists, proponents of alternative medicine, unions opposed to NAFTA, antiwar activists, Hispanic separatists and immigration opponents alike, gun rights defenders, pro-lifers alongside gay militants in San Francisco, leftist radicals in Berkeley, and far-right tax resisters. Each of these elements could have their own reasons for desiring secession with each disagreeing with all on many, perhaps even most, issues. Some of these differences might be dealt with pragmatically through the decentralization of state politics to the local and then to the community or neighborhood level. A movement like this in California could then align itself with a similar movements in the South, or Alaska, or New England, or wherever. Black militants in the inner cities might even become the inadvertent allies of white separatists in Idaho and vice versa. Anarchists, as keepers of the anti-state faith, might serve as facilitators of dialogue between disparate antigovernment groups, mediators during the course of negotiations occurring during the process of coalition building, and coordinators of joint activities and actions around common issues and purposes.

There exists throughout the United States a huge variety of groups and movements who are hostile to the state in many ways, particularly the federal government. Most of these would not qualify as anarchists or even libertarians in any consistent or pure sense. Yet they are collectively a potential source of support for a radical populism with an explicitly anti-state bent and a potential goldmine of activist manpower. Revolutions are typically made not by majorities but by impassioned minorities. The government's Vietnam War effort was effectively stalled by an antiwar movement involving no more than five percent of the US population. Only five percent of the population of the thirteen colonies favored independence from Britain when it was initially declared. Only two percent participated in the military efforts of the revolutionaries. By the time independence had been won only a third had come to favor it. Anti-statists have not even begun to consider the possible strategic alliances that might come into being through greater outreach efforts. Those whom with we might make common cause include Muslim and Arab-American groups opposed to the US government's use of funds looted from American taxpayers to subsidize the tyrannical state of Israel,[7] religious cults harassed and persecuted by government agencies, "hate" groups attacked through trumped up lawsuits and hate crimes laws, poor inner-city minorities whose family members are being herded into the state's massive prison industry via the drug war,[8] advocates of minority self-help and self-determination like the Nation of Islam, American Indian groups fighting for their land rights, small farmers plowed under by state-subsidized agribusiness cartels and federal lending programs,[9] citizens militia groups, and common law advocates. These are just a few examples.

The elimination of the state will occur when enough anti-state causes triumph that the state can no longer maintain its aura of legitimacy. The convergence of a myriad of single-issue movements into a broader coalition organized around the common demand for the decentralization of power, with anarchist militants serving as its intellectual and activist vanguard, would seem to be the proper means of tying together the various threads of independently emerging anti-state sentiments into a unified quilt capable of smothering and extinguishing the monster of Leviathan altogether. In the years and decades leading up to the final assault on the state, four essential concerns might become the primary focus of the leadership corps of the revolutionary forces. The first of these would be the creation of alternative infrastructure that would be

---

7   Particularly disgusting has been the support of some Objectivists and "libertarians" for the state of Israel. It seems inconceivable that a racist, theocratic, imperialist, national socialist military dictatorship could be defended by ostensible champions of free market economics and the intellectual ideals of the Enlightenment. Do Palestinians or Lebanese have any "natural rights"?

8   The "prison-industrial complex" is no myth. See Joel Dyer, *The Perpetual Prisoner Machine: How America Profits from Crime* (Boulder, CO: Westview Press, 2000).

9   See Joel Dyer, *Harvest of Rage: Why Oklahoma City Is Just the Beginning* (Boulder, CO: Westview Press, 1997), and James Bovard, *The Farm Fiasco* (San Francisco: ICS Press, 1989).

in place and ready to take over those social functions abandoned by the state, including the issuance of units of exchange backed by a precious metal standard, provision for dispute resolution through an arbitration or common law system, an independent educational system, associations formed for the care of the elderly, the disabled, and the otherwise infirm, entrepreneurial endeavors serving as a model of an alternative to state-created and subsidized corporate systems, popular organizations for the handling of consumer interests, cooperative health clinics, and other similar institutions. Second, an alternative media would be necessary for the dissemination of propaganda favorable to the anti-state movement in order to counter the pro-state propaganda generated by the establishment media. Shortwave and pirate radio broadcasts, public access television programs, websites, and independent publishing services are no doubt the embryo of such a phenomenon. Ultimately, anti-statists should aspire to obtain a network of independent television and radio stations of their own, perhaps emulating the numerous forms of religious media currently in existence.

The last two concerns are also the most controversial. One involves the relationship of the anti-state movement(s) to local political institutions. Most contemporary anarchists favor a position of total non-involvement with state institutions, even local ones, and consequently shun voting, lobbying, and other forms of "working within the system."[10] While the enthusiasm for this position is understandable, I am not sure that it is

---

10 I am not sure this total rejection of political action is consistent with anarchist history. Both Pierre-Joseph Proudhon and Johann Most served in the French and German parliaments respectively. One of Proudhon's fellow deputies was the proto-libertarian and free-market economist Frédéric Bastiat, whose book *The Law* remains an anti-statist classic. During the era of classic Spanish anarchism, anarchists were regularly elected to mayoral positions in local towns and villages. During the Republican era, anarchists participated in Spanish national elections when it was strategically advantageous, although they never fielded candidates of their own. During his 45-year career as an anarchist, Murray N. Rothbard paid careful attention to both national and local elections, ran for governor of California on the Peace and Freedom Party ticket in 1968, endorsed Norman Mailer's New York Mayoral campaign in 1969, initially supported the Libertarian Party and wrote much of its platform, and even endorsed major party candidates with antiwar leanings, including statists like Adlai Stevenson and nationalists like Patrick Buchanan.

practical. Certainly, the efforts of groups like the Libertarian Party to field candidates for President are absurd. Yet grassroots local governments are far more accessible to the average person and far more responsive to public pressure. The seizure of local political institutions by secessionist oriented forces, constantly under pressure by a grassroots anti-state movements, might serve to create antagonisms between localities and the central state resulting in a loss of perceived legitimacy and the emergence of a situation where an alliance of seceding communities and regions could "pull the rug out from under" the federal empire. Note that I am not claiming that local secessionist politicians could be trusted as custodians of the liberty of the people. Such a scenario would only be feasible if such politicians were under enormous pressure from intermediary institutions and popular organizations existing independently of government at any level.

Finally, there is the question of what to do when the state attempts to maintain power by means of direct armed force. This is a question many anarchists shy away from but it is an immensely important one. Bloodless political change is always preferable but not always possible. On this question, the patriot militia movement of the 1990s had it right. During the time leading up to the final confrontation with the state, the formation of locally-based citizen militias, guerrilla forces, paramilitary outfits, contracted mercenary organizations, established on a decentralized model and combined with underground cells and lone wolf fighters, will no doubt be indispensable.[11] On this matter, I am a hawk. It will also be necessary to obtain the sympathy of a substantial number of international forces capable of providing economic, diplomatic, and, if necessary, military support to the anti-government forces à la French and Spanish support for the first generation of American revolutionaries.[12]

---

11 For excellent commentary on military matters, see Bill Bridgewater, "Armed Revolution Possible and Not So Difficult," http://attackthesystem.com/armed-revolution-possible-and-not-so-difficult/.

12 Reactionary, theocratic, monarchical France declared war on behalf of the colonies hoping to see its rival England undermined. Similarly reactionary Spain provided enormous assistance to the American revolutionaries for the same reasons although

Fidelity to Patrick Henry's famous proclamation, "Give me liberty or give me death!" is likely to be not only a moving sentiment but a practical necessity in the battle against the state.

formal support was not declared for fear of inspiring similar revolutions among Spain's colonies in the New World. Holland also declared war on England during this time. Probably the best sources of international support for an antigovernment movement in the United States would be nationalist, separatist, anti-imperialist, and anti-globalist tendencies in all nations, whatever their ideology, and rival states to the US regime such as China. Britain's "National-Anarchist" movement has developed the best ideas thus far on the question of international alliances against US imperialism and globalism.

Fourth Generation Warfare, and the Decline of the State:

An Examination of the History of the Decline of the State's Monopoly on Violence and War

Introduction

World events of recent years have brought to the forefront of public attention and intellectual debate the matter of what is commonly called "terrorism." Efforts at merely defining this provocative term have proven difficult, and no consensus exists among scholars as to what "terrorism" actually is. The standardized cliché that "one man's terrorist is another man's freedom fighter" appears to have some actual basis in fact given the ideologically charged nature of many efforts at summarizing the core characteristics of terrorism. Can all individuals or organizations who engage in extra-legal violence for political purposes objectively be classified as "terrorist"? Or do such actors need to engage in a narrower set of behaviors, such as inflicting injury or death upon persons not directly involved in whatever "cause" or "struggle" the alleged "terrorists" may be motivated by, in order to validly earn the "terrorist" label? Is the term "terrorism" itself appropriate when describing non-state actors who engage in political violence? Does this label signify any characteristics at all that are unique to those to whom it is being applied, or is the "terrorist" label merely a subjective ideological construct?[1]

---

1   For a comprehensive overview of modern terrorism, see the following sources: Anthony M. Burton, *Urban Terrorism: Theory, Practice and Response* (London: Western Printing Services, 1975); Christopher Dobson and Ronald Payne, *The Terrorists: Their Weapons, Leaders and Tactics* (New York: Macmillan, 1979); Jay Robert Nash, *Terrorism in the Twentieth Century* (New York: M. Evans and Co., 1998).

Of course, the use of physical threats and raw violence towards the achievement of political ends by rulers and the ruled alike has been commonplace since time immemorial. Political history is to a large degree the story of palace coups, massacres, purges, insurrections, and other incidents of violence occurring outside the context of any formalized legal infrastructure. However, "terrorism" as it is commonly perceived of by contemporary Westerners certainly carries with it the imagery of particular kinds of actions such as bombings, assassinations, hijackings, and deliberate destruction of physical infrastructure carried out by persons devoted to the achievement of some political program through the use of such tactics and doing so in a manner that is frequently indistinguishable from that of common criminals so far as established legal norms are concerned. An examination of the history and evolution of modern Western "terrorism" would indicate that this lay perspective is indeed rooted in fact. However, it is inappropriate to associate extra-legal political violence with ordinary criminality. To understand why this is so, it is necessary to first understand the relationship between "terrorism" and the modern institution of the state as it has evolved in the Western nations and subsequently been exported to other parts of the world.

As will be shown below, political governance underwent a major transformation in the Western world in the eras between the early Renaissance period and the rise of modern nationalism in the nineteenth century. The foremost characteristic of this transformation was the emergence of government as a corporative as opposed to personalized conception. Parallel to the development of this impersonalized, bureaucratized manifestation of government was the decline of the older polycentric order of Europe whereby powers that were previously shared by a variety of institutions (including war powers) were now concentrated into the hands of the corporative state. The state then claimed for itself an exclusive monopoly on the use of political violence. Over time, the state evolved from its role as a means to an end (the maintenance of order) to an end unto itself. This latter process transpired from the time of the French

Revolution to the explosions of the "total wars" of the twentieth century.

Beginning in the late nineteenth century, the state's monopoly on political violence and war began to meet challenges from contending ideological currents and organizational forces. One of the earliest manifestations of this trend was the advent of so-called "propaganda by the deed," a term given to the tactics of the classical Anarchists, an ideological tendency that ironically denied not only the legitimacy of the state's monopoly on violence but the legitimacy of the state in its entirety. Though the classical Anarchists of the "propaganda by the deed" period effectively died out as a political or ideological force following their defeat in the Spanish Civil War and the eclipsing of radical labor movements by the Second World War, their tactics were appropriated and utilized by a wide variety of dissident political currents in Europe and the Americas during the postwar period. Such currents originated from all over the geographical and intellectual spectrum. Some were "far Left," others "far Right." Some were religious in nature, others avowedly secular. Some consisted of indigenous Europeans or Americans, others originated from the Third World. Some killed or bombed indiscriminately, others were more selective. Indeed, the only common denominator to be found among postwar Western "terrorist" groups is their resolute opposition to one or another of the manifestations of modern liberalism and its foundations: bourgeois commercialism, neocolonialism and liberal imperialism, relative cosmopolitanism, rapid technological expansion, and parliamentary forms of government.

Following the collapse of the Soviet Union and the end of the Cold War, the Western liberal model has achieved unprecedented hegemony and taken root in an expanded number of nations. The elimination of the Soviet Union as a constraint on liberal imperialism has been accompanied by a predictable rise in militarism on the part of Western liberalism.[2]

---

2   Noam Chomsky, *Deterring Democracy* (New York: Hill and Wang, 1992), 9–64.

Furthermore, the universalist presumptions and economic determinism of liberalism, combined with the ongoing process of the globalization of capital, have propelled the liberal powers, particularly the United States, towards the pursuit of unprecedented and unchallenged global hegemony. That this state of affairs should meet with resistance from many of the world's peoples is no surprise, particularly those peoples whose cultural foundations are the most antithetical to liberalism, i.e., those of the Islamic world. Interestingly, pockets of resistance to liberal global hegemony have arisen within the First World as well, including the United States.

Much of conventional opinion regards the practice of modern "terrorism" as originating from ordinary criminal motivations, ideological extremism, mental illness, or moral deficiency on the part of its perpetrators. Accusations of this type are frequently selective, uninformed, and ideologically biased. In this article a dissenting point of view will be presented. "Terrorists" will be described as non-state political and military actors engaged in the rational application of ordinary principles of realpolitik. This application includes the process of mounting a challenge to the state's claimed monopoly on political violence. The methods utilized are not fundamentally different ideologically, morally, or psychologically from those of state actors. Instead, the kinds of "terrorist" groupings to be examined will be shown to be representatives of a new stage in the evolution of modern war (so-called "fourth generation war"). Additionally, an examination of modern military history, contemporary military theory, and the dramatic expansion of both the scale and success of so-called "terrorist" entities will demonstrate both the rise of such entities as major political contenders and the decline of the state as a monopolist of political violence.

1. The Rise of the Modern State and Its Monopoly on Violence (1300–1800)

The Dutch-Israeli military historian Martin van Creveld, in his seminal work *The Rise and Decline of the State* (1999), describes the origins and development of the modern conception of the state as it emerged during the fourteenth through the nineteenth centuries in Western Europe. Van Creveld emphasizes the importance of distinguishing the state from government per se. What are the characteristics that are unique to the state are not necessarily to be found in government generally? The most important of these is the notion of the state as a legal person unto itself. The state has a legal and institutional life of its own that exists above and beyond its individual members or subjects and is self-perpetuating even as its personnel change. The state is a corporate body, but unlike other corporate entities (business corporations or religious and educational institutions) the state regulates and externally establishes the conditions of operation for other kinds of corporate bodies, maintains for itself an exclusive territorial monopoly and a monopoly on particular attributes of public authority ("sovereignty"), and is recognized by and interacts with other state entities in a way that non-state entities do not.[3]

Van Creveld points out that political government was carried out with varying degrees of formality by tribes, chiefdoms, city-states, and empires before the rise of the state. Typically, ownership and rule went hand-in-hand. Those who acquired ownership of land and resources, by whatever means, also ruled over those who lived upon the land.[4] An important contribution of the Greek cities and the later Roman Republic to the eventual rise of the state was to separate ownership from rule. The operation of the machinery of government existed independently of the private property of owners and individual rulers. One could lose one's

---

3   Martin van Creveld, *The Rise and Decline of the State* (Cambridge: Cambridge University Press, 1999), 126–54.

4   Ibid., 1–58.

political position without losing one's personal wealth in the process. However, the political arrangements of antiquity did not conceive of government as an institution independent of its individual members. Van Creveld cites Thucydides' claim that "the city *is* its men" and Cicero's description of the *res publica* as "an assembly of men living according to law."[5]

With the collapse of the Roman Empire in Western Europe and the emergence of the subsequent feudal era, a historically unique set of arrangements came about that created the conditions necessary for the rise of the state. Van Creveld observes that unlike previous disruptions of centralized authority and the dispersion of power into the hands of localized rulers, the medieval feudal rulers who comprised the Holy Roman Empire found themselves in the position of having to share power with the Church. The Church was a massive institution unto itself. The Pope maintained his own seat of authority in Rome, while the domain of the Emperor moved from place to place. The Pope also possessed his own armed forces and the Church maintained many privileges of its own that preserved its independence from secular authority. Out of the cracks in the overlapping authority of Church and Emperor came the monarchies which formed the basis of future states. The monarchs' persistent struggle against the powers of the Church, the Holy Roman Empire, the independent cities, and the feudal nobility proved successful over the long term, and the time of absolute monarchs began.[6]

Van Creveld describes the process by which these centralized monarchies began laying the foundations of the state by building a bureaucratic infrastructure for administrative purposes.[7] The bureaucracy eventually became a power unto itself and began to challenge the power of the monarchy, the Church, and the centers of authority to be found in the broader society. The bureaucracies' powers of collecting both information and taxes

---

5   Ibid., 57.

6   Ibid., 59–117.

7   Ibid., 127–54.

from the citizenry at large transformed its relationship to the citizenry. The emergence of a bureaucratic infrastructure with the power of taxation subsequently made it possible for the bureaucracy to gain a monopoly over the raising of armed forces and making war, an activity that had previously been largely privatized. The growth of regular armies, along with internal police organizations and penal institutions, cemented the concentration of authority into the hands of the bureaucracy. By the end of the eighteenth century, the bureaucracy had grown to the point where it crystallized into the person of the state.[8]

During the centuries of its evolution, the state was accompanied by the parallel development of a radically altered intellectual culture, one which gradually came to deny the previous theological foundations for political legitimacy in favor of a more pragmatic secular concern for the obtainment and preservation of order. As the state grew, the power and influence of intermediary institutions such as the Church, the aristocracy, the individual monarch, the patriarchal head of the household, and the slave master diminished. Particularistic attachments along with traditional systems of rank and privilege began to decline. Rulers and authority figures came to be seen as ordinary persons whose powers and privileges were derived from their official positions rather than any intrinsic virtue, wisdom, or superiority of their own. As traditional hierarchies began to vanish, subjects began to be seen less in terms of their ascribed status and more as individuals in terms of their relationship to the universal authority of the state. Egalitarian doctrines arose whose effect was to extend political rights to ever-growing groupings of citizens (classes, religions, ethnicities) within the state. This leveling of traditional hierarchies, combined with the disruptions and dislocations generated by the industrial revolution, caused the state to grow ever-more powerful.[9]

Van Creveld examines the transformation of the state from a

---

8   Ibid., 184–88.

9   Ibid., 170–83.

means to an end (the preservation of order and the protection of life and property) to an end unto itself. The intellectual framework in which this occurred involved the marriage of the state with nationalism.[10] The glorification of the nation-state and the transfer of traditional particular, provincial, or parochial loyalties to the state first found full expression in the French Revolution. Traditional religious sentiments were replaced with the quasi-deification of the state and the nation. State ceremonies, rituals, and pageants began to take on quasi-religious symbolism and expressions of reverence. This trend was manifested in particularly spectacular ways by the totalitarian regimes of the twentieth century, but was also observable in less extravagant ways in the liberal states such as France, England, and America. Conscripted, popular armies became the norm and to give one's life in the fight for one's country was elevated to the level of the highest ideal. The state strengthened its control over civil society not only by means of its police and penal institutions but also through assuming control over education, welfare services, banking, and other sectors of social and economic life as well. This unprecedented dominance on the part of the state afforded individual states the means with which to wage war against one another with previously unheard of levels of death and destruction.[11] Ironically, the state, whose original purpose had been the maintenance of peace, became an agent of unparalleled disorder. Martin van Creveld thus describes the legacy of the modern state:

> In return for fostering technological development which made possible a much-augmented standard of living the state exacted protection money. Essentially it consisted of unlimited blood and treasure, a development which climaxed during the first half of the twentieth century. Reveling in total war, the state demanded and obtained sacrifice on a scale which, had they been able to imagine it, would have made even the old Aztec gods blanch.[12]

10   Ibid., 189–204.

11   Ibid., 205–62.

12   Ibid., 262.

2. Anarchists versus the State and Propaganda by the Deed: Early Challenges to the State's Monopoly on Violence (1885–1915)

As previously mentioned, the use of violence to promote political ends has always existed in some form or another. The actual use of the term "terrorism" began during the time of the French Revolution. The term was brought into common use by the English political philosopher Edmund Burke, who denounced the "terrorism" of the French revolutionaries.[13] What is of importance to the thesis outlined in this article is not political violence per se, but the manner by which the use of such violence has arisen in the modern Western world and its relationship to the modern state and the future of the modern state. What is distinctive about modern terrorism is not that it is "terrorism" but that it occurs within the context of an institutional framework where a single corporative entity (the state) claims a monopoly on the use of violence as opposed to one where the waging of war by private individuals and groups is expected and where private acts of violence (such as assassination) are standard political tools.

The popular image of "terrorism" in its contemporary form is traceable to the tendency of nineteenth-century revolutionaries to engage in political assassinations. Such tactics were utilized by a number of ideological tendencies (for instance, Irish nationalists), but by far the most notorious and stereotypical of such tendencies were what would now be called the "classical anarchists."[14]

There is a certain amount of irony in the fact that among the earliest challengers to the modern state's monopoly on violence would be an ideological tendency that denies the very legitimacy of the state itself, as opposed to the legitimacy of a particular type of state or a specific state policy or action. Although fairly

---

13   Geoffrey Nunberg, "Head Games, It All Started With Robespierre; Terrorism: The History of a Very Frightening Word," *San Francisco Chronicle*, October 28, 2001.

14   Burton, *Urban Terrorism*, 17–34.

obscure today, the classical anarchists were in their time a rather large movement, considering the radical nature of their ideas, involving millions of people and maintaining a presence in most countries, not only in Europe and North America but also in Russia, Asia, Latin America, and even Africa. As might be expected, the anarchists were a diverse and often eccentric lot. Their ranks included everything from labor militants to organizers of utopian colonies, proto-feminists and homosexuals to those who synthesized anarchist militancy with the machismo common to Latin cultures, quasi-Marxists to extreme individualists, and pacifists and extreme idealists to proponents of terrorism or what was called "propaganda by the deed."[15]

The concept of "propaganda by the deed" was formulated by the anarchists as a means of describing their notion of leadership by method of "direct action" as opposed to conventional political outlets like political parties. Not all efforts at "direct action" or even "propaganda by the deed" involved violence. Sometimes these terms took on milder connotations, such as the creation of alternative institutions (for example, worker cooperatives or independent schools) that the anarchists hoped would be a model for the broader transformation of society. However, these terms eventually came to be identified by the public at large and many anarchists alike as mere synonyms for acts of political violence. There were many such incidents. The most notorious of these were the regicides carried out by the anarchists. In his study of the origins of urban terrorism, Anthony M. Burton observes that over a thirty year period in the late nineteenth and early twentieth centuries, the anarchists assassinated a head of state or cabinet official approximately once every eighteen months. The most well-known attacks of this type were the assassinations of Tsar Alexander II of Russia, President Carnot of France, King Umberto of Italy, Empress Elisabeth of Austria, and President William McKinley of the United States.[16]

15   Paul Eltzbacher, *Anarchism: Exponents of the Anarchist Philosophy*, trans. Steven T. Byington, ed. James J. Martin (New York: Chip's Bookshop, Booksellers and Publishers, 1958 [1900]).

16   Marie Fleming, "Propaganda by the Deed: Terrorism and Anarchist Theory in Late

The actual political and intellectual theories of the anarchists were more sophisticated than what they were often given credit for, and not all anarchists approved of the actions associated with "propaganda by the deed."[17] Indeed, the anarchists included within their ranks many rather innovative thinkers, including the pioneer sociologist and leading anarchist militant Peter Kropotkin, the economist Pierre-Joseph Proudhon, the geographer Élisée Reclus, and other individuals of similar caliber. Some anarchists opposed violent actions outright, and others felt somewhat ambivalent about the question. However, some anarchist leaders were unabashed champions of armed insurrection and overthrow of the existing bourgeois order by any means necessary. The majority of anarchists did not simply oppose the state and its laws and institutions. They were also social revolutionaries of a type and bitterly denounced the frequently deplorable working conditions the laboring classes of the day were subjected to, a characteristic they shared with socialists and progressives of all stripes. Political violence was not merely an end unto itself but an act of revolt against political and economic situations regarded as unduly oppressive and unjust.[18]

Of the leading personalities of classical anarchism, the one who was perhaps most representative of the stereotype of the anarchist as the terrorist madman was the German-American Johann Most. By the time of his emigration to America in 1882, Most had already served time in Germany's Reichstag (as a socialist deputy) and in Germany's prisons (as a treasonous socialist revolutionary). Deciding that socialism lacked the revolutionary fervor he desired, Most became an anarchist. As editor of the anarchist publication *Freiheit* (German for "Liberty"), Most was an incessant preacher of violent revolution.[19] He was at

Nineteenth-Century Europe," in *Terrorism in Europe*, ed. Yonah Alexander and Kenneth A. Myers (London: Center for Strategic and International Studies, 1982), 8–28.

17 April Carter, *The Political Theory of Anarchism* (New York: Harper and Row, 1971).

18 Richard Suskind, *By Bullet, Bomb, and Dagger: The Story of Anarchism* (New York: Macmillan, 1971).

19 Frederic Trautmann, *The Voice of Terror: A Biography of Johann Most* (Westport, CT:

times described as a "terrorist of the word" with his writings characterized as "like lava shooting forth flames of ridicule, scorn and defiance . . . and breathing hatred."[20] The title of one of Most's published works provides a sufficient description of his general outlook: *Science of Revolutionary Warfare: A Manual of Instruction in the Use and Preparation of Nitro-glycerin, Dynamite, Gun Cotton, Fulminating Mercury, Bombs, Fuses, Poisons.*[21] Most was based in Chicago, location of the Haymarket incident of 1882, when a bomb was thrown into a crowd of persons, killing eight policemen. Though no actual perpetrator was determined, eight anarchist militants were prosecuted for incitement. Four were executed and a fifth committed suicide while awaiting the gallows.[22]

Anarchists were predictably regarded by the authorities of the day as mere deviants and criminals. Two interesting works that survive from the Haymarket period bear this out. One of these, *Anarchy and Anarchists: A History of the Red Terror and the Social Revolution in America and Europe* was written by Michael J. Schaack, a Chicago police captain who supervised the investigation following the Haymarket bombing. Schaack describes the anarchists with language resembling that of the "international communist conspiracy" rhetoric that later came to be popular in the United States during the 1950s:

> Let none mistake either the purpose or the devotion of these fanatics, nor their growing strength. This is methodic—not a haphazard conspiracy. The ferment in Russia is controlled by the same heads and the same hands as the activity in Chicago. There is a cold-blooded, calculating purpose behind this revolt, manipulating every part of it, the world over, to a common and ruinous end.[23]

Greenwood Press, 1980).

20 Suskind, *By Bullet, Bomb, and Dagger*, 45.

21 Burton, *Urban Terrorism*, 27.

22 Suskind, *By Bullet, Bomb, and Dagger*, 1–17, 44–59.

23 Michael J. Schaack, *Anarchy and Anarchists: A History of the Red Terror and the Social Revolution in America and Europe* (New York: Arno Press, 1977 [1889]), 688.

The other work in question, *The Rise and Fall of Anarchy in America*, by an unidentified author using the name "George N. McLean," describes the Haymarket incident and the subsequent investigation, trial, and executions. Included is a section with the subtitle "The Anarchist's Fatal Delusion," providing the following characterization of the anarchist:

> Under the fascination of rose-tinted delusion whose fatal mists obscure the mental and moral realm of thought, many become criminals, goaded on by blind infatuation which persevered in becomes a passion all-absorbing in its nature. In the blindness of their infatuation they seek to immortalize their names by a bold and base attempt at the subversion of law and order.[24]

So much for the prosecution. In assessing the incendiary rhetoric and violent behavior of the anarchists from the perspective of a historian, context is immensely important. Yes, the anarchists could be violent at times, but so could their opponents. The labor battles of the era often approximated the idealized "class war" preached by radicals of the day. Violence was common on both sides, and utilized not only by labor militants, but also by strikebreakers, "scabs," policemen, soldiers, and state militiamen. Many acts of violence carried out by the anarchists were done in response to repression of dissent or lethal action against labor organizers and striking workers carried out by the forces of the state and business interests. The anarchists' antigovernment rhetoric, in the context of the present era, often mirrors that of contemporary political conservatives. Many of the issues championed by the anarchists, such as the right of labor unions to organize, the right to birth control, and freedom of political speech, are now mainstream and frequently uncontroversial. So were the anarchists really criminals and deviants as their enemies proclaimed, or were many of them simply people whose thinking was ahead of its time?[25]

---

24   George N. McLean, *The Rise and Fall of Anarchy in America* (New York: Haskell House Publishers, 1972 [1890]), 267.

25   Robert Graham, *Anarchism: A Documentary History of Libertarian Ideas, vol. 1, From*

The importance of the classical anarchists for the purposes of this article is not their specific beliefs, but their role as one of the earliest and most famous political tendencies that sought to overthrow the modern liberal states that have taken root in the Western world over the last one and a half centuries. The anarchists would eventually fade from the scene, but many other groups would subsequently arise that would utilize tactics identical to those associated with "propaganda by the deed." The anarchists offered an alternative to liberal-democratic capitalism that contained a vision of decentralized confederations of autonomous worker communes and farming villages. Future insurrectionists would possess alternative political visions of their own. These visions would be widely divergent, but their common denominator would be a hatred of the values of modern liberal society.

Anarchy to Anarchism (300 CE to 1939) (Montreal: Black Rose Books, 2005).

3. Liberalism and Anti-Liberalism: Political Violence by Non-State Actors in the Postwar Era (1945–89)

Insisting it is the lack of freedom that fuels terrorism, Bush declares, "Young people who have a say in their future are less likely to search for meaning in extremism." Tell it to Mussolini and the Blackshirts. Tell it to the Nazis, who loathed the free republic of Weimar, as did the communists.

"Citizens who can join a peaceful political party are less likely to join a terrorist organization." But the West has been plagued by terrorists since the anarchists. The Baader-Meinhof Gang in Germany, the Red Brigades in Italy, the Puerto Ricans who tried to kill Harry Truman, the London subway bombers were all raised in freedom.

"Dissidents with the freedom to protest around the clock," said the president, "are less likely to blow themselves up at rush hour." But Hamas and Islamic Jihad resort to suicide bombing because they think it a far more effective way to overthrow Israeli rule than marching with signs . . .

—Patrick J. Buchanan, September 10, 2006[26]

We need a Revolution, be it fascist, communist or Islamic, please God(s), save Portugal from big money democracy, I'm willing to support anything other than this.

—Portuguese revolutionary nationalist, September 10, 2006[27]

Political violence by non-state actors declined in the West during the period between 1914 and 1945. The labor battles that had

---

26   Patrick J. Buchanan, "America's Ideologue in Chief," Vdare.com, September 10, 2006, http://www.vdare.com/buchanan/060908_chief.htm.

27   Email to author via Yahoo! discussion list, September 10, 2006.

characterized previous decades were overshadowed by the fury of the First World War. In some countries, particularly the United States, the war effort was used as a pretense for the repression of dissident political movements under the guise of suppressing "sedition", and preserving national unity. Structural changes implemented by Western governments during the interwar period had the effect of either co-opting or subjugating labor unions and the Socialist parties. In some countries, particularly those of Central and Eastern Europe, the newly emergent fascist and communist movements often maintained violent quasi-military organizations of their own, but these soon came to either dominate the state (such as the German Nazis or Italian Fascists) or suffer repression when their enemies were able to seize political power (such as the Communist parties in countries where right-wing authoritarian regimes came into being). The atmosphere of total war that accompanied the Second World War had the effect of diminishing conflict between states and non-state actors, and the conflict of this type that did take place (the resistance in France, for example) primarily pitted indigenous resistance forces against the forces of direct foreign occupation. Prior insurrectionary forces like the anarchists were overrun by the hegemony achieved by Communism on the political Left following the Bolshevik Revolution of 1917 and the increased respectability, cooptation, and "mainstreaming" of the labor movements of the various Western nations.

The defeat of the Axis powers in 1945 and subsequent American occupation of Western Europe, the region from where the state first originated, assured for that region the pre-eminence of liberalism. Martin van Creveld observes that while the corporative state was subsequently exported to other regions following its initial rise in Western Europe, particularly Eastern Europe, Russia, and Latin America, it was in the nations of the Anglosphere that the state became most firmly established.[28] It was in these nations that a particular ideological expression of the state, liberalism, became the most pronounced. How

---

28   Van Creveld, *The Rise and Decline of the State*, 263–331.

can liberal states be best described? The irreducible minimum qualities would be a parliamentary form of government of some sort, a commercial-capitalist-bourgeois economic foundation, an expansive technological base, a relatively cosmopolitan cultural atmosphere, and, since at least the mid-twentieth century, an extensive public sector managerial bureaucracy. Additionally, the defeat of the Axis forces in the Second World War, the resulting occupations of Western Europe by the United States and Eastern Europe by the Soviet Union, and the emergence of the Cold War between the two great superpowers had the effect of reducing Europe to the status of de facto colonies or vassalages to one of the two Cold War contenders. Also, the unprecedented level of international power achieved by the United States in the postwar era combined with its ongoing rivalry with the Soviet Union, brought about a drastic expansion of American intervention into conflicts between other states and into the internal politics of other states.

The presence of this arrangement in the Western world in the latter half of the twentieth century means that political violence exercised by non-state actors during this period, at least in the West, amounted to acts of violence against the United States and its protectorates, client states, or de facto colonies in Europe, Latin America, and, because of the symbiotic relationship between the United States and Israel and the propping up of the Saudi oil cartel by the United States, the Middle East. In examining this phenomenon, it is once again essential to point out that the concern of this article is not the question of political violence per se or even non-state political violence (so-called "terrorism") but the relationship between political violence carried out by non-state actors and states who claim to possess a legitimate monopoly on such violence and the effect of this relationship on the evolution of warfare and the likely future of the state. During the postwar era, liberal and/or American hegemony was challenged by an amazing variety of organizations, groups, and tendencies with grievances, ideologies, agendas, and strategies of their own, and some of them rather colorful to say the least.

In 1982, Dennis Pluchinsky observed that Western Europe had become the focus of terrorist activity and that 33 percent of terrorist actions between the years of 1968 to 1980 had occurred in this region. Latin America achieved a close second place with 21 percent.[29]

These non-state armed resistance forces can be broken down into roughly the following classifications: First World Marxist, Third World Marxist, nationalist, separatist, religious, racialist, traditionalist, and ecologist and/or technophobic. Each of these, of course, could be broken down into several sub-categories of their own. In 1992, Stephen E. Atkins identified more than eighty major organizations involved in violent resistance to Western states and/or puppet regimes in Europe, North and South America, and the Middle East.[30] Many of these organizations are fairly well-known. Among those who can be considered "First World Marxist" are Germany's Red Army Faction (the Baader-Meinhof Gang), Italy's Red Brigades, and America's Weather Underground. These kinds of insurrectionary groupings typically claimed hostility to Western imperialism, neocolonialism, capitalism, and racism, and profess solidarity with leftist revolutionaries, or "Third World Marxists," whom they see as their counterparts in the lesser developed regions. Most of the more significant armed, militant leftist groups from the Third World have, during the postwar era, originated from Latin America. These included El Salvador's Farabundo Martí National Liberation Front (FMLN), Nicaragua's Sandinista National Liberation Front (FSLN), Peru's "Shining Path" (a popularized term for the Communist Party of Peru-Maoist), Colombia's Armed Forces of the Colombian Revolution (FARC), and the "Zapatista" peasant revolutionary force of the Mexican state of Chiapas.

29 Dennis Pluchinsky, "Political Terrorism in Western Europe: Some Themes and Variations," in *Terrorism in Europe*, ed. Yonah Alexander and Kenneth A. Myers (London: Center for Strategic and International Studies, 1982), 40–78.

30 Stephen E. Atkins, *Terrorism: A Reference Handbook* (Santa Barbara, CA: ABC-CLIO, 1992), 99–136.

Some groups wished to achieve the independence of a particular national entity from a foreign colonial power (for example, the Irish Republican Army). Others desired the separation of a particular region from a larger state entity (such as the Basque autonomists). Still other factions maintained religious motivations, usually of an extreme fundamentalist or strongly orthodox nature (for instance, various Islamic "terrorist" groups, the Falangists of Spain, or the violently anti-abortion militants in the United States). Some desired the independence or separation not of territorial entities or "nations" per se, but of racial and ethnic groupings in a biological sense. One such faction, an American neo-Nazi group simply called "The Order," carried out a series of armed robberies during the 1980s for the purpose of establishing an "Aryan" homeland in the US state of Idaho.[31] Particularly interesting has been the rise of militant resistance groups in recent decades committed to violent or extra-legal actions on behalf of environmental causes. Indeed, the US Federal Bureau of Investigation currently classifies environmental and "animal rights" militants as the primary domestic terrorist threat within the United States.[32]

Following the collapse of the Soviet Union and the end of the Cold War in the late 1980s and early 1990s, a new target emerged that became the source of much hostility on the part of armed militant or "terrorist" organizations worldwide. This target was the unprecedented global hegemony achieved by the United States following the demise of its only true rival. Lacking the constraining force of the Soviet Union, the United States was afforded a freer hand in its capacity to impose its desired liberal-capitalist order on the entire world. This effort has been met with resistance by a wide range of forces, many of them the same organizations that opposed Western states or Western neocolonialism during the postwar period. The globalization

---

31 Kevin Flynn and Gary Gerhardt, *The Silent Brotherhood: Inside America's Racist Underground* (New York: Free Press, 1989).

32 Charley Reese, "Let's Get Real," Populist Party of America, December 2, 2006, http://www.populistamerica.com/let_s_get_real.

of capital is offensive to dissidents worldwide for a variety of reasons. Some regard globalization as a force for greater exploitation of labor, particularly in Third World countries. Others are concerned about environmental destruction. Still others are concerned about the erosion of traditional cultural, religious, ethnic, national, racial, and regional identities.[33] The most zealous and effective opponents of the unipolar domination of the United States and its program of liberal-capitalism have, of course, been the Islamic fundamentalists.[34] However shocking such incidents as the hijackings and destruction of September 11, 2001, may have been to people the world over, it is also true that many of the world's peoples share many of the concerns that drove some individuals to such extreme action. As William S. Lind explains:

To many of the world's peoples . . . [the global triumph of liberal capitalism] . . . represents Hell, and they will fight it literally to their dying breath.[35]

This is true even of some within the United States itself. The journalist Joel Dyer described the US militia movement of the 1990s in the following terms:

Following [the killing of dissidents by federal agents at] Ruby Ridge and Waco, the antigovernment movement focused on the creation of militias. With its military arm in place, the movement's next push came in the form of common-law courts. As the sovereignty concept took hold across the nation, antigovernment adherents began to form organizations that encompassed all of these antigovernmental elements—sovereignty, courts and militias. The goal is that each organization should become

---

33 Michael Hardt and Antonio Negri, *Empire* (Cambridge, MA: Harvard University Press, 2000).

34 Jane Corbin, *Al-Qaeda: In Search of the Terror Network That Threatens the World* (New York: Thunder's Mouth Press/Nation Books, 2003).

35 William S. Lind, "Forcing the World to Be Saved," Antiwar.com, January 21, 2006, http://www.antiwar.com/lind/?articleid=8422.

self-sufficient, able to fully govern its membership with no assistance from the outside world. It's as if there are thousands of independent countries operating within the border of the United States . . . Regardless of their differences, which are substantial, these groups realize that they must ultimately support each other to avoid being crushed by the federal government . . . These self-governing antigovernment bands range in size from a dozen people to several thousand . . . The actions of these supposedly sovereign groups are often in direct conflict with the laws of the United States, which they no longer recognize . . . The longer it exists, the stronger it grows, as more and more people are choosing to opt out of the federal system, whose taxes make the difference between a family's eating or sending its children to bed hungry . . . The government's refusal to recognize the sovereignty of these pockets of patriots is understandable: That would lead to anarchy.

A new breed of other elements within the movement—representing perhaps yet another step in the movement's evolution—is also seeking foreign funding. One of my contacts, whom I will call "Tom" since he spoke on the condition of anonymity, told me that he is actively seeking money abroad. Tom's antigovernment organization, which has established dialogue with Mexico's Zapatistas, South America's Shining Path guerrillas, and the Nation of Islam, is the antithesis of the [Christian] Identity-driven groups. But don't mistake Tom for a leftist—he's not. His vision of America is similar to that of the sovereigns, with small pockets of self-governed individuals living in regions outside of any federal authority. "If blacks want to live separate from whites," says Tom, "they should have that right. I don't think that's necessary, but people should be allowed to choose how and where they live." Tom says that the American government is responsible for creating the conditions worldwide that have spawned the sort of radical organizations his group communicates with in other countries, so it's only natural that today's antigovernment movement should consider them as allies. In line with this vision, he says: "Who knows? Maybe someday we'll have a standoff in Texas . . . and the Zapatistas will come to our defense. It could happen."[36]

---

36 Joel Dyer, *Harvest of Rage: Why Oklahoma City Is Just the Beginning* (Boulder, CO: Westview Press, 1997), 191, 247.

4. Fourth Generation Warfare and Non-State Military Actors (1989–)

The historiography and historical narrative presented thus far provides the necessary background for the direct examination of the core thesis of this article, i.e., that the state's historic monopoly on violence and war has declined and been rendered archaic as a result of successful challenges to that monopoly by so-called "fourth generation" military forces. The concept of "fourth generation warfare" was first outlined in 1989 by the American military historian William S. Lind.[37] The "generational" division of types of warfare is used to describe the evolution of war since the rise of the state. Lind traces the beginning of the state's monopoly on warfare to the end of the Thirty Years War in 1648 with the Treaty of Westphalia. From that point on, wars were fought by states against states. The era of "first generation" warfare reigned from the time of Westphalia until the time of the American Civil War of 1861–65. "First generation" militaries were characterized by their emphasis on formality and a military culture oriented towards rank, order, and discipline. Battles often took on the character of formal gamesmanship, open-air fighting, and maneuvers involving the movement of large numbers of soldiers simultaneously. During the time of the US Civil War, the "orderliness" of battles began to dissolve and became more chaotic. The second and third generations of warfare each arose as a response to this change.

"Second generation" warfare was devised by the French during the First World War. The "second generation" approach to battle maintains the traditional emphasis on rank, structure, and top-down decision-making. The strategic emphasis is on artillery and firepower, attrition, and occupation. The aim is to inflict large-scale casualties on the enemy. The "second generation" approach continues to dominate American military strategy to date. "Third generation"

---

37   William S. Lind, Keith Nightengale, John F. Schmitt, and Gary I. Wilson, "The Changing Face of War: Into the Fourth Generation," *Marine Corps Gazette*, October 1989, 22–26.

warfare also had its origins in the First World, although it was invented by the Germans rather than the French. The emphasis of the "third generation" is on maneuvers and innovation by the lower ranks. Junior officers were permitted, for example, to disregard orders from superiors if those orders proved ineffective at getting the job done. The highest duty of the combat officer was to achieve victory by any means necessary, even if it meant altering or even abandoning battle plans formulated by commanders. Firepower was also replaced by speed as the focus of "third generation" warfare, and encirclement and dislocation of the enemy, rather than attrition, became the objective of battle. "Fourth generation" warfare represents the shift from wars between states to wars between states and non-state actors, a process Lind regards as the most important change in the nature of war since the initial obtainment of the monopoly on war by the state with the Treaty of Westphalia.[38]

To some degree, the guerrilla warfare tactics developed during the anti-colonial wars of Asia during the postwar era, such as those led by Mao Tse-tung in China and Ho Chi Minh in Vietnam, serve as prototypes for "fourth generation" warfare.[39] However, these do not completely qualify as "fourth generation" in nature as they do not represent a complete break from the notion of war as combat between states, but qualify as conventional civil wars with two factions within a state fighting for supremacy, conventional revolutions where one state replaces another, or where a colonial power and its domestic puppet government are regarded by the insurgents as illegitimate and are expelled with the assistance of other states. It is with the rise of contemporary Islamic "terrorism" that fourth generation warfare really comes into its own. The Al-Qaeda organization, for example, is a completely privatized, non-state military entity that managed to carry out

38   William S. Lind, "Understanding Fourth Generation War," Antiwar.com, January 15, 2004, http://antiwar.com/lind/index.php?articleid=1702.

39   Mao Tse-tung, "On Guerrilla Warfare" (1937), in *Selected Works of Mao Tse-tung*, vol. 9, http://www.marxists.org/reference/archive/mao/works/1937/guerrilla-warfare/. See also Cecil B. Currey, "Senior General Vo Nguyen Giap Remembers," *Journal of Third World Studies*, October 2003, http://www.findarticles.com/p/articles/mi_qa3821/is_200310/ai_n9337860.

an unprecedented attack on the American mainland, inflicting casualties on a level comparable to the Japanese air raid on Pearl Harbor in 1941. Likewise, the present-day "insurgent" forces with which the United States is at war in Iraq do not represent a particular state, nor do they necessarily represent any specific would-be successor state. Instead, they represent religions, tribes, clans, ethnic groups, familial networks, ideologies, and causes that exist independently of any recognizable state formation.

An interesting case study of a "fourth generation force" is the Hezbollah organization of Lebanon.[40] Hezbollah's entry into the war between Israel and Hamas during the summer of 2006 marks the first time a "fourth generation" force has actually conducted an outright military invasion of an actual state. This proved to be a case where a "fourth generation" entity was able to match the firepower of a state military force and outmaneuver them. Hezbollah was also able to engage Israel in air and naval battles with rocket attacks capable of destroying Israeli planes and ships. Hezbollah did all of this while the Lebanese state sat by unable to defend itself against a massive air assault by Israel. Hezbollah is a particular well-developed fourth generation entity in that it maintains not only an independent military force but also an elaborate system of private social services, religious and educational institutions, and hospitals as well. Such a model is a likely prototype for the way in which fourth generation forces will evolve in the future. Such forces will continue to arise from strange places. A story in the April 26, 2005, issue of the *Washington Times* reports:

> Brazilian drug traffickers have teamed up with Columbian rebels to smuggle narcotics through Paraguay, creating a lucrative new channel for distribution to the United States and Europe . . .

---

40 Nir Rosen, "Hizb Allah, Party of God," Truthdig, October 3, 2006, http://www. truthdig.com/report/print/200601003_hiz_ballah_party_of_god. See also William S. Lind, "The Summer of 1914," On War #175, July 18, 2006, http://www.d-n-i.net/lind/ lind_7_18_06.htm.

Using a precisely orchestrated system of flights from the Columbian jungle, Marxist rebels from the Revolutionary Armed Forces of Columbia, or FARC, are shipping 40 to 60 tons of cocaine annually to farms in Paraguay owned by Brazilian drug lords, who then put the cocaine in cars and small trucks and drive them across the nearly unmonitored border into rural western Brazil . . . in return for arms, dollars and Euros from Brazilian traffickers [for the FARC].[41]

Observes William S. Lind:

How long will it be before and other Islamic non-state forces make their own alliances with the drug gangs and people smugglers who are experts in getting across America's southern border? Or use the excellent distribution systems the drug gangs have throughout the United States to smuggle something with a bigger bang than the best cocaine?

Just as we see states coming together around the world against the non-state forces of the Fourth Generation, so those non-state forces will also come together in multi-faceted alliances. The difference is likely to be that they will do it faster and better. And, they will use states' preoccupation with the state system like a matador's cape, to dazzle and distract while they proceed with the real business of war.[42]

---

41   Carmen Gentile, "Drug Smugglers, Rebel Join in Hand," *Washington Times*, April 26, 2005.

42   William S. Lind, "More on Gangs and Guerrillas vs the State," Military.com, April 28, 2005, http://www.military.com/Opinions/0,,Lind_042805,00.html.

5. Fourth Generation Warfare and the Decline of the State (1975–)

Martin van Creveld argues that without the monopolization of war as the primary function of the state, it would have been very difficult for the state to achieve the level of dominance that it eventually did. It was for the purpose of waging war that the state initially instituted its programs of bureaucracy-building and taxation, and its provision of health, education, and social welfare services were intertwined with the development of its war making capacities, thereby creating a type of "welfare-warfare" state. These features, combined with the state's monopoly over money, land, and other economic resources, fused with a legitimizing ideology in the form of nationalism, served to turn the state into the mighty (or, some would say, monstrous) entity that it eventually became. How could such an entity eventually lose its monopoly on war?

Van Creveld traces this phenomenon to five principal sources. First, the advent of nuclear weaponry and modern "weapons of mass destruction" has significantly raised the costs of interstate warfare. The gains of such warfare are now overshadowed by its risks and costs. What does it profit a nation to conquer other nations but lose itself to massive nuclear retaliation? Just as the warfare state has been excessively costly, so has the welfare state. Even the most prosperous regimes have found it difficult to maintain its established levels of social spending without the use of deficits and the acquisition of public debt. A wide consensus exists among policy makers that "trimming the fat" from public budgets will become a necessity at some point, though politicians and political interest groups do their best to delay the day of reckoning.

A third challenge to the state's hegemony has been the internationalization of technology and innovations in the fields of technology and communications that make instantaneous commercial transactions possible by parties on all corners of the globe. The effect of this can only be to weaken dependence on national governments. Still another factor is the failure of the state to fully take root and stabilize itself in many parts of the world, notably Africa, Asia, and Latin America. The disorder generated by the failure of the state in those regions has begun to spread to other regions as well (for example, the importation of Central American crime gangs into North America and African refugees into Western Europe). Lastly, there is the decline of nationalistic ideology and a greater unwillingness on the part of citizens to sacrifice themselves on behalf of their respective states. For instance, van Creveld observes that nearly all states that have abolished military conscription have found it impossible to reinstate it due to overwhelming public hostility.[43]

Whither the state? Van Creveld suggests that the state as it has been described in this article maintains three essential attributes: a corporative as opposed to personalized institutional expression, exclusive territorial monopoly, and a monocentric rather than polycentric concept of "sovereignty" (and hence a monopoly on violence, war making, and also on rule or "law"). Van Creveld argues that the breakdown of the state will result in a proliferation of entities that are, like the states they replace, corporative in nature but also polycentric and extra-territorial. Most importantly, the state's monopoly on violence will be forfeited and warfare in the future will likely be smaller-scale, more localized, and waged by groups whose territorial boundaries (if any) will be less clearly delineated. This new order will be neither a restoration of the medieval world that yielded to the state at the dawn of modernity, nor will it be the decentralized or libertarian utopia of the anarchists, though it may resemble both of these more closely than does the now-fading traditional state order. Will such a world be a better or worse place than the one that we are accustomed to? That would seem to be a matter of perspective. Van Creveld prefers to answer this question with a verse from Mao, who gave the following answer when asked what might follow a nuclear war:

---

43   Van Creveld, *The Rise and Decline of the State*, 336–414.

"The sun will keeping rising
trees will keep growing
and women
will keep having children."[44]

Perhaps this quote from Albert Einstein would be equally appropriate:

"I never think of the future. It comes soon enough."[45]

---

44   Ibid., 415–21.

45   *The Expanded Quotable Einstein*, ed. Alice Calaprice (Princeton, NJ: Princeton University Press, 2000), 18.

6. Historiography of the Decline of the State's Monopoly on Violence and War

The Pre-State Era (Before 1300)

Government is personalized and identified with a particular individual or group. The rulers are believed to have achieved their basis on the basis of divine providence or their superior wisdom and virtue. The Greek cities and the Roman Republic serve as a prelude to the development of the state by separating the concepts of ownership and rulership.

The Rise of the State (1300–1648)

The monarchies of Western Europe achieve victory over the competing powers of the Church, nobility, city-states, and the Holy Roman Emperor. The monarchs achieve a monopoly on violence and war.

The Emergence of the State as a Corporative Entity (1648–1800)

The monarchies proceed to build a bureaucracy for the purpose of waging war. This bureaucracy, with its monopoly on taxation and information, forms the basis for the corporative state. Political theory develops in response to previous theological justifications for political authority. Government is conceived of in secular, pragmatic terms with an emphasis on the need to preserve order and protect life and property. The bureaucracy grows to the point where it overshadows the monarchy and becomes the state itself.

The Fusion of the State and Nationalism (1800–1945)

Beginning with the French Revolution, the state is glorified not as a means unto an end but as an end unto itself. The state expands its activities into the areas of health, education, and welfare. Conscripted armies become the norm. The combination of large popular armies, technological advances, gargantuan state bureaucracies, and ideological nationalism creates a situation that erupts in the form of the large-scale international wars of the first half of the twentieth century.

Early Challenges to the State's Monopoly on Violence (1885–1915)

Revolutionary groups begin using assassinations and bombings as a tactic. The classical anarchists assassinate the head of state of five major countries and many lesser officials over a thirty-year period. Violent battles between radical labor groups, state forces, and private vigilantes become common.

The State at Its Apex (1914–45)

Violence by non-state actors is temporarily eclipsed by the First and Second World War, the Bolshevik Revolution, internal repression within different countries, and the cooptation of labor movements by twentieth-century governments. "First generation warfare" of the type that developed after the Treaty of Versailles in 1648 gives way to "second generation warfare" invented by the French during the First World War. The Germans respond by developing "third generation warfare" during the same period.

Continued Challenges to the State's Monopoly (1945–89)

The defeat of the Axis powers results in the division of Europe into blocs of colonies controlled by the United States and the Soviet Union. The rise of the Cold War and American power escalates US intervention into the Third World. Armed resistance groups form in Europe, Latin America, the Middle East, and North America to resist US imperialism. These groups are ideologically divergent and frequently hostile to one another. Their only commonality is their opposition to US hegemony and its program of liberal-capitalism. These armed resistance groups continue the tactics of bombings, assassinations, hijackings, and other methods used by their nineteenth-century predecessors like the anarchists. These groups begin to form the basis of "fourth generation warfare" where states and non-state organizations wage war against one another. A transitional phase between second or third and fourth generation warfare takes place during the guerrilla wars of Asia during the Cold War period.

The Dominance of Fourth Generation Warfare (1989–)

The collapse of the Soviet Union ends the Cold War and its related "hot wars," such as those of Central America. The United States now achieves unchallenged and unprecedented hegemony. Resistance forces, acting independently of states, escalate their wars against US imperialism. Included in this are not only attacks against US targets abroad or US allies and interests, but attacks within the US mainland as well, whether by domestic insurgent forces (such as the US militia movement or so-called "eco-terrorists") or by foreign organizations waging war against the United States (such as Al-Qaeda).

The Decline of the State (1975–)

The state begins to recede and its primary function, the waging of war, is rendered too costly by the advent of nuclear weapons. The economic costs of the welfare state also contribute to an implosion of the state. The rapid development of communications and transportation technology renders the state less necessary for the facilitation of trade. The failure of the state to fully consolidate itself in certain regions leads to the spread of disorder elsewhere. Public confidence in the state begins to diminish.

Armed Struggle Against the State

Note: The material contained in this article is intended for purposes of education and discussion only. Neither the author nor the American Revolutionary Vanguard organization accepts responsibility for the misuse of this material. Neither advocates unlawful activity of any sort.

Perhaps no political question is more controversial than the matter of when it is acceptable to take up arms against the state under which one is a subject. The American Declaration of Independence, no doubt one of the most significant documents in the history of political philosophy and political struggles, sought to address the central questions that must be considered when armed revolt against the established political order is undertaken. The Declaration recognizes that revolutionaries, out of "a decent respect to the opinions of mankind," should fully articulate and be fully forthcoming concerning their specific reasons for instigating rebellion and the specific objectives which they hope to achieve by means of their revolutionary efforts. While recognizing that "governments long established should not be changed for light and transient causes" and that "mankind are more disposed to suffer while evils are sufferable than to right themselves by abolishing the forms to which they are accustomed," the Declaration maintains that at times "it becomes necessary for one people to dissolve the political bands which have connected them with another." The central question involves the matter of when political conditions have degenerated to the point where a revolutionary endeavor "becomes necessary."

A number of perspectives exist on the question of armed rebellion against the state. Participants in current antigovernment movements in the United States come from a variety of cultural and ideological backgrounds and bring with them certain conventions and traditions. Many of those attracted to grassroots populist movements have fairly conservative social and cultural values. A central feature of traditional conservatism is an emphasis on order as an overriding value. Conservatism typically regards suffering under unjust laws and government actions to be superior to the threat of chaos that often accompanies the breakdown of political authority. A good number of American conservative-populists also think of themselves as nationalists. The US Constitution is seen as almost divinely inspired. The emotional impulse of many of these people is to regard open rebellion against the state as "unpatriotic," "un-American," or "treasonous." Much of this seems to be rooted in the culture that developed in America during the Second World War era. In those days, the norm was to "rally around the flag pole" in support of the government's war effort against the evil Axis forces. The perceived justice of the Allied crusade against the Axis alliance combined with the perceived benevolence of Roosevelt's New Deal as a means of coping with the social and economic disasters associated with the Great Depression served to inculcate in many Americans the idea of an enlightened and virtuous American regime deserving of loyalty, reverence, and obedience. These attitudes are still quite common among the older generation and among the cultural groups that have been most isolated from and least impacted by the cultural revolution of the 1960s.

Strong nationalistic currents that serve to erect a certain taboo against defiance of the state are reinforced by the strong Christian traditions found among many conservative-populists. Most religions generally teach that obedience to civil authority is a good thing and some Christian clergymen will often refer to biblical passages that speak of the "powers that be" as having been ordained by God for the sake of preserving peace and order in society. So among many "traditional" cultural groups there is a strong religious as well as nationalistic impediment to resistance to the state. At the same time, however, it is also possible to stand some of these cultural norms on their head and use them to *support* the idea of rebellion against political authority. After all, the American Revolution, an event that is glorified both in the educational system and in popular culture, involved armed overthrow of the existing political order. Resistance to tyrannical rulers is an idea that is deeply ingrained in American traditional culture. The revered Declaration of Independence is, in fact, a revolutionary decree. Deified figures from American history such as George Washington and Thomas Jefferson led an armed revolution against the state under which they lived. The constitutional "right of the people to keep and bear arms" is considered sacred by many cultural conservatives, even those who know practically nothing about the rest of the Constitution's contents.

Religious traditions and icons can be used in a similar manner. The Bible is full of stories of oppressed people engaging in revolt against political tyrants. Egyptian pharaohs, Babylonian kings, and Roman emperors are depicted as evil, vicious, satanic oppressors. The key for contemporary revolutionaries is to liken enemy political figures to biblical villains such as Herod or Nebuchadnezzar and to compare the current American regime to the evil empires of ancient Rome or Babylon.

In addition to grassroots conservative populists and religious traditionalists, many libertarians are also to be found among the ranks of current opponents of the government. This tradition includes a powerful axiom against the "initiation of force" to achieve political goals. A problem here is that many libertarians use this axiom as a basis for what amounts to virtual pacifism. However, libertarians typically revere the American "founding fathers" who engaged in violent revolution against the state. Libertarians are also typically younger, less religious, and less nationalistic than cultural conservatives, so this obstacle does not seem insurmountable.

Nonviolence is also a strong current among opposition groups on the left. This phenomenon seems to be largely rooted in the influence of religious pacifists such as Mahatma Gandhi and Martin Luther King on contemporary leftists. Some of it is also no doubt traceable to mere personal cowardice. A few acts of violent state repression of the Kent State/MOVE/Ruby Ridge/ Waco variety against leftists would hopefully wake many of them from their love affair with pacifism. Meanwhile, some of the more committed advocates of nonviolence on the left have demonstrated their willingness to confront the police and be arrested in acts of "nonviolent civil disobedience" so the situation does not appear entirely hopeless.

If ever there was a political situation where armed revolution would be justified, it would have to be the contemporary United States. A statement of this type will understandably seem incongruous to persons reared on sophisticated propaganda about the "land of the free and home of the brave." However much power these illusions may hold over people who cling to them, some heavy doses of reality ought to prick their respective balloons.

One source of contemporary nationalistic sentiments is the tremendous and quite justifiable pride that many Americans feel concerning their nation's revolutionary origins and traditions of liberty. However, it is essential to recognize that the classical American republic of the revolutionary era no longer exists and has long been overthrown by an amalgam of corporate, bureaucratic, and military interests. While strands of the original US Constitution, such as the free speech clause of the First Amendment, survive in part, the bulk of the provisions of the Bill of Rights, particularly the Fourth, Eighth, Ninth, and Tenth Amendments have been de facto repealed. So by traditional constitutional standards, and certainly by the libertarian standards of the political philosophy outlined in the Declaration of Independence, the current American regime is unconstitutional, illegal, immoral, and illegitimate. This regime has nothing in common with the federal republic outlined in the Constitution whatsoever. The current American regime is an oligarchy ruled by corporations and elite financial interests, bureaucrats, media bosses, and a professionalized political class. This oligarchy maintains the outward forms and symbols of the classical republic solely for the purposes of thought control of the average citizen and creating an appearance of legitimacy. A necessary task for revolutionaries is to demonstrate to the broader public the thoroughly unconstitutional, illegitimate, and essentially un-American nature of the current regime.

The present American regime is not so much a national government as a world empire. While many of those with antigovernment sentiments have correctly condemned the emerging system of global governance, the so-called "New World Order," via institutions such as the United Nations, International Monetary Fund, World Bank, World Trade Organization, North American Free Trade Agreement, etc., it must be recognized that the domestic American oligarchy and ruling regime are the primary instigators and beneficiaries of the developing global order. Simply put, there is no "UN" without "US." Like the Romans of two thousand years ago and the British of two hundred years ago, the US ruling class maintains an international empire that engages in unchallenged, unrivaled, and unparalleled world domination. In this respect, King George Bush II has much in common with an earlier King George from the American revolutionary era. The consequences of America's half century of world domination for the rest of the world have been devastating. Nearly four million killed in the American-sponsored Indochinese wars of the 1960s and 1970s. Six million killed in subversion, destabilization, and counter-insurgency campaigns orchestrated by the CIA and its corporate controllers.[1] Millions, including hundreds of thousands of children, dead from the genocidal sanctions imposed on Iraq. Brutal oppression of the Palestinian people by the American client state of Israel.

---

1   The figure of six million has been independently arrived at by a number of scholars including Peter Dale Scott, John Stockwell, Johan Galtung, and Noam Chomsky.

Hundreds of thousands of Central Americans killed in the CIA-sponsored wars of the 1980s. The economic exploitation of the oil-producing nations of the Middle East and the subsequent destabilization of the region. The exportation of armaments to rival combatants worldwide and the resulting escalation of local wars. The economic stranglehold placed on Cuba. Hundreds of thousands of Timorese slaughtered by the US-backed, armed, and financed Indonesian regime. The American support for the genocidal Khmer Rouge in the 1980s. Thousands killed in the America air assault on Serbia. The list goes on and on.[2]

The current regime's domestic performance has been quite heinous as well, though not nearly as destructive at its international actions. The United States maintains the world's largest prison population with millions incarcerated in federal and state penitentiaries, local jails, juvenile detention facilities, military concentration camps, psychiatric prisons, and labor camps. Millions more are in the direct clutches of the state via the probation and parole system. Most of these people are victims of cultural persecution or political repression, such as those imprisoned for drug "offenses," or poor people arrested for relatively minor economic or property crimes and unable to afford attorneys and bail bondsmen or, simply put, to buy their way out of jail. Government thugs ranging from federal agents to metropolitan police regularly kill unarmed civilians with impunity. Many more are robbed and assaulted, harassed and threatened by the state's goon squad commonly referred to as "law enforcement." Millions of traditional farmers have been run off their lands by state-supported agribusiness cartels. Repressive housing regulations guarantee a large homeless population that is subsequently criminalized under loitering and vagrancy laws. State-subsidized prison construction, private profiteering from the war on drugs, and corporate use of prison labor has created a new system of chattel slavery. A full-frontal assault on

---

2   *Killing Hope: U.S. Military and CIA Interventions Since World War II* (Monroe, ME: Common Courage Press, 2003) by William Blum is probably the best introductory work to the murderous effects of US foreign policy on the citizens of the Third World. The works of Noam Chomsky are a virtual cornucopia of information on these matters.

all traditional civil liberties is now underway by means of the "terrorism" hysteria. The average person works nearly half the year just to cover tax debts. Mounting public debts and liabilities guarantee an eventual economic meltdown. Monopolistic health care cartels have effectively priced medical treatment out of the range of working people. The ongoing process of currency devaluation and the looting of social security funds by improvident politicians threaten to completely destroy the retirement security of the present generation of workers. The economic base of the working class is being depleted as domestic manufacturing is being moved to "Third World" nations where nineteenth-century-like wage slavery prevails and cheap labor can be exploited. The war on drugs, gun laws, the anti-crime hysteria, and the police state has criminalized minority youth en masse. Meanwhile, efforts by the ruling class to buy the loyalties of minority elites via social engineering schemes have reduced white workers and students to second-class citizens in many areas of life. The America of the future looks to be a bankrupt police state with a Third World-like class structure, in a perpetual state of war, undergoing persistent terrorist assaults and riddled with ethnic and cultural strife.[3]

It is important to remember that the first generation of American revolutionaries engaged in armed revolt against the British Empire over far less egregious state actions. Mostly they were concerned about minor taxation without representation, unreasonable restrictions on trade, and sporadic government intrusions such as the Quartering Act. The American founders would no doubt regard the present state system as a hideous monster of a tyranny. Fortunately, the regime has not yet been able to fully extinguish freedom. It is difficult for the regime to impose formal censorship as this would be in conflict with the interests of the powerful media corporations.[4] The deeply embedded American gun

---

3 The writings of James Bovard document in much vivid detail acts of repression carried out by the US regime domestically. Thomas Sowell has described efforts by the state to breed ethnic conflict. See also Democracy: The God That Failed (New Brunswick: Transaction Publishers, 2001) by Hans-Hermann Hoppe.

4 Contrary to conventional wisdom, the First Amendment to the US Constitution has not

culture has greatly hindered efforts at civilian disarmament. Some apologists for the state use these examples of remaining freedoms as an excuse for demanding public support for the state. However, the time to take action against a tyrannical government is not after freedom has been completely abolished. By then it is too late, as the residents of Nazi Germany and Soviet Russia learned the hard way.[5] The time for action is before the state is fully able to consolidate its power in a totalitarian manner. This means that, in contemporary America, the time for action is now. The United States will not be able to undergo another thirty to fifty years of current statist expansionism without succumbing to the full apparatus of totalitarianism.

Most people generally prefer that political change take place in a peaceful manner and rightfully so. Change that occurs with the least amount of violence, bloodshed, and societal disruption and dislocation is obviously the kind of change that is likely to be the most beneficial to the average person. Armed actions against the state should never be undertaken solely for the purpose of gratuitous violence, the emotional satisfaction that comes with revenge, or simply "to make a statement." Indeed, revolutionary organizations should shun persons who demonstrate such motivations as dangerous security risks and possible provocateurs. Military actions against the state must be done for defensive or purely strategic purposes only. While such military actions should certainly not be pursued in a reckless

---

been a reliable protection for free speech. During the First World War, Eugene V. Debs was sentenced to twenty years imprisonment for criticizing the war. Two nineteen-year-old girls in Colorado were sentenced to five years hard labor for handing out antiwar pamphlets. The US Supreme Court never applied the First Amendment with anything even remotely approaching consistency until the middle part of the twentieth century—about the same time that the mass media (publishing, television, and radio) started to become a powerful interest group.

5   For a description of the parallels between the early days of Nazi repression and current political conditions in the United States, see Nazi Justiz: Law of the Holocaust (Westport, CT: Praeger, 1995) and Drug Warriors and Their Prey: From Police Power to Police State (Westport, CT: Praeger, 1996), both by Richard Lawrence Miller. Another interesting general study is William L. Shirer's The Rise and Fall of the Third Reich: A History of Nazi Germany (New York: Simon and Schuster, 1960). In the 1950s Shirer remarked that the US would be the first nation to go fascist democratically.

or imprudent manner, it also needs to be recognized that no ruling class ever steps down without a fight. Recall the fate of the Chinese students at Tiananmen Square, the peasants of El Salvador, or the Branch Davidians at Waco. At the end of the day, all of the lobbying, voting, petitioning, letter writing, ballot initiatives, demonstrations, speech-making, leafleting, class action lawsuits, jury nullifications, strikes, boycotts, construction of alternative institutions, passive resistance, and "non-violent civil disobedience" in the world will not be sufficient to dislodge those who have a vested interest in maintaining the status quo. The former rulers of the Soviet Union knew their system was a failed and dying dinosaur. Yet they clung to their sacred Marxist-Leninist dogma and bureaucracy to the death. The rulers of the corporate states of the West will no doubt do the same. This is particularly true of the American ruling class which has an empire to defend. If global tyranny and domestic police statism are to be successfully resisted and defeated, then the next wave of American revolutionaries must be prepared to fight and win.

The rules of war that apply to states are also binding upon anti-state revolutionaries as well. Those who undertake the task of a war of liberation against a tyrannical state must conduct themselves according to the highest standards. Every possible precaution should be taken to avoid injury or damage to the person or property of innocents. Persons taken as prisoners of war, from the highest to the lowest, should be treated as well as conditions of war permit. Military actions should be pursued only when there is a reasonable chance for success and when there is some genuine strategic or defensive purpose involved. Those who involve themselves in such actions must be prepared to face full responsibility for their actions and fully consider the very likely consequences. Execution, lengthy terms of imprisonment, or death in combat are the frequent fates of those who engage in armed struggle against the state. Generally, revolutionaries are worth more to their movement alive and in civil society rather than dead or in prison. So caution is obviously of the utmost importance.

A campaign of armed struggle against the state would likely take place over a lengthy period of time and involve several distinct stages. Different types of armed struggle would be employed at each stage in the fight. The earliest stages would primarily involve acts of tyrannicide or strategic bombings carried out by individuals or small groups. Larger guerrilla actions against broader targets would follow. The final stage would involve popular insurrection and militia self-defense. It must be kept in mind that any discussion of these matters is entirely theoretical. There is simply no way to predict all of the many variables that would factor into an actual revolutionary situation. There is no "operators' manual" for the prosecution of an armed struggle campaign. Individual situations must be evaluated on a case-by-case basis and individual persons must rely on their own value judgments. The purpose of this article is not to provide instruction or give orders as to how an armed struggle effort should be carried out. Rather, the goal is to construct a theoretical model of what a hypothetical armed struggle in the United States would look like. Therefore, what follows is intended for education and discussion only and is certainly not intended to be any sort of "game plan," "instructions," "orders," or "advice" for potential revolutionaries to follow.

Revolutions are never made by the majority. When the American war of independence from Great Britain began, only about five percent of the population of the colonies thought secession from the British Empire to be a good idea. By the time independence had been won, only about thirty percent had come over to the side of the revolutionaries. To use a more recent example, only about five percent of the US population participated in the movement to oppose the US war in Vietnam. The complaint of most Americans was that the government was not fighting the war even harder than they were. Yet the efforts of this minority of protestors and antiwar activists severely weakened the government's war efforts. Those who seek to depose an established regime will always be in the minority during the initial stages of the struggle. Most people prefer security and familiarity to sweeping changes in the social order. Most people acquire their notions of right and wrong from cues taken from peers or perceived authority figures, so revolutionaries are always initially perceived as criminals or troublemakers. This is particularly true of revolutionaries who take up arms against an established regime. Typically, when an armed struggle commences, the revolutionaries are frowned upon by the general public who regard them as extremists, terrorists, and fanatics. The state will seek to engage in further repression for the sake of its own preservation and to expand its own power, and the general public will acquiesce. However, the repression eventually expands to the point where "ordinary" citizens start becoming the victims of the repression, thereby generating an increased loss of public confidence in the state.

An interesting example of this is the American War on Drugs. This war has been going on in various forms for nearly a century. However, the current level of intensity of this war has its roots in the Reagan administration's police state ambitions during the 1980s and has been continued by subsequent administrations. Initially, most Americans enthusiastically supported the drug war as is common when the state targets a socially disapproved of scapegoat for persecution. However, the increased repression involved in the drug war began to spill over into other areas of society. The militarization of law enforcement traceable to the drug war led to the attacks on gun owners and religious minorities and Waco and Ruby Ridge. Asset forfeiture laws created as a means of fighting the drug war have subsequently been used against other persons caught in the web of federal regulatory agencies. This state of affairs has generated a wider dissatisfaction with and hostility to the federal regime among many of the same population groups who were initially strong supporters of the drug war and still are in some cases. It can be plausibly argued that the creation of the militia movement, for example, is directly traceable to the drug war as it was the spillover effects of the drug war that led to the antigovernment militancy of those who formed the militia movement.

The purpose of the early stages of armed struggle is to wear down and weaken the regime by disrupting state activities, psychologically paralyzing state functionaries, removing individual tyrants, and generating a loss of public confidence in the regime. The American regime is largely an oligarchy of transnational corporate interests, career bureaucrats, and professional politicians. However, these interests would be powerless without the various layers of stooges whom they employ to carry out their directives. The symbolic assassination of a head of state is strategically useless as such characters are nothing more than easily replaceable figureheads in modern state systems. Instead, direct engagement of those involved in the day-to-day "nuts and bolts" operation of the machinery of statist oppression is likely to be the most fruitful course of action. Without the vast armies of police, district attorneys, judges, prison administrators, media propagandists, inspectors, regulators, and tax collectors who do their dirty work, the plutocrats, media bosses, and politicians would be powerless. The system's stooges are generally more easily located and eliminated than the oligarchs themselves. Wearing down the state's oppressive machinery through a war of attrition could paralyze the ruling class politically.

Again, it must be remembered that military actions against the state should be strategic or defensive rather than symbolic if they are going to be effective. For example, not all judges are equally tyrannical. Physical elimination of the most tyrannical judges would have the dual effect of curbing the worst excesses of the abuse of state power through removing individual perpetrators and providing serious psychological incentive to other judges not to cross certain lines. If more moderate, mild-mannered judges were to observe some of their more tyrannical colleagues simply disappear Jimmy Hoffa-style, then they might certainly consider becoming less tyrannical themselves. The same is true of the police. Indiscriminate, random attacks on uniformed patrol cops would be ineffective as cops would have no means of knowing how to alter their behavior to avoid becoming the target of such an attack. Some cops are relatively honest and decent. Others are scum who engage in police brutality and the framing of suspects. If individual cops of this type were to be physically eradicated their less heinous comrades would know what types of behavior they should avoid.

Most serious, organized state repression is not carried out by ordinary uniformed patrol cops. Instead, this repression is the domain of special police units such as SWAT teams, narcotics, firearm, gang enforcement and vice units, political police (formerly called "red squads"), and federal paramilitary forces such as the FBI, DEA, and BATF. In an armed struggle campaign against state tyranny, *all* police agents of these types would be legitimate military targets. Mere membership in such units indicates a willingness to disregard the rights of others. The identification, tracking, and elimination of such individuals would necessarily be a primary component of the armed struggle effort. Another effective tactic might be the destruction of the facilities that headquarter tyrannical government agencies. Such objectives could even be achieved without the loss of life. The Weather Underground bombings of the late 1960s and early 1970s did not involve even a single injury. The Weathermen would plant a bomb and then give notice in time for the building in question to be evacuated. So the bombing of buildings owned by government or corporate enemies need not involve massacres of the Oklahoma City variety.

As the rebellion spread and gained more converts and recruits, larger guerrilla operations against enemy targets would become possible. Raids conducted against police stations, courthouses, the headquarters of enemy government agencies and corporate entities, prisons, media centers, legislative buildings, and, eventually, military bases would serve the purpose of disrupting the day-to-day operations of the system for the purpose of rendering the state machinery dysfunctional. Police stations that constantly have to been on guard in case of a guerrilla attack will have fewer personnel and resources with which to conduct investigations, arrests, stings, entrapment schemes, infiltration of political organizations, etc. Court operations that are consistently disrupted by such attacks will have less time to herd human chattel into the prison-industrial complex. Raids on prisons resulting in the freeing of prisoners, the elimination of administrative personnel, and the destruction of facilities will prove quite costly to prison-industrial profiteers. Some corporate officers and government agents would no doubt be inspired to resign from their jobs in the face of guerrilla attacks. Assaults on media centers would likely throw a wrench in the propaganda machinery of the ruling class. During the Los Angeles uprising of 1992, probation and parole offices were attacked and their records destroyed. Police precincts were similarly attacked. Actions by large groups need not even involve violence to be effective. For example, in urban areas where corporations, elite civic organizations, and class interests work to repress the economic activities or civil liberties of the poor, a nighttime torchlight march of masked crowds of poor people and dissidents through gentrified districts or outside the homes or offices of leading class enemies would no doubt be somewhat effective at intimidating and deterring such individuals and groups.

The most important phase of the armed struggle would occur during the days when the state is on the verge of collapsing. By this time the regime will have lost credibility in the eyes of the general public and large popular revolutionary organizations will have previously been organized. The most effective revolutionary strategy would probably be to seize political power at the local or regional level, and then secede from the central government. A number of past revolutionary experiences are instructive as to what kinds of scenarios might come about in a revolutionary situation. The American Revolution of 1776 came about through the radicalization of colonial governments and a declaration of independence from the British crown. Similarly, the election of hard-line separatists or revolutionaries to local town councils and regional assemblies could result in a new large scale secessionist project resembling the colonial secession from Britain or the

Southern secession in the days leading up to the beginning of the American Civil War. The Spanish Revolution of 1936 involved an insurrection by popular militias. The Libyan Revolution of 1969 came about through a coup instigated by radicals who had infiltrated the military. The anti-Communist revolution in Eastern Europe of 1989 occurred largely through passive resistance, popular non-compliance, and the loss of state legitimacy.

Armed struggle against the US regime would likely commence following several waves of mass demonstrations, civil disobedience, strikes, riots, formal declarations of independence by regions and localities, and direct armed confrontations with the state of the Waco variety. The armed forces of the revolutionary struggle would be drawn from a variety of sources, including militias created by popular organizations ranging from labor unions to churches to gun clubs, mercenaries hired by sympathetic groups and individuals, public militias organized by sympathetic local governments, defector units within the state's armed services, local and state militia units, sheriff's departments and National Guard that have defected or been redirected by superiors, armed outlaw groups like street gangs, motorcycle clubs, or prison gangs, and troops donated by sympathetic foreigners, perhaps even foreign governments.

Three overriding principles would have to be adhered to during the course of the struggle. A primary strategy of the government would be to attempt to crush the revolution by "starving out" the opposition. This would include the shutting down of utility, transportation, and communications systems within areas that served as strongholds for the revolutionary forces. It would be essential that in the days, months, and years leading up to the collapse of the central government the revolutionary and popular organizations begin preparing for such a scenario. Large and readily available supplies of food, medical gear, clothing, heating and energy sources, vehicles and vehicle maintenance equipment, fuel, communications equipment, ammunition and weapons would be essential. The ideal weapons for popular militias would be those that are easily maintained, transported, and resupplied with ammunition. This would include semi-automatic handguns, high-powered sniper rifles with a good scope, and ordinary shotguns sawed off as low as possible. Grenades and landmines stolen from the military or provided by foreign sources would also be quite useful. The government's arsenal of atomic weapons would be useless in combating a domestic insurgency but the government would likely employ the use of chemical weapons and poison gases. Any sort of equipment that could be used to counter potential attacks of this type would be important.

It would also be vital that the revolutionary forces be organized as a decentralized militia confederation. This would be necessary in order to prevent the recentralization of power following the defeat of the state, safeguard against potential treachery at the top, and avoid the potential for the government to crush the revolution by "cutting off the head." The revolutionary forces would not need to "win" a civil war against the regime. They would simply have to "not lose." It would be futile and foolish to confront the state's armed forces directly. The correct military strategy would be to wear down the government's forces through a war of attrition of the Viet Cong/mujahideen variety. The American colonists achieved victory through a strategy of this type. The Southern independence forces lost the civil war of 1861–65 largely because of their efforts to carry out a traditional military campaign which they were not equipped or qualified to do. Let's learn from their mistakes.

www.ingramcontent.com/pod-product-compliance
Lightning Source LLC
Chambersburg PA
CBHW071639270326
41928CB00010B/1975

* 9 7 8 1 9 1 0 8 8 1 4 4 6 *